Rudolf Otto
and the
Concept of Holiness

ಠ

Rudolf Otto
and the
Concept of Holiness

ða

MELISSA RAPHAEL

CLARENDON PRESS · OXFORD
1997

Oxford University Press, Great Clarendon Street, Oxford OX2 6DP

Oxford New York

Athens Auckland Bangkok Bogota Bombay
Buenos Aires Calcutta Cape Town Dar es Salaam
Delhi Florence Hong Kong Istanbul Karachi
Kuala Lumpur Madras Madrid Melbourne
Mexico City Nairobi Paris Singapore
Taipei Tokyo Toronto Warsaw

and associated companies in
Berlin Ibadan

Oxford is a trade mark of Oxford University Press

Published in the United States
by Oxford University Press Inc., New York

British Library Cataloguing in Publication Data

Data available

Library of Congress Cataloging-in-Publication Data
Rudolf Otto and the concept of holiness / Melissa Raphael.
Based on the author's thesis (doctoral).
Includes bibliographical references and index.
1. Otto, Rudolf, 1869–1937—Contributions in doctrine of the Holy.
2. Holy, The—History of doctrines—20th century. I. Title.
BL48.R28   1997   200'.92—dc21   97–489
ISBN 0-19-826932-3

1 3 5 7 9 10 8 6 4 2

Typeset by Graphicraft Typesetters Ltd., Hong Kong
Printed in Great Britain on acid-free paper by
Bookcraft (Bath) Ltd., Midsomer Norton

To my father

Acknowledgements

I would like to thank Professor Keith Ward for his challenging and careful supervision of the doctoral thesis on Rudolf Otto's concept of holiness that was to set the foundations for this book. I greatly appreciate his supporting the publication of this book, as did Professor Ursula King, who has inspired, encouraged, and assisted myself and many others in our careers. I am also grateful to Peter Byrne who read the manuscript at an earlier stage and, like the anonymous readers for Oxford University Press, made a number of useful suggestions for its improvement. Thanks are also due to the Revd Stanley Rudman, Head of the Centre for the Study of Religion at Cheltenham and Gloucester College of Higher Education, for kindly reducing my teaching load towards the end of this project, to my husband Michael for his support and practical assistance, and to my 2-year-old daughter Verity whose priorities and sense of humour have kept this work in perspective.

Contents

Abbreviations

Works by Rudolf Otto

FN   *Freiheit und Notwendigkeit, ein Gespräch mit Nicolai Hartmann über Autonomie und Theonomie der Werte* (Tübingen: J. C. B. Mohr, 1940)

IH   *The Idea of the Holy*, trans. J. W. Harvey (New York: Oxford University Press, 1958; orig. pub. 1917)

IRG   *India's Religion of Grace and Christianity Compared and Contrasted*, trans. F. H. Foster (London: SCM Press, 1930)

KGSM *The Kingdom of God and the Son of Man*, trans. F. V. Filson and B. L. Woolf (London: Lutterworth Press, 1938; orig. pub. 1934)

MEW   *Mysticism East and West*, trans. B. L. Bracey and R. C. Payne (New York: Macmillan, 1976; orig. pub. 1926)

NR   *Naturalism and Religion*, trans. J. A. Thomson and M. B. Thomson (London: Williams & Norgate, 1913; orig. pub. 1904)

PR   *The Philosophy of Religion Based on Kant and Fries*, trans. E. B. Dicker (London: Williams & Norgate, 1931; orig. pub. 1909)

RE   *Religious Essays: A Supplement to 'The Idea of the Holy'*, trans. B. Lunn (London: Oxford University Press, 1937)

Works by other authors

COH   O. R. Jones, *The Concept of Holiness* (London: Allen & Unwin, 1961)

RO   P. C. Almond, *Rudolf Otto: An Introduction to his Philosophical Thought* (Chapel Hill, NC: University of North Carolina Press, 1984)

ROR   R. F. Davidson, *Rudolf Otto's Interpretation of Religion* (Princeton: Princeton University Press, 1947)

Note

Several linguistic features of this study require explanation. First, I refer to God as 'he'. This is not because I think the divine personality is male in character, but because convention and logic demand that any discussion of the biblical 'God' should use the pronoun 'he'. By and large, God's relationship with the world is depicted in the traditionally male gender roles of king, father, and judge. Any use of 'she' for God in this book would therefore be a confusing misidentification and a pointless linguistic gesture.

Second, I often use the phrase 'biblical theology'. I recognize that this generalization is an artificial synthesis of plural theologies and diverse texts, but have used the phrase as a Western religio-cultural context for the concept of holiness in which, if not strictly continuous, the meanings of words like 'salvation', 'sin', 'history', and 'God' are basically held in common. Third, although I have used the terms 'Old Testament' and 'New Testament' of the Jewish and Christian scriptures, I do not mean to indicate any supersession of the 'Old' by the 'New'. Again, for the sake of clarity, I use these terms because Otto and the majority of his commentators have done so.

Introduction

The twentieth-century history of the concept of holiness is largely unintelligible without reference to that advanced by Rudolf Otto in *The Idea of the Holy*. For nearly eighty years this text has been used as a yardstick against which subsequent studies of holiness have declared and defined their own position. Like other books which have achieved classic status, *The Idea of the Holy* 'exceeds the rules by which any single discipline would claim it',[1] and it has left its mark not only on the history of religions but also on twentieth-century philosophy, psychology and aesthetics of religion, biblical studies, and theology. In its own time, *Das Heilige*, translated in 1923 as *The Idea of the Holy*, sparked methodological and theological debates that remain central to contemporary religious studies. Most scholars would agree with Lorne Dawson that while *The Idea of the Holy* is often philosophically and ethnographically undeveloped, the numinous remains 'a constantly recurring referent of "talk of religion"',[2] and that Otto's conceptualization of transcendence has helped and continues to help 'to formally demarcate and focus religious studies as a discipline'.[3] There are historical as well as academic reasons for this. Otto had a strong influence on a number of highly influential scholars who, like Joachim Wach, emigrated from Nazi Europe and took up academic posts in America, exporting with them the Ottonian definition of

[1] L. Poland, 'The Idea of the Holy and the History of the Sublime', *Journal of Religion*, 72 (1992), 175.
[2] L. Dawson, *Reason, Freedom and Religion: Closing the Gap between the Humanistic and Scientific Study of Religion* (New York: Peter Lang, 1988), 205.
[3] Ibid. 206.

religion as the experience of the holy as, in Wach's terms, the 'trunk' rather than a 'branch' of religion.[4]

More generally, *The Idea of the Holy* occupies a distinctive place in the twentieth-century history of ideas. This one, relatively short text encapsulates a period in which religion was most particularly on the defensive. Before Otto wrote *The Idea of the Holy*, he was concerned (like Schleiermacher before him) that secularism was eroding religious faith and the authority of religious discourse and institutions among the intelligentsia. *Naturalism and Religion* (1904) attempted to establish the autonomy and irreducibility of religion against both scientific reductionism and natural theology, both of which, he claimed, rationalize away the darkness and confusion of life as lived.[5] *The Idea of the Holy* is an unequivocal expression of romantic hostility towards modernity's accelerating industrialization and its corrosion of religious values. Few religious scholars have resisted secularization and reductionism more passionately than Otto. He did not merely complain of secularization: as we shall see, *The Idea of the Holy* deploys drastic methodological and rhetorical measures whereby religion is effectively removed from encroachment by the natural—that is, from any discourse produced by human culture. As Wayne Proudfoot has observed, Otto rules out a priori any naturalistic explanation of religion, and guarantees the inviolability of religious experience by claiming, in effect, that if a religious experience can be explained, it is not a religious experience.[6]

Otto's polemics against secular materialism might have been less vehement today, when religion has shown itself to be far more robust than scholars of the early and mid-twentieth century thought it would be. So too, since the end of the Second World War, rationalism has been widely discredited as producing the psychological and technical capacity for killing on an unprecedented scale, and there has been a

---

[4] D. Hay, 'Scientists and the Rediscovery of Religious Experience', in U. King (ed.), *Turning Points in Religious Studies* (Edinburgh: T. & T. Clark, 1990), 236.

[5] *NR* 5–7.

[6] W. Proudfoot, *Religious Experience* (Berkeley: University of California Press, 1985), 118.

rapprochement between (postmodern) science and contemporary spirituality that Otto could not have foreseen.[7] But
The Idea of the Holy is not only a testament to religion's
turn-of-the-century engagement with modernity; it also marks
a period of transition between nineteenth- and twentieth-
century modernities. Otto was engaged in at least two intra-
religious struggles: one between nineteenth-century romantic
and liberal Protestants over the embourgeoisement of Christianity, the other over the status of Christianity in a colonial
world of 'other' religions. The eighteenth- and nineteenth-
century history of religions had demonstrated that 'primitive'
religion was indeed religion (rather than barbarism), even if
it was less 'evolved' than Christianity. *The Idea of the Holy*
both supports the nineteenth-century evolutionists' quest for
the trans-historical origin and essence of religion and for evidence of its evolutionary fulfilment in European Christendom,
and at the same time is a witness to that quest's decline. The
text bears vestiges of nineteenth-century confidence in 'vast
comparisons and synthetic pattern-making';[8] yet the vestiges
are just that: whilst loyalty to his own faith compelled him
to argue that Christianity is the religion most evolved from
the crude *sensus numinis*, it is also, on that count, the less
'purely' religious.

Although Otto was 48 when *Das Heilige* was published,
his thought belongs more to the twentieth century than to
the nineteenth. The intellectual and cultural period which
produced *The Idea of the Holy* also produced the modernist works of Joyce, Proust, Bartok, Schoenberg, Lawrence,
Mann, and Freud. The efflorescence of modernism has been
dated between about 1910 and 1915—a very few years in
which 'the whole world of representation and of knowledge
underwent a fundamental transformation'.[9] And in many
ways *The Idea of the Holy*—an introverted, fragmentary text,

---

[7] For a good illustration of this process see D. R. Griffin (ed.), *The Reenchantment of Science: Postmodern Proposals* (New York: State University of New York Press, 1988).

[8] E. Sharpe, *Comparative Religion: A History* (London: Duckworth, 1975), 174.

[9] D. Harvey, *The Condition of Postmodernity: An Enquiry into the Origins of Cultural Change* (Cambridge, Mass.: Blackwell, 1990), 28.

dislocated from the continuities of a single tradition and permeated by a sense of crisis—exemplifies and contributed to
what is sometimes called the romantic period of modernism.

However, I am not sure that Otto, who in 1923 (and again
in 1931) declined to promote his period's tendency 'towards
an extravagant and fantastic "irrationalism"',[10] would have
been altogether delighted to find *Das Heilige* referred to by
Mircea Eliade as one of 'the important events' in the great
'irruptions' of early twentieth-century irrationalism. Eliade
ranks the Ottonian numinous with Freud's discovery of the
unconscious, Bergson's *élan vital*, Lévy-Bruhl's analysis of the
pre-logical, mystical mind, 'as well as the artistic revolutions
of Dadaism and surrealism'.[11] Yet, wherever Otto would have
located his style and his loyalties, *The Idea of the Holy* is a
modernist departure from traditional ways of representing the
divine. Here the numinous, the non-rational element of the
holy, is, in itself, unrepresentable—it is derived from no myth
or story—and yet it is perceptible in unlimited cultural and
religious forms. And in common with avant-garde artists and
psychologists of his time, Otto refuses to suppress explosive,
primal religious emotion, making unorthodox comparisons
between religious and sexual instincts and attempting to release religious feeling from the constraints of tradition.[12]

At the same time, the work anticipates postmodernity's
distrust of discourses penned by pseudo-omniscient subjects
of whom nothing is known but their name. Otto's authorial
personality is stamped on the text. He and his readers are
undoubtedly the subjects of their own experience; neither
Otto nor any other authoritative subject is permitted to arrog-
ate the articulation of numinous experience on the reader's
behalf. Otto does no more than suggest analogies that might,
or might not, nudge the reader into recognition of the numinous. Certainly, Otto's project is characteristically modern
in its claim to timelessness and its pursuit of the universal
and the general—qualities whose value postmodernism has

---

[10] See Sharpe, *Comparative Religion*, 166.
[11] M. Eliade, *The Quest* (Chicago: University of Chicago Press, 1969), 46.
[12] *IH* 46.

precisely set in reverse.[13] But the disembodiedness of Cartesian reasoning is absent here: religious truth is born of a reaction to God that is experienced in the body and through all the senses—just as postmodern spirituality is insisting it should be. For Otto, numinous awe is an emotion that, in a recurrent phrase, 'breaks out' almost like sweat on the skin; it produces an 'inward shuddering' and 'seems to penetrate to the very marrow, making the man's hair bristle and his limbs quake'.[14] In this sense, Eric Sharpe was right to observe that 'Rudolf Otto's English translator was foolish (or at least unwise) to render *Das Heilige* as "The *Idea* of the Holy". An imperative does not become an idea without losing much of its force.'[15] So too, to present holiness or the numinous as a primarily intellectual event overlooks the somatic qualities of this form of religious knowing.

In that *The Idea of the Holy* represents a confluence of classically modern preoccupations, the romantic criticism of modernity, and elements that anticipate postmodernity, it is not a period piece; indeed, it eludes precise classification within the history of ideas. And perhaps more intriguingly, the text is almost unclassifiable because it produces an impression of its standing outside the temporal flux. The contemporary reader is both fascinated by and distrustful of its transcendental content and method; for, in a postmodern academic climate, no one can fail to be aware of the contextual and perspectival nature of theory. But Otto is committed to a far more ambitious and subtle project than a commentary on religion in his time, or even to the use of the category of the numinous to tell the story of religious evolution. Rather, as Lynn Poland has observed, Otto aims 'to uncover the "original" element of the numinous present in every manifestation of religious awareness, early and late. As for Freud, and like many modernist literary works, ontogeny recapitulates phylogeny; Otto's "origin" is timeless and repeatable.'[16]

---

[13] See S. Toulmin, *Cosmopolis: The Hidden Agenda of Modernity* (New York: Free Press, 1990), 30–5, 186–92. [14] *IH* 14, 16.

[15] E. Sharpe, *Nathan Söderblom and the Study of Religion* (Chapel Hill, NC: University of North Carolina Press, 1990), 211.

[16] Poland, 'Idea of the Holy', 186.

The Idea of the Holy invites its readers, irrespective of their time and place, to apply their intuitive faculties and 'any deeply felt experience' to their reading of the text, so as to construct their own sense of the numinous from these and from the allusions Otto sets before them. (If readers cannot or will not involve themselves in the process of coming to recognize the reality of the *sensus numinis*, they are told to put the book aside.[17]) But for those who become 'insiders' to the text, a rapport is established between them and Otto in a manner quite untypical of modern scholarly texts. Read as Otto wants it to be read, the text will both evoke and excite numinous consciousness. As Poland notes, 'the work is not only about religion; it is also, willy-nilly, religious writing. The numinous must be experienced to be understood, Otto insists; his task is not simply to analyze a religious phenomenon but to produce it in his readers.'[18] Similarly, Leon Schlamm suggests that *The Idea of the Holy* is an attempt not only to evoke numinous experience through a process of associated feelings, 'but also to assist in the recovery of memories of numinous experience long since forgotten and thereby to convince his readers of the reality, vitality, value and authority of religious experience'.[19]

In a collection of funeral eulogies published a year after Otto's death,[20] the Archbishop of Uppsala remarked that the greatest aspect of Otto's work was the degree to which his personal convictions were expressed in his theoretical work. And it was precisely this strenuous, impassioned quality of *The Idea of the Holy*, and Otto's expectation that his readers' receptivity and responsiveness would match his own, that first attracted me as a postgraduate student to Otto's work. For me, as a Jew who had been academically trained in Christian theology, Otto made new connections between the biblical testaments, and furnished my spirituality with the numinous elements in which *halakhah* seemed to me to be deficient. Although orthodox Judaism is virtually constituted

[17] See *IH* 8.   [18] Poland, 'Idea of the Holy', 175.
[19] L. Schlamm, 'Numinous Experience and Religious Language', *Religious Studies*, 28 (1992), 551.
[20] *Rudolf Otto: Gedächtnisfeier* (Berlin: Verlag A. Töpelmann, 1938), 33.

6

by its concept of holiness, it has little need of private, non-rational spirituality or impulsions outside the religious experience inherent in the content and daily practice of Torah. Torah's legal jurisdiction over the whole of life seemed to leave little room for the *unheimlich*—especially for women like myself. In orthodox Judaism women's sacral sphere is a non-numinous domestic one, whereas the male sacral sphere of public worship can, on occasion (such as on Rosh Hashanah and Yom Kippur) have markedly numinous elements. I have argued elsewhere that women's numinous experience cannot be the same as men's, and that feminism has much to object to in Otto's evocation of numinous value.[21] However, *The Idea of the Holy* is so socially and historically disengaged that it cannot help but be (at least notionally) indifferent to the gender of its reader, of divinity (because God's 'wholly otherness' is transcendent and deconstructive of any such rational and anthropomorphic distinctions), and to any gendered division of labour. In other words, studying *The Idea of the Holy* did not exclude me as a woman in ways that other texts had done.

Moreover, whilst Otto's concept of holiness is heavily dependent on Western philosophical categories and his own Lutheran tradition, it is never parochial. The close relation of his phenomenology and his theology entails that Otto imposes no obligation of choice between one's own tradition and another, or any of the tests of spiritual loyalty that a Jew studying Christian theology is likely to face. By its nature as the non-rational element of the holy, the numinous is resistant to subsumption into dogma or the sectarian interests of religious institutions.[22] Later, in my research for this book, the inclusivity of *The Idea of the Holy* encouraged me to interpret Otto's theological position using not only Christian discourse on the holy, but also some of the Jewish discourse that my background inclined me to supply.

Whilst it may not have been Otto's theological intention, he does, phenomenologically, give an account of religious

---

[21] M. Raphael, 'Feminism, Constructivism and Numinous Experience', *Religious Studies*, 30 (1994), 511–26.　　　　[22] See *RE* 41.

experience without privileging grand religious narratives or their chief actors. (Perhaps it is Otto's refusal to tell any stories that has, for many, disqualified *The Idea of the Holy* from theological status.) By making numinous consciousness a non-rational human faculty not limited to (male) persons set apart by a male God, Otto's concept of holiness proposes an egalitarian anthropology that implicitly questions the history of religions whose decisive events have converged upon particular prophets, messiahs, and saints set apart or appointed to the status of holiness. Otto's anthropology presupposes not only that these figures are fully human (which for Jews is not controversial) but that humanity's potential for such decisive encounters with the divine is ontologically grounded and unobstructed by any notion of intrinsic sin. Because numinous consciousness is, according to Otto, spontaneous and immediate, dispensatory mediation of the holy by particular (male) religious authorities is not a requirement of the religious life. Revelation begins with a private reaction to the divine presence. Otto's evocation of the numinous makes no claim on any positive authority, and the heterodox genesis of *The Idea of the Holy* during his revelatory travels to North Africa, India, and the Far East before the First World War is widely known.[23]

An Outline of Otto's Position in The Idea of the Holy

It would be helpful for those readers who are unfamiliar with Otto's work if I were to outline his concept of holiness here. Holiness, in Otto's work, is a combined category. That means that it contains two sorts of elements: rational and non-rational. The primary element, or 'moment', of holiness is a pure reaction to the divine which is, like its object, unthinkable and unspeakable, because it is unlike any other possible experience. The state of mind and the object of this experience are characterized by the word 'numinous' to denote

---

[23] See R. F. Streetman, 'Some Later Thoughts of Otto on the Holy', *Journal of the American Academy of Religion*, 48/3 (1980), 368; H. Rollmann, 'Rudolf Otto and India', *Religious Studies Review*, 5 (1979); *RO* 17, 23.

that they refer to an as yet unspecified divinity—a numen. But as the numinous emotions are thought through, they are gradually accommodated in the religious scheme whose experiential foundations they have provided. The numinous is schematized or completed as the holy when it has become sufficiently delineated to give a structural and moral dynamic to a given religious system; that is, when numinous consciousness has been replaced by the content provided by collective—'natural' that is—ordinary, rational intra-mundane consciousness. It is not numinous consciousness that changes or is transmuted in its assimilation into the rational world-view, but the subject's developing sense of the meaning of that original numinous experience. Natural experiences of mystery, terror, or sublimity cannot 'become' numinous experiences, despite their being analogous to numinous experience; numinous experience is itself irreducibly other.[24] Holiness, then, contains within itself a *sui generis* category that is peculiar to religion and defines the essence of religion: the *sensus numinis*—the feeling of the divine.

Like Schleiermacher and his successors, Otto finds the essence of religion in the emotions evoked by an immediate sense of the divine. Using his phenomenological knowledge of the holy from the history of religions, Otto characterizes the essence of diverse divinities and the essence of diverse human reactions to divine presence as the numinous: the *mysterium tremendum et fascinans*. As the numinous is indefinable or 'wholly other', any analysis of the holy arises indirectly from analysis of the subject's own feeling response to the *numen praesens*—the sense of the presence of the numen or deity. Since the numinous cannot strictly be described, Otto offers instead a number of analogical adjectives and phrases to evoke the experience. Typical numinous emotions might be a feeling of uncanniness, of being awed to the point of being horrified, but also utterly captivated.

The valuation of the numinous presence is not derivable from any other experience of value. It is not merely a special form of value continuous with moral goodness or the

---

[24] *IH* 27.

aesthetic sublime, though the latter, by its nature, arouses closely analogous emotions. 'Strong' numinous experience (to use Keith Yandell's phrase for a type of numinous experience that goes beyond the mere sense of the uncanny and is phenomenologically described as an apparent experience of God[25]) evokes what Otto calls 'creature-feeling' in human beings. 'Creature-feeling' encapsulates the feeling of the numinous as a revelation of 'wholly other' value that stimulates an overwhelming sense of personal finitude and cosmic insignificance. When worldly power allows persons or political systems to forget their creaturely contingency, numinous experience shakes the subject into a recognition of the profanity of his or her hubris—a condition of having transgressed the limits of creaturehood and so provoked numinous wrath. Numinous experience is therefore more than an experience of mere self-depreciation; as I shall argue in my two final chapters, the numinous carries within it its own prophetic and juridical possibilities.

However, it is important to Otto that the reality of the holy is not simply inferred from religious sensibility, however powerful. If the holy were only an inference, reductionist philosophy and psychology of religion might justly claim that these emotions have a natural origin. Otto pre-empts any such move by arguing that the natural world is the occasion of numinous experience, but not the cause. The objective presence of the numen is recognized by the soul's supernatural capacity to 'divine' the numinous manifestation by pure intuition, or what Kant's disciple Jakob Fries called *Ahndung* (an archaic form of the contemporary term, Ahnung).

The Controversies Surrounding Otto's Work

Otto and Karl Barth were the two most influential theologians of their time: Otto's *Das Heilige* and Barth's *Römerbrief* 'set the theological agenda for many years, though in different

---

[25] K. Yandell, *The Epistemology of Religious Experience* (Cambridge: Cambridge University Press, 1993), 16.

directions'.[26] None the less, many in the German and British theological establishment of the inter-war years gave Otto's concept of holiness a less enthusiastic reception than they might have done. Otto was a Professor of Systematic Theology at Breslau from 1914 until 1917, and then held a similar post at Marburg from 1917 until his retirement in 1929. In the confessional atmosphere of theology in Europe in the first three decades of this century, Otto's comparativism aroused suspicion of his theology from the outset. In this climate, his reputation as an innovative scholar and translator of Hindu devotional texts did not inspire confidence in his theology. His colleague Karl Barth, though appreciative of the transcendental otherness of numinous value, made a firm distinction between the Gospel and religion, and regarded the category of 'religion' with which Otto was concerned as 'tantamount to unfaith'.[27]

For Otto, numinous consciousness prepared the ground for knowledge of the God revealed in the Bible, the reading of which is 'always determined by contemporary ideas and by the imagination of the individual'.[28] The result—that special historical revelation becomes subsequent upon private non-rational experience—was unpalatable to conservative theology. The neo-Orthodox theologian Emil Brunner contended that if Otto's Christological confession on the closing page of *The Idea of the Holy* was meant seriously, then 'all that is in the preceding two hundred pages is beside the mark'. Brunner and others like him regarded Ottonian divination of an inclusivist 'holy' as contradicting the Christian vision of 'man' as the recipient of special revelation. For Brunner, mere 'awareness' of 'something divine' is not relevant to the challenge of Christian faith.[29] And Rudolf Bultmann and his students held Otto in little higher regard, attacking what they considered to be Otto's irrationalism and the deficiencies of his Christology and his exegetical method.[30]

---

[26] T. Ludwig, 'Otto, Rudolf', in M. Eliade (ed.), *The Encylopedia of Religion* (New York: Macmillan, 1987), xi. 139.

[27] Streetman, 'Some Later Thoughts', 378.   [28] *RE* 30, 38.

[29] E. Brunner, *The Mediator* (London: Lutterworth Press, 1934), 69 n. 1.

[30] *RO* 5-6. M. Lattke, 'Rudolf Bultmann on Rudolf Otto', *Harvard Theological Review*, 78 (1985), 356, 359-60.

The illiberal theological climate of Marburg from 1921 until the late 1930s harmed Otto's reputation, and, as Philip Almond and Michael Lattke have shown, reduced his influence on German theology during the first half of this century. But not all the controversy over Ottonian theology can be attributed to the ascendance of dialectical theology. Christian theology as a whole would be likely to take exception to certain features of the Ottonian scheme. A number of British theologians contemporary with Otto (and who needed little excuse for hostility to German thought) were also concerned that numinous experience was more macabre than Christian: that it had the ring of natural religion, and it appeared to obviate any immediate need for faith or commitment to the Church. The generous span of Otto's theory of religion made theologians apprehensive that his understanding of holiness would include sub-Christian elements. These fears were not groundless. Undoubtedly, numinous consciousness is not, in itself, an entirely reliable foundation for Christian theology. In *The Idea of the Holy* Christianity becomes an instance, rather than the pre-condition of, the holy; and revelation becomes, in Otto's hands, what Mircea Eliade would call a hierophany: indispensable for religion, but without theological particularity.

Above all, many theologians were doubtful that the putatively universal object of numinous experience could ever adequately conform to a biblical model of God. Indeed, Otto's denial that the essence of Godhead is rational—that is, either conceptually comprehensible, personal, or consisting in knowable values—would be problematic for any theologian wanting to put Otto's concept of holiness to work in the biblical tradition wherein God is experienced and imaged as a divine person. As we will see in Chapter 3, Otto suggests that 'God' is a concept, while the divine in-itself is a fearfully non-rational numen—a fact of which, Otto believed, mysticism, Hinduism, and 'primitive' religions have long been apprised.[31] This emphasis on divine holiness as something essentially horrifying but compelling has not satisfied

---

[31] See *IH* 62.

theologians whose intention is not only to articulate faith but also to commend God as a rationally justifiable object of worship, experience of whom is conducive to a transformation that is fundamentally moral in character.

Otto's making theology subsequent on numinous experience remains phenomenologically, epistemologically, and theologically controversial. The present generation of liberationist and ecological theologians, who insist that the sacred is relational in character and not exclusive of any profane other, are rather less concerned about the moral status of the holy in abstraction than about Otto's pervasive dualism—especially his virtual identification of creatureliness with profanity and his apparently ascetic depreciation of flesh and world in *Religious Essays*. Although emancipatory theology is, like Otto, methodologically committed to experiential theology, it finds 'creature-feeling' too disempowering and negative a footing for theory and praxis.

The Ottonian concept of holiness is not only theologically controversial; philosophers and phenomenologists of religion have long debated whether Otto was successful in framing an adequate typology of primary religious experience (even if only of Western religion) or whether, in fact, numinous experience is not as phenomenologically comprehensive a category as Otto believed it to be. So too, Otto's dichotomization of the moment of religious experience and its interpretation has recently been contested. There are epistemological objections to the notion, typified in Otto's work, that the diversity of religious experience can be reduced to one perennial moment of pure consciousness regardless of its historical, conceptual, and linguistic context; it is now more customary to regard context and experience as mutually informing.

Published within two years of each other, *Das Heilige* and Karl Barth's *Römerbrief* both created a sensation at the time of their publication. Yet Barth's work has attracted sustained scholarly attention, while Otto's has not. In the early 1950s Joachim Wach wrote that 'while innumerable books, articles and reviews have been devoted to Karl Barth and his theology, very few monographs or studies have been dedicated to Rudolf Otto and his teachings'.[32] Robert Streetman's survey of the American and English theological journals published during the period in which Otto was writing reveals 'shockingly little discussion, or review, of his works'. And it is in light of such neglect that Streetman urges other scholars of the late 1970s to join him 'in the attempt to reappropriate Otto's legacy for our time'.[33] In an age of minute and voluminous scholarship, it is surprising that Otto should have had only two full-length books in English devoted to his work. Of these valuable studies, to which this study is greatly indebted, one, Robert F. Davidson's *Rudolf Otto's Interpretation of Religion*, is concerned with Otto's understanding of religion as such, and not with his concept of holiness. It was published in 1947, and therefore cannot address issues of contemporary theological concern or assess the criticism of Otto in the second half of this century. The other full-length study is much more recent. Published in 1984, Philip Almond's *Rudolf Otto* is primarily interested in the relation of Ottonian phenomenology of religion to the metaphysics of Jakob Fries.[34]

Since Otto's death in 1937, and particularly since the publication of Almond's study, there has been a steady flow of articles discussing the various facets of Otto's work, but there has been no sustained analysis in English of Otto's theological and philosophical contribution to the modern history of the concept of holiness—the task of the present study. By drawing together the scholarly commentary on Rudolf Otto from 1917, when *The Idea of the Holy* was first published in German, to the present, I will offer a critical examination of the context and theological ramifications of Otto's concept of holiness. As such, this book is not and could not be about only one text, *The Idea of the Holy*, however important a text it might be. On the contrary, in the first chapter I establish some of the customary meanings and usages of the English

---

[32] J. Wach, *Types of Religious Experience* (London: Routledge & Kegan Paul, 1951), 210.   [33] Streetman, 'Some Later Thoughts', 381.
[34] For reviews of *RO*, see C. Williamson, *Journal of the American Academy of Religion* (hereafter referred to as *JAAR*), 53/8 (1985), 473–4; J. Boozer, *International Journal for Philosophy of Religion*, 23 (1988), 43–5.

word 'holiness', after which I go on to show how Otto's concept of holiness relates to developments in the concept of holiness over the last hundred years. Without wanting to suggest that Otto's theology is in every way the best of all possible theologies, Chapters 3–6 interpret, on Otto's own terms, how his concept of holiness actually works—not just as a theory in limbo—but in creative interaction with those theological issues with which Otto himself was particularly concerned: namely, the holiness of divine personality, the relation of holiness to the moral good, and the meaning of numinous experience. It is only in the last chapter and Conclusion that I give a freer reading of *The Idea of the Holy*, exemplifying how the Ottonian model of holiness is adaptable to theological discourses that have developed in the last thirty years.

The Classification of Otto's Work

The Idea of the Holy represents an original and creative synthesis of theology and the history of religions. But Otto's academic reputation has suffered from the methodological idiosyncrasies that have also made *The Idea of the Holy* a classic. As Philip Almond has shrewdly remarked, in his own time Otto was too much a historian of religion for the theologians, and too much a theologian for the historians of religion.[35] The same holds true today: Kurt Rudolph, who argues that the methods used in the history of religions should be scientific rather than experiential or theological, names Otto as one of those highly influential historians of religion who have set a precedent for 'historians of religion [who] display an increasing propensity to wander in directions that are not scientific'.[36] Of course, phenomenologists such as Chantepie de la Saussaye and Raffaele Pettazoni's criticism of insufficiently scientific, self-validating, and self-interpretative methods of studying religion would not be confined to Otto himself;

[35] P. Almond, 'Rudolf Otto: Life and Work', *Journal of Religious History*, 12 (1983), 319.
[36] K. Rudolph, *Historical Fundamentals and the Study of Religions* (New York: Macmillan, 1985), 37, 44.

theirs is, after all, a criticism of a whole twentieth-century tradition of non-rational, non-reductionist approaches to the phenomenology of religion. This is a tradition of which Otto may have been a founding father, but one which is more normatively defined by Gerardus Van der Leeuw, W. B. Kristensen, C. J. Bleeker, Mircea Eliade, and Wilfred Cantwell Smith.[37] None the less, as one of the earliest, best-known, and most passionate advocates of understanding the affectivity of religion through one's own affectivity, Otto has been one of the main targets of its criticism.

Theologians have commonly regarded Otto as more of a phenomenologist of religion than a theologian; yet, strictly speaking, his work pre-dates phenomenology proper: that is, the scholarly tradition instituted by Van der Leeuw, among others, on the basis of Husserlian phenomenology.[38] Otto's work does not fully employ methods typical of the phenomenology of religion. Whilst he practises a form of eidetic vision—attempting to penetrate to the numinous essence of religious phenomena—there is little evidence of epochē; his judgement of religious phenomena is rarely suspended—indeed, he tends to rank them (however ambiguously) as more or less mature, or more or less 'purely' religious. Of course, Otto's sympathy with religion as such and his search for religious meaning across a variety of traditions is clearly proto-phenomenological, but he was far less interested in the taxonomy and observation of religious phenomena than in the metaphysical values which sustained them.

Otto was as 'personally wedded' to his speculation as any other theologian, and used the history of religions as a source from which to select material that corroborated his own view of religion.[39] Whilst Otto shares in that phenomenological tradition of meta-empirical exposition without which, arguably, there can be no correlation of a particular religious phenomenon with the world-view it represents,

---

[37] See Dawson, *Reason, Freedom and Religion*, 152, 2.
[38] See W. Oxtoby, 'Holy, Idea of the', in Eliade (ed.), *Encyclopaedia of Religion*, vi. 437.
[39] H. D. Lewis and R. L. Slater, *The Study of Religions* (Harmondsworth: Pelican, 1969), 12 f. See also Streetman, 'Some Later Thoughts', 381 f.

Otto's account of holiness seems to be more illustrated than produced by the phenomenology of religion. With some justification, then, Mircea Eliade preferred that Otto be classified as a philosopher of religion working 'first-hand' with the documents of religious history.[40] Notwithstanding the phenomenological and psychological *substantiations* of his argument, Otto's thought is grounded in metaphysical, theological, and ontological assumptions. For Otto, God is not a rational object of knowledge: only the feeling of holiness can (indirectly) yield a sense of what God is like. The human capacity for numinous consciousness (rather than Christs's Incarnation or any other event in revelation) discloses the essence of what it is to be a human created in the image of God. As the soul represents a form of ontological continuity with divinity, Otto believes that the *sensus numinis* is the closest we will ever come to experiencing God, who, as the object of the most basic spiritual apprehension, is numen before he is named 'God'.

On these methodological grounds I have chosen to classify and interpret Otto's concept of holiness as a form of philosophical theology, and to show that numinous experience is a useful category of theological analysis. Despite the widespread view among theologians and biblical scholars that Otto's work is of a generalized significance to the history of religious studies, I argue that the object of his research, the holy, is, or should be, at the heart of theology. Malcom Diamond has suggested that it is only John Harvey's translation of the German title of Otto's work *Das Heilige* into *The Idea of the Holy* that has led people to believe that Otto was interested in the human concept of holiness, whereas he was, in fact, concerned more with 'The Holy'—that is, God.[41] This is, in some ways, a fair observation, and one which usefully conveys the point that in Western discourse holiness is meaningless without reference to its origin and definitive state in God. However, *The Idea of the Holy* never gets as far

---

[40] Eliade, *Quest*, 23.
[41] M. Diamond, *Contemporary Philosophy and Religious Thought* (New York: McGraw-Hill, 1974), 86.

as an explicit theology—it is, as its subtitle, 'An Inquiry into the non-rational factor in the idea of the divine and its relation to the rational' indicates—an inquiry into the non-rational factor in our idea of the divine. It is Otto's later work that theologically completes what he began in *The Idea of the Holy* and which will help to complete my own theological exposition of his work.

The numinous element of the holy is preliminary to theology, but holiness, the completed category, is an anchor concept of all theistic discourse. God is worthy of worship (rather than absolute admiration) only if he is holy. Holiness is the defining characteristic of divinity, the essential quality of God's attributes. Humans may, by analogy, ascribe virtues and capacities to God that are infinitely amplified forms of those they enjoy themselves. But holiness is not the projection of a human virtue. It is *sui generis*, and belongs to and defines God who is ontologically unique. Listing Otto's criteria for the holy being we call God, Richard Swinburne concludes that if such a being exists, he 'would not merely be worthy of men's worship; he would have most, and probably all, of the properties which make up holiness, classically described by Rudolph [*sic*] Otto in his *The Idea of the Holy*'.[42] Holiness represents the peculiarity of God; yet also in its non-rational numinous element, holiness indicates a plural, inclusive construction of the divine that cannot be doctrinally foreclosed, making it a useful focus for theistic discussions in these times of complex theological negotiation.

The awesome nature of the Ottonian numen may forbid intimacy between the believer and the object of faith, but there is little despair in Ottonian theology, which is, after all, founded upon the possibility that God's call to holiness— 'For I am the Lord your God; consecrate yourselves therefore, and be holy, for I am holy (Lev. 11: 44 (RSV))'—can be answered. Without turning God into a superman and humans into gods, Otto reunites God and humanity by his spiritual ontology, according to which the human senses are open to the numinous. Whatever the failings of Otto's religious

---

[42] R. Swinburne, *The Coherence of Theism* (Oxford: Clarendon Press, 1977), 292.

epistemology, his theory that God creates persons who are able to sense God as *praesens* mitigates the alienation narrated by the story of the Fall. Whilst God is not an object of ordinary knowledge, he is, none the less, an object of spiritual experience by virtue of our being ensouled human beings.

Holiness in Late Modernity

I have not written this book for the sake of Otto's reputation. It is more important that his work be assessed for its relevance to contemporary spiritual and theological concerns. Ewart Cousins has discussed how a resurgence of interest in spirituality has been one of the major events of contemporary religious life. Cousins defines spirituality as 'the experiential dimension of religion in contrast with formal beliefs, external practices, and institutions', and as being concerned 'with the relation of the person to the divine, the experience of the divine, and the journey of the person to a more intimate relationship with the divine'.[43] If Cousins is right that these are the defining characteristics of modern spirituality, then Otto's contribution remains an important framework for its study and practice.

That Otto's theological style is more evocative than analytic,[44] and that, as a Lutheran, he assumes that religion is primarily an inner experience,[45] may be, for different reasons, attractive to postmodern spiritualities for which institutionalized religious observance and the grand narratives their communities represent have become secondary or even irrelevant to private spiritual experience. Whilst Otto was not a guru of alternative religion and did not advocate the end of religious traditions, his conviction that the sacred was available to the most and least sophisticated religious thought, and regardless of piety, would now be of greater

---

[43] E. Cousins, 'Spirituality in Today's World', in F. Whaling (ed.), *Religion in Today's World* (Edinburgh: T. & T. Clark, 1987), 306.
[44] P. Almond, *Mystical Experience and Religious Doctrine* (Amsterdam: Mouton, 1982), 119.   [45] *ROR* 5.

and wider interest than it would have been in the inter-war years. Since the 1960s theology and spirituality have become ever more troubled by the modern desacralization of the environment and of consciousness; holiness always was at the heart of theology and spirituality, but now in the spiritual, political, and ecological conditions of the end of this century, it is crucially so. Nationalism, religio-ethnic animosities, and far-Right militias are surfacing in the wake of the disintegration of the Communist bloc and mass unemployment. The times are not altogether unlike those in which Otto worked to build good international relations between the religions and so foster world peace. In 1921 he set up and worked closely with the Inter-Religious League, though not with the support of all his contemporaries. (Otto, Tillich, and Nathan Söderblom have been named as the only Christian theologians of their period to have shown a genuinely empathetic attitude to other religions;[46] Söderblom, himself regarded as a liberal, came to consider Otto's ecumenism as unfortunately syncretistic.[47])

Yet even the end of the Second World War and an increasing sense of the tragic failure of Christendom to make any significant intervention in the events of the Holocaust did not make the inter-faith movement either religiously or academically respectable. As Marcus Braybrooke remembers, at the 1958 Tokyo conference of the International Association for the History of Religions (IAHR), J. C. Bleeker reminded his audience that the purpose of the IAHR was a scientific one, and firmly distanced the IAHR from the ecumenical movement and from the World Congress of Faiths. Even in the mid-1960s all faiths services could be picketed, and those committed to inter-faith dialogue suspected of being eccentric theosophists.[48]

Since then, however, the inter-faith movement has grown considerably, and with the help of scholars like Wilfred

---

[46] F. Whaling, *Christian Theology and World Religions: A Global Approach* (Basingstoke: Marshall, Morgan & Scott, 1986), 6.

[47] Sharpe, *Comparative Religion*, 257.

[48] M. Braybrooke, 'Religious Studies and Interfaith Developments', in U. King (ed.), *Turning Points in Religious Studies* (Edinburgh: T. & T. Clark, 1990), 132 f.

Cantwell Smith and John Hick has carried forward Otto and others' belief in dialogue as a means of promoting peace and solidarity among the traditions. 'Strong' numinous experience—which is to be found in Christianity, Judaism, Islam, and Bhakti Hinduism[49]—might well be a categorical ground for such honourable efforts. For if, in Nathan Söderblom's words, 'religious is the man to whom something is holy',[50] then the numinous, as the common ground of different responses to, and conceptions of, the Holy (One), has an inclusivity that is favourable to the globalism that many historians of religion, theologians, and believers have, over the last ten years or so, wanted to be the new context for religious discourse. Wilfred Cantwell Smith's attempt to articulate global theological categories that are Christian (but unbounded by Christianity) and to apply them creatively to the situation of global ecological and spiritual crisis is, I think, an endeavour Otto would have whole-heartedly supported.[51] Numinous consciousness denotes a non-rational spiritual orientation that, by its nature, might constitute what Huston Smith would call a 'primordial tradition':[52] the non-rational basis of a perennial theology which would unify different religions but which would not preclude cultural loyalties to given traditions or awareness of their incommensurably different truth claims.

So too, Otto's counsel that religion steer a path between the extremes of authoritarian rationalism and mystical libertarianism remains important today. In his own time, Otto recognized that the holy had been almost moralized out of existence. In puritanical religious circles the same domestication of holiness as moral or ascetic virtuosity is likely to prevail. But Otto's conviction that the holy is the source and summary of all values, and at the same time an *extra*-mundane

---

[49] Yandell, *Epistemology of Religious Experience*, 16.

[50] N. Söderblom, 'Holiness: General and Primitive', in J. Hastings (ed.), *Encyclopaedia of Religion and Ethics* (Edinburgh: T. & T. Clark, 1913), vi. 731.

[51] See W. Cantwell Smith, *Towards a World Theology* (Philadelphia: Westminster Press, 1981).

[52] See H. Smith, *Forgotten Truth: The Primordial Tradition* (New York: Harper & Row, 1976).

category, protects the mysterious otherness of the holy, and ensures that the category is inexhaustible by any socio-historical condition and remains open to the future.

Otto's concept of holiness holds the rational and non-rational elements of religion in creative tension, and as such it has a corrective function as a *via media* through the contemporary religious situation. Generally speaking, the Western religious spectrum is becoming polarized. At one end of the spectrum, fundamentalisms are flourishing, and at the other, syncretism, eclecticism, and other forms of religious tourism are being practised (often for good reasons) under the umbrella of the New Age movement. Otto may well have regarded the New Age sense of the uncanniness of certain sacred texts, rituals, and sites as evidence of the endurance of numinous consciousness, despite modernity's best attempts to demystify or suppress it. But for him, 'miracle and legend and the whole dream world of pseudo-mysticism', while originating in the numinous excitement of the imagination, are a 'mere substitute for the genuine thing, and they end in a vulgar rankness of growth that overspreads the pure feeling of the *mysterium* as it really is and chokes its direct and forthright emotional expression'.[53] Otto recognized that religion degenerates without clear critical thinking—something that, arguably, both the extremes of inclusivism and exclusivism lack. For he also had little time for unbending dogmatism; the numinous is not amenable to fixing in systems whose rationalism dispels the mysterious.[54] Some forms of Christian fundamentalism, although non-rational in so far as they emphasize spirit over intellect, domesticate the numen by over-familiar, colloquial forms of prayer, and so fail to show proper humility to the sheer ontological otherness of the divine. Fundamentalism exercises authority by virtue of its certainty that the whole of life can be accommodated and resolved within its own salvific scheme. And Otto would have judged that kind of certainty as he did other such forms of pseudo-omniscient theology in his own time: as over rationalized and therefore deficient in the numinous

[53] *IH* 77.   [54] *NR* 373.

awe and humility that he considered to be the essence of true religion.

Whilst it seems clear that Otto's work has a prophetic function within the religious criticism of religion, it is not, however, renowned for its political relevance. Among others, Christine Wenderoth has claimed that *The Idea of the Holy*, in sundering the numinous from history and social utility, 'appears to put the transformative quality of religion seriously in question'.[55] Certainly, belief in the socially transformative qualities of religion would not have been unknown to Otto. Apart from the merely moralistic tendencies of the nineteenth-century concept of holiness, Anglo-American evangelicalism had exemplified an activist theology which identified Christian service with the strenuousness of social reform. And in the same year that *The Idea of the Holy* was first published, 1917, Walter Rauschenbusch published his *Theology for a Social Gospel*, presenting a systematic argument for the relevance of Christian theology to the social injustices of his time, and sharply criticizing unworldly mysticism as ultimately self-centred escapism.[56] Rauschenbusch was arguing that the purer the Christianity, the deeper would be its passion for justice and love of humankind.

Otto, by contrast, steadfastly refused to reduce religion to any project or function—even, implicitly, a liberative function. He was not concerned with the political causes or consequences of numinous experience; indeed, he considered any causal or functional account of numinous experience falsely reductive:

The criterion of the value of a religion as religion cannot ultimately be found in what it has done for culture . . . It can only be found in what is the innermost essence of religion, the idea of holiness as such, and in the degree of perfection with which any given religion realizes this.[57]

---

[55] C. Wenderoth, 'Otto's View on Language: The Evidence of *Das Heilige*', *Perspectives in Religious Studies*, 9 (1982), 43. See also Bernard Meland's similar point in his article 'Rudolf Otto', in M. Marty and D. Peerman (eds.), *A Handbook of Christian Theologians* (Cleveland: World Publishing, 1965), 189.

[56] W. Rauschenbusch, *Theology for a Social Gospel* (Nashville, Tenn.: Abingdon, 1981), 103.   [57] *IH* 173.

Otto did, however, acknowledge that religious impulses have affinities with moral and emotional impulses, and part of the purpose of this book is to counter the widespread impression that because the numinous is not reducible to any function, it is therefore relevant only to the phenomenology of mystical or private religion. I argue instead that numinous consciousness of the absolute inconsequence of the creature before the Creator is not a derogation of human life as such, but rather, in the context of the exploitation and violation of God's creation, is primarily a *sui generis* religious emotional reaction to the hubristic exercise of power and whose articulation is integral to prophetic theology. In a Western, biblical context, numinous consciousness can be completed as faith that the holy stands in judgement on the profanity of hubris: the ambition to subordinate God and God's creation to the human project.

1

The Concept of Holiness

Whilst theists are generally agreed that holiness is the essential quality of God's attributes,[1] derivative holiness, as an experience and as a quality of things and places, is more variously understood. So before turning to Otto's understanding of holiness, it is necessary, for the sake of clarity, to attempt to define holiness, or at least to outline in what sense the word is being used in the present study. However, it should be borne in mind that Otto would reject a strict definition of the holy, since its numinous essence cannot be rationally conceived, but only evoked.[2] And since he held holiness to be a *sui generis* category of reality, it cannot be defined; there is nothing else in terms of which it can be described. I shall attempt to evoke the meaning of holiness by two means: first, by exploring the semantics of the words 'holy' and 'holiness', and second, by offering an analysis of the ontological status of holiness.

The Semantics of Holiness

It should be noted here that the word 'holy' will be semantically differentiated from the word 'sacred'. John Harvey, who translated Otto's *The Idea of the Holy* into English, regarded the two words as synonyms, but found the word 'holy' more evocative of the numinous than 'sacred'.[3] But the choice of terms is surely less arbitrary than that. English, unlike most

[1] See e.g. J. G. Davies, *Every Day God* (London: SCM Press, 1973), 46; J. Macquarrie, *Principles of Christian Theology* (London: SCM Press, 1966), 192; *MEW* 133.   [2] *IH* 5; Davies, *Every Day God*, 14.
[3] Harvey's own appendix, *IH* 216.

25

other languages, differentiates between 'sacred' and 'holy'. A person might read the Holy Bible, but not the Sacred Bible. Although the words are often used synonymously, 'holy' will be understood here as a participant religious term, while 'sacred' will be regarded as a phenomenological term that can be used descriptively by those outside a given religious community as well as confessionally.[4] P. S. Minear summarizes this type of distinction between the sacred and the holy when he notes that 'sacredness points to human activity oriented towards God; holiness to God's activity oriented towards people'.[5] Of course, for Otto, the German word *heilig* refers indifferently to the participant's term 'holy' and the observer's term 'sacred'. This allows him to speak both from within religious experience, as a theologian, and from without, as a comparativist.[6] But since English is privileged to have two terms for the one German word, I will use the word 'holy' in preference to the more secularized 'sacred', as being truer to Otto's own existential participation in his subject.

In offering an introductory analysis of the meaning and categorical status of holiness I will differentiate between two approaches to understanding holiness. The first approach may be given the shorthand title 'meaning-as-use'. Here the meaning of holiness as a predicate and a category is given in the terms that theologians have employed for it in the history of their discourse. The second approach may be called the 'analytical'. By this approach, I will attempt to elucidate the ontological status of holiness, using the concept of a salvific relation between God and the world as a hermeneutical key. This latter is the more truly Ottonian, since he argues that holiness can be discussed only within the non-natural categories of religious meaning and supernatural reference.

The English word 'holy' comes from the Old English *hálig*, where *hál* means 'whole'. The *Oxford English Dictionary*

---

[4] See Oxtoby's discussion of this issue, 'Holy, Idea of the', 434–6. See also *idem*, 'Holy [The Sacred]', in P. Wiener (ed.), *Dictionary of the History of Ideas* (New York: C. Scribner's Sons, 1973), 511 f.; Davies, *Every Day God*, 123–6; *ROR* 81; P. S. Minear, 'The Holy and the Sacred', *Theology Today*, 47 (1990), 5–7; H. W. Turner, *Rudolf Otto: The Idea of the Holy* (Aberdeen: H. W. Turner, 1974), 9.

[5] Minear, 'Holy and the Sacred', 6.   [6] Oxtoby, 'Holy, Idea of the', 436.

of 1933 divides agreed usage of the word into three main categories: as an attribute of God, as an attribute of things deriving their holiness from their association with God, and as the attribute of persons and actions obedient to the divine will.[7] So too, a *concept* of holiness is a set of ideas of which 'holy' is the agreed name. If one has a concept of holiness, the words 'holy' and 'holiness' become a convention and a capacity for correct use of the word in a sentence. The concept becomes a structure in which one accommodates a number of ideas about holiness and which orders them into a coherent and meaningful whole.

Similarly, a set of criteria for canonization can be assembled which might provide Catholics with a model of human holiness.[8] Or conversely, the institutional procedures whereby desecration is dealt with alerts people to the sanctity of a consecrated building.[9] Such definitions of holiness may have adumbrated the condition which characterizes objects called holy such that, armed with the requisite logic and theology, a person might be able to pick out or think about a holy object in distinction from other sorts of objects.

The meaning of the word 'holy' can be understood within the 'grammatical' rules and conventions of theology. The meaning of holiness is, as Patrick Sherry says, 'interlocked with a whole theological system'. As part of a theological, rather than, say, an empirical system, the term 'holy' must indicate 'that facts about human life and history are being interpreted in terms of something beyond them'. As such, he continues, we cannot just point to something and say '*that* is what it [holiness] is'.[10] Often people can be taught the meaning of terms by pointing to an object to which the term refers. We can of course point to the use of 'holy' in

---

[7] See B. M. Leiser's article, 'The Sanctity of the Profane: A Pharisaic Critique of Rudolf Otto', *Judaism*, 20 (1971), 89, for an analysis of the grammatical behaviour of the word 'holy'.

[8] See the collection of articles proposing such criteria in C. Duquoc and C. Floristàn (eds.), *Models of Holiness* (New York: Seabury Press, 1979).

[9] See e.g. J. T. Gulczynski, *The Desecration and Violation of Churches* (Washington: Catholic University of America Press, 1942); M. D. R. Willink, *The Holy and the Living God* (London: Allen & Unwin, 1931), 90–2.

[10] P. Sherry, *Spirits, Saints & Immortality* (London: Macmillan, 1984), 44.

theological discourse or texts, but that may tell us no more than what the four letters of 'holy' mean in current or ancient usage.[11] Or again, if it is argued that holiness is associated with talk about God, then theological convention can dictate the function, role, and logic of the word 'holy'. But limiting meaning to usage tacitly disposes of abstract propositions about holiness as a self-subsistent, publicly available reality.[12]

So the problem of the ontological categorization of holiness is not easily resolved. As will be shown, neither a purely grammatical analysis of holiness in language nor an empirical analysis of holiness as a putatively substantive quality of things will penetrate the *mysterium* of the holy. Adopting Otto's theological realism, it can be argued that the actuality of holiness-in-itself is purely transcendental: the reality named by the word 'holy' is no more a possible object of knowledge than the divinity which it defines.

The Ontological Status of Holiness as Manifest in Persons and Things

Despite the structural differences between the theological metaphysics of Paul Tillich and those of Otto, Otto would not quarrel with Tillich's summary statement that

The sphere of the gods is the sphere of holiness. A sacred realm is established wherever the divine is manifest. Whatever is brought into the divine sphere is consecrated. The divine is the holy.[13]

I shall take the position that a holy thing is, in Tillich's words, 'a bearer of unconditioned meaning', presupposing that 'in reality there is a specifically sacred sphere that stands over against the secular'.[14] Bearing in mind Otto's belief that the

---

[11] See Willink, *Holy and Living God*, 17.
[12] This is also true where the recognition of the sacred is limited to the observation of human patterns of behaviour. See W. Comstock, 'A Behavioural Approach to the Sacred: Category Formation in Religious Studies', *JAAR* 49/4 (1981), 638.
[13] P. Tillich, *Systematic Theology* (London: SCM Press, 1978), i. 215.
[14] P. Tillich, *What is Religion?* (New York: Harper & Row, 1969), 81.

holy cannot be taught but only 'awakened in the mind',[15] and his instruction to analyse 'the feeling which remains where the concept fails',[16] none the less it seems worthwhile to suggest, in images at least, how the ontological and metaphysical status of holiness might be described.

It would be relatively straightforward if holiness were simply a metaphysical category with no connection to the *Lebenswelt*: to matter or mundane categories. It would be helpful if the logic of holiness were like that of, say, heaven. For if it is analytically true of the word 'heaven' that it is a reward of religious virtue—a state of bliss subsequent to death and judgement—then 'heaven' cannot be literally predicated of earthly experiences. To say, then, that a kitchen, a playing field, or even the most magnificent of religious buildings is 'heaven' (rather than heavenly) would be false. Holiness, however, straddles the categories of time and eternity. As Otto and, later, Eliade and Tillich recognize, holiness belongs to the divine sphere, but is none the less an experienced phenomenon. Eliade finds the hierophany to be 'a reality that does not belong to our world, in objects that are an integral part of our natural "profane" world'.[17] Furthermore, in Tillich's words, holiness is open to phenomenological description, making it a 'cognitive doorway' to the understanding of both religion and the divine.[18] And as a 'doorway', holiness is trans-categorical. Its residence is neither fully of heaven or earth. Thus M. D. R. Willink:

> The holy, being an invasion or point of contact from a higher order into ours, runs back into that order to which it belongs and is lost to our present sight, so that we apprehend more than we comprehend, and more than can be brought into an adequate definition.[19]

That this participation in time and eternity is the clue to the salvific efficacy of holiness as a medium of divine–human

---

[15] *IH* 7.   [16] *IH*, 'Foreword by the Author to the First English Edition'.
[17] M. Eliade, *The Sacred and the Profane* (New York: Harcourt Brace & World, 1959), 11.
[18] Tillich, *Systematic Theology*, i. 215. For comments on this supposition see G. Marcel, 'The Sacred in the Technological Age', *Theology Today*, 19 (1962), 27.
[19] Willink, *Holy and Living God*, 110 f.

relations will become clear. And although, categorically, the holy will not, so to speak, sit still, the very impossibility of a full empirical analysis of holy objects can actually give us a clue to the transcendent nature and value of holiness for religious people.

There is, of course, a sense in which the holy is not anything at all. For if the holiness of things is the sign of a relation to the divine, then the significance of that relation must not be mistaken for the object itself. From a Protestant or Jewish perspective, to say that a material object is intrinsically holy is the beginning of idolatry. Holiness is only mediated in and by the world, whether in human consciousness or natural objects. In the Old Testament, because God's distinction lies in being imageless, little provokes such furious divine jealousy, or 'calls forth such threats of dire catastrophe', so readily as idolatry.[20] Holy people or objects remain as natural objects, but are at the same time concentrations of symbolic power. As mediums or ciphers of that power, their own significance is negated or relativized by their supernatural reference. Their power becomes demonic rather than holy if they are allowed to appropriate that divine power to command fear and veneration for themselves.[21] Thus Emil Brunner: 'Even the most horrible idol tells us something about the secret of the Holy.'[22]

If an entity is categorized by its cause and origin, it can be stated without hesitation that holiness originates in the very abyss of the Godhead. Therefore, at whatever remove, holy things belong to the category of divine things. Holiness cannot be reified—it is not a quality of objects, but a spiritual 'seal of approval' marking its inclusion in the divine scheme. As such, although it is attributed to concrete objects of sense experience, those objects are experienced as such only in the

[20] I. Efros, *Ancient Jewish Philosophy: A Study in Metaphysics* (Detroit: Wayne State University Press, 1964), 8. See also A. B. Davidson, *The Theology of the Old Testament* (Edinburgh: T. & T. Clark, 1904), 150; Exod. 20: 4; Deut. 4: 15–19, 5: 8.

[21] Tillich, *Systematic Theology*, i. 218. See also i. 216; *idem, The Protestant Era* (London: Nisbet, 1955), 123; S. Spencer, 'Religion, Morality and the Sacred', *Hibbert Journal*, 28 (1930), 351–3.

[22] E. Brunner, *Man in Revolt* (London: Lutterworth Press, 1947), 180.

spiritual, intuitive discernment of faith. In this connection, it is telling that archaeologists identify sacred objects by default: if the object is clearly useless—that is, it is not something like a comb or a spear-head—it is often labelled 'cult object for religious purposes'.[23]

What holiness *is* cannot be said in the sense that I might say what a beach or a deck-chair *is*. It may be that one can only skirt the peripheries of a definition of holiness with a good deal of symbolic and mythological language, perhaps defining pre-conditions for an object to be holy, but not actually saying what holiness as such is like.

Two further considerations must be borne in mind when attempting to establish the ontological status of holiness. First, holiness cannot be 'handled'. The holiness of a thing is not 'detachable' in the way that a stain can be rinsed out of a piece of cloth. And the psycho-biological reaction to a holy object or situation may show no discernible difference from that of other psychic events.[24] Although more subtle, it is still inadequate to say that an object is holy because of its psychological effect on those handling or worshipping it. To reduce holiness merely to the measure of its psychological effect is to say something about the human mind rather than the category itself. Certainly, the power mediated by a holy object might be called 'awesome' as it precipitates an emotion best described as 'awe'. To say that holiness is awesome adds to our categorical knowledge of holiness *as experienced*, but not to holiness-in-itself, which is not dependent on the emotional response it may or may not evoke.

It seems, then, that the holiness of an object cannot be analysed apart from the salvific function of the object. Second, holiness is, following Otto, supra-conceptual or, as he prefers, 'non-rational'. So the concept of holiness cannot be taught as mathematics might be taught in the experience of dealing with quantities of objects. There are no scientific procedures whereby holiness can be differentiated from that

---

[23] S. Clark, *The Mysteries of Religion* (Oxford: Blackwell, 1986), 8.
[24] See C. Windquist and D. Winzenz, 'Altered States of Consciousness: Sacred and Profane', *Anglican Theological Review*, 56 (1974), 181–9.

which is not holy, and even attempting to design them would be a denial of its transcendent otherness, and a category mistake to boot.

The ontological status of holy objects and persons is no different from that of any natural object of the same class: they can all be perceived as natural objects by sense experience. Moreover, the object, whether it is a *Sefer Torah* or an icon, is not revered for its natural qualities, but for its translucence as a 'window' to the mystery, power, and value of the holy.[25] Although the holiness of things cannot be perceived through sense experience, by manifesting the sacred, an object becomes something else whilst continuing to remain itself.[26] But what precisely the object becomes and how it has become so remain open to question.

S. S. Acquaviva has spoken of how the hierophanic object 'ceases to be what it was and acquires a new character': it is ontologically transformed.[27] Whilst Jewish and Protestant theology would be wary of associating holiness with any transubstantiatory function, to claim that a person is spiritually transformed by reunion with the divine through the operation of holiness is not controversial. This is because a person, who is both a material object and an agent of consciousness, is trans-categorical in the way that a rock or a piece of wood is not.

Realists would want to say that the holiness of a time, place, person, or object subsists independently of their own propositional acts. Yet holiness is not an item in the world. It has no natural explanation, no material, substantive instance, no quantity.[28] Nor is it a predicate of things in the way that 'redness' or 'softness' might respectively be predicated of ripe tomatoes or cats' fur. There are no procedures by which holiness might be recognized, either by sceptic or sacramentalist, as a quality of objects. There is no perceptible factor common to holy objects, but only a common disposition towards them that can be summarized as a special sort of

---

[25] See Eliade, *Quest*, 52.   [26] Eliade, *Sacred and Profane*, 12.
[27] S. S. Acquaviva, *L'Eclipse du sacre dans la civilisation industrielle* (Tours: Mame, 1967), 61 f.; quoted in Davies, *Every Day God*, 26.   [28] See *COH* 16–26.

respect. There is no sensory quality common to holy objects such as smell, colour, or audibility, however sublime each of those might be. There is no apparent molecular difference between a vial of holy water that has been blessed and that from a household tap. Objects do not vibrate with holiness. This leaves us with a choice. Either the predicate 'holy' is semantically superfluous, since it contributes nothing to the empirical description of a thing and is not involved in establishing its existence,[29] or the predicate is retained by arguing that an empirical analysis of holiness is a category mistake.

For an Orthodox theologian, an icon's holiness is not merely a ritual or linguistic convention. The holiness of an icon does not simply reside in the habitual use to which it is put. Arguably, it is not enough to say that an icon is holy because it has a function in religion. Rather, it has a function in religious devotion *because* it is perceived as holy. On the other hand, its holiness is not a magical ingredient of the wood and paint. It is, for Jews and Protestants at least, 'superstitious' to treat an object with special consideration because of supposed powers resident in the object itself.[30] The holy object may offer access to supernatural power, but only as a medium.

Withdrawn from a reliquary, a saint's knuckles will look and feel identical to the knuckle bones of any human skeleton. But a Catholic will have a different psychological response to them than a Jew offered the same bones to handle. This implies that the holiness of the bones resides not in the bones themselves but in the relationship of the bones to the theology or metaphysics of the subject. That a Catholic may feel reverence and a Jew mere curiosity or repugnance seems to show that holiness is not a quality of objects but, at least in part, a quality of how the object is perceived interacting

[29] See D. Bastow, 'Otto and Numinous Experience', *Religious Studies*, 12 (1976), 166.

[30] A 'superstitious' idea of the holy is undoubtedly still a part of living religion. In Y. Eliach, *Hasidic Tales of the Holocaust* (New York: Oxford University Press, 1982), 92–4, the Berkowitz family recount how their survival was ensured by carrying their holy books with them at all times. Cf. e.g. G. Van der Leeuw, *Religion in Essence and Manifestation* (London: Allen & Unwin, 1938), 37–42; K. Thomas, *Religion and the Decline of Magic* (London: Weidenfeld & Nicolson, 1971), 51, 53.

with a vast network of largely inherited metaphysical and religious assumptions. O. R. Jones makes a related contribution to this point. He argues that people are aware of holiness not as an extra quality of things but as something intellectually discerned in an object. He gives the example of the meaning of the word 'useful' in conjunction with a lawnmower. The usefulness of the lawnmower is not 'seen' in the same way as the colour of its paint might be seen. It is in the intellectual sense of the word 'see' that its usefulness is discerned —that is, when a 'whole complex of facts' about lawns and machinery has been grasped.[31] Similarly, while holiness may be related to certain observable phenomena such as paintings, graves, or persons, their significance as holy is dependent not on observable features so much as on an intellectual discernment of their relationship to certain structures of belief.

Holiness and the Category of Relation

It may be that the concept of 'possession' or 'belonging' holds a clue to the nature of holiness.[32] As Flesseman contends, 'strictly speaking holiness can only be attributed to God himself; only he is holy. But all things which in some way belong to the divine realm become holy too.' An object or person is holy, then, in becoming God's 'special possession'. To become a possession of God, the object must be separated from profanity: 'for nothing which is unholy can be in the presence of the divine'.[33]

The image of a holy object, person, or stretch of time as God's possession illuminates its particular significance for theology, since possessions reflect the character and

---

[31] COH 24.

[32] It is noteworthy that shamans and prophets are referred to as spiritually 'possessed'. Cf. COH 92–7. But where Jones finds the meaning of holy things to be in their participation in the 'personal wholeness' of the divine, I point only to their relation to specific historical acts of divine will. See also Willink, Holy and Living God, 20.

[33] E. Flesseman, 'Old Testament Ethics', Student World, 57 (1964), 220.

preferences of their owner. In the mundane world, a person's property may represent an extension of her or his personality. This is particularly so in the sentimental value and interest attached to personally significant items of a dead woman or man's effects such as letters, photographs, and diaries. A more melodramatic example of the ability of possessions to reveal the character of their owners might be that of a photograph of an unknown woman found in the pocket of, say, a deceased film star. Such a photograph possesses far greater significance as the treasured possession of a great celebrity than the same picture on sale at a flea market, where there is no evidence of its intimate relation to the life history of a notable person.

Theologically, holy things and persons may stimulate the sense of the divine presence in the world. They present the divine will to history. Holiness is, then, a relational quality of things that participate in both divine consciousness and its reception in history.[34] Like the film star's treasured photograph, an object's significance lies in its intimate relation to its owner, or, in this case, to that divine power which has taken possession of its being.[35] That holiness is relational rather than substantial is the insight driving Otto's marriage of holiness and the emotions. It must be stressed, however, that the judgement of manifested holiness as a category of relation is not a purely philosophical judgement, but is dependent on the way holiness is understood within the concepts of revelation and divine will.

It has been shown that the holiness of things is best explained in terms of a person's relation to what the thing *signifies*.[36] This is not a variant of the 'dispositional' argument, in which holiness describes only a subject's attitude towards an object. Holiness is operational between two conscious

---

[34] See H. Ringgren, *The Prophetical Conception of Holiness* (Uppsala: Universitets Arsskrift, 1948), 13. He supports Baudissin in saying that the holy does not denote a quality, but a relation to divinity and the divine sphere. See also J. E. Fison, *The Blessing of The Holy Spirit* (London: Longman, Green & Co., 1950), 43; J. Z. Smith, *Imagining Religion: From Babylon to Jonestown* (Chicago: University of Chicago Press, 1982), 55. [35] Cf. *COH* 50, 91.
[36] See Davies, *Every Day God*, 125 f., for a parallel understanding of holiness as a relational category; Davidson, *Theology of the Old Testament*, 145 f.

parties, God and a human being, with the initiative understood to have come from God. However, as more a product
of the divine salvific initiative than of its historical reception,
holiness is originally a supernatural category. The holy object,
whether a person or a thing, is a symbol or 'pointer' towards
the transcendent, a symbol whose relation to the holy has
the power to awaken the sense of the holy as such. So the
holiness of ritual and natural objects is not an ordinary predicate, but consists in the relationship of the object to the
transcendent reality of which it is a fitting symbol.[37]

Spiritual (and often physical) welfare has traditionally been
considered to be dependent on a correct relation to the holy.
If an object has been hallowed by God, then it is important
not as a locus of power that might be harnessed and put to
work for human advantage, but as a vehicle of the divine
presence and will. Holiness is God's communication to the
created world. In the biblical scheme it is non-rationally
received by what Otto would call 'numinous experience', then
'translated' into the concepts wherein 'heaven' and earth
are shown in the crisis of engagement. This encounter of
the finite and the eternal is then accommodated within the
rational or conceptual structures of covenant, exhortation,
sacrifice, and proclamation. So by venerating the object as
holy, whether it be a person, a text, or a natural phenomenon, women and men participate in the history of salvific
mediation between God and themselves.

The Bible does not confine holiness to God's own nature.
By covenant and exhortation, God's holiness is, in Mackintosh's quaint phrase, 'perpetually striving to convey itself to
His frail and polluted children'.[38] By appointment to holiness,
God is present in and related to the world by his will and
command; the holiness of persons and things is a witness to
God's glory. Here, holiness, as the extension of divine will
into history, is not the panentheistic diffusion of God in
creation. Rather, in the course of salvation history, God's

---

[37] Cf. A. Grossman, 'Holiness', in A. A. Cohen and P. Mendes Flohr (eds.),
Contemporary Jewish Religious Thought (New York: Free Press, 1988), 390.

[38] H. R. Mackintosh, *The Christian Apprehension of God* (London: SCM Press,
1929), 156.

holiness may become manifest in the world in designated hallowed forms. That these hallowed forms are 'approved' by God does not alter their physical properties. The holiness of things like the Torah, prophets, saints, rituals, holy scriptures, or icons resides in their being vessels of divine self-revelation: they are public witnesses to God's holiness for a given community of faith. The holy object becomes, so to speak, God's property.[39] And since in some real sense God has initiated its separation from profane objects, its holiness is more than just a human way of seeing or using an object with special respect. To faith, holy things are holy because they belong to God, entailing their objective, rather than subjective, holiness.

The holy object mediates a message, whether it be a prophetic warning of judgement against those who violate what belongs to God, a gospel, or a set of commands. Holy things become signs or pointers to the transcendent. In order to mediate the salvific message, the *evangelion*, they come to participate in the reality to which they point. Their holiness is thereby instrumental in the processes of revelation in salvation history. On God's side, the holy object conveys his will to humanity; on humanity's side, the holy thing becomes a means to love, venerate, and obey God. The reverence shown to a holy thing is ultimately referred back to the object of worship: the holy thing's creator and appointee.

Christian and Jewish theology teaches that God created humans to be holy like himself, and that the purpose of life is to attain this end.[40] Appointed by God, holy things have expressive power as vehicles of supernatural meaning, and are a means to the achievement of personal holiness, as demanded by God. Holiness is received in what Otto has called 'numinous experience': a mystery of such intense value that the self is entirely subsumed within it. The absolute claim of holy value means that to those participant in its story, death is preferred to the possible violation of a holy thing.

---

[39] That the holy belongs to God, either by a human sacrificial gift or by its issuing from the divine sphere, is an ancient biblical idea. See Ringgren, *Prophetical Conception of Holiness*, 7, 11; *COH* 90–7.

[40] Sherry, *Spirit, Saints and Immortality*, 72. See also e.g. Lev. 19: 2.

As historically decisive in the relationship between God and humanity, the perception of the holiness of objects appointed by God as instruments of his self-revelation is more than a merely aesthetic judgement.[41] There is, however, a second class of holy things which create what Otto calls a 'numinous impression'. This may take a variety of forms. For example, participation in a momentous and solemn religious assembly may stimulate the sense of the holy.[42] It might also be stimulated by the atmosphere of locations associated with religion, such as the darkened interior of a cathedral or a neolithic stone circle. Or, more generally, a certain quality of light or a sublime landscape or piece of music which is without explicit theistic reference might, in a preliminary and diffuse way, stimulate intuitions of a numinous realm of meaning and value.[43] The sense of holiness stimulated by these situations or objects is primarily a religio-aesthetic event. This class of holiness does not mediate the 'Word' but may, in H. D. Lewis's words, 'help in an outstanding way to induce the religious mood and prompt its distinctive insights'. A landscape, for example, may become 'a focus of religious experience'. Its wildness, vastness, serenity, or remoteness may, writes Lewis (following Otto), establish 'an association between natural fact and religious concept'.[44] I would add that the more religiously diffuse sense of holiness described here, or in any of Otto's haunting examples, arises from their association with a given idea of God.[45] Certain personalistic emotions attributed to God, like wrath or love, may be symbolized for the individual subject by the form or atmosphere of the object or scene as it moves the spirit: 'this inborn capacity to receive and understand' numinous impressions.[46] So, for example, meditation on land that has

[41] M. Scheler, *On The Eternal in Man* (London: SCM Press, 1960), 316.

[42] *IH* 60 f.

[43] See W. A. Claydon, 'The Numinous in the Poetry of Wordsworth', *Hibbert Journal*, 28 (1930), 603, 607, 609.

[44] H. D. Lewis, *Our Experience of God* (London: Allen & Unwin, 1959), 179 f. On p. 180 Lewis strenuously rejects on Otto's behalf those popularizers of Otto's work who make 'misleading allusions to the alleged numinous quality of certain things and places'.   [45] See *IH* 40–9, 60–71.

[46] *IH* 61.

been devastated by agricultural monoculture or acid rain might evoke the sense of what the world is like when divine holiness has been exiled by technological desacralization and environmental destruction; contemplation of a new-born child or a fruit-laden orchard, that of the presence of holiness in blessings.

This area of our discussion is not problematic. Although an important privilege of, and stimulus to, the life of religion, these aesthetic events are considered by biblical theologians, including Otto, to be feelings *associated* with the numinous and therefore preliminary (and sometimes incidental) to the category of holiness as previously discussed.[47] The place, object, or situation may be a powerful metaphor for the holy or numinous, and may propose a concept of holiness, which being itself non-rational, cannot be conceived other than by metaphor. But the religio-aesthetic experience, though a part of the spiritual life as a whole, is not understood by most theologians as an instance in which God is present in the direct expression of his will as revelation. The religio-aesthetic impression is a private intuition: an aesthetic judgement stimulating spiritual self-transformation and possibly readiness for the reception of full divine revelation.[48]

In sum, the ontological character of holiness has been described as a metaphysical category of relation. It can be conceived as a non-natural, non-material attribute of objects or states of personal being which have been ontologically transformed through their appointment by God as mediums of the salvific relationship in the history of his self-revelation. It is when objects and persons 'belong' to God that they create what Otto calls a 'numinous impression'. Personal holiness is to be distinguished from the holiness of things, since the human personality is ontologically 'fitted' to receive holiness

---

[47] See *IH* 42. See also A. Hardy, *The Divine Flame* (London: Collins, 1966), ch. 5, 'The Numinous, the Love of Nature and the Inspiration of Art'.

[48] Cf. Tillich, *Systematic Theology*, i. 216. Despite correctly calling Otto's work 'theology', Tillich mistakes Otto's concept of holiness as sharing Schleiermacher's tendency to deny that holiness belongs to the sphere of the divine and to locate it in the realm of the aesthetic-emotional. This is inaccurate. In fact, Otto never treats the aesthetic as more than a preliminary to religion proper, and the emotions are significant only as a key to religious perception of the divine object.

by virtue of its soul and conscience. Unlike holy objects, holy people are not merely 'requisitioned' to the salvific scheme. On the contrary, even if God wills it, it is only by the passion of their own will to holiness that people attain a form of likeness to God. Admittedly, in what that likeness might consist is obscure, since 'likeness' to a category lying outside possible knowledge undermines any hope of conceptual precision.[49]

Holiness defines deity: it qualifies all other divine attributes. Yet its enigmatic quality rests in its being both essential and communicable as an attribute of divine consciousness in extension.[50] God's will, command, revelation, and creation are all functions of his self-projection in time and space. Whatever participates in the extension of divine consciousness is holy. As the expression of divine will and consciousness, holy things are symbols of ultimate *sui generis* value. Otto holds the value of holiness to be non-rational or non-conceptual—whereas the values of goodness and beauty, so often mistaken for holiness itself, are conceivable and culturally relative. Holy value is first apprehended as the *mysterium tremendum*, and cannot be described in itself. Rather, it is 'contained' by the symbolic theological structures discussed above. The holy is inevitably articulated in the rational categories of the mind and of mundane experience that evoke, rather than describe, the nature of holiness.

[49] See Duquoc and Floristàn, *Models of Holiness*, p. vii.
[50] Cf. Mackintosh, *Christian Apprehension of God*, 156.

2

Das Heilige in Context

For at least two decades, Otto's *The Idea of the Holy* brought the concept of holiness to greater prominence in academic and popular circles than it had previously enjoyed. Of course Otto did not discover the category of the holy. The originality of Otto's work and its place within theistic belief cannot be measured, therefore, without due attention to developments in the concept of holiness both prior and subsequent to his work. This chapter will survey the history of the concept of holiness in twentieth-century theology and biblical criticism (rather than the phenomenology of the sacred), for it is the theistic dynamics of Otto's work with which I am concerned.

Holiness and the History of Religions

The concept of holiness largely owes its existence as a concept to the development of a new discipline: comparative religion. It was comparative religion, or the science of religion, which provided philosophical theology with its present generic understanding of holiness as a metaphysical category rather than, as previously, a mode of spiritually desirable behaviour. As will be shown, late nineteenth-century comparative accounts of holiness as a cross-cultural and trans-historical 'essence of religion' were a major catalyst in the shift in application of the concept of holiness. In addition, Wilhelm Windelband's essay on holiness as a metaphysical value,[1] and

[1] W. Windelband, 'The Sacred', in *An Introduction to Philosophy* (London: T. Fisher & Unwin, 1921; orig. pub. 1898), 323–33.

then Otto's subsequent use of the word 'holy' as a noun, have been strongly influential.

The ground for speculative interest in the holy had been prepared in the sixteenth and seventeenth centuries. Exploration, trade, and Christian missions to the East and to the Americas were bringing back material (if less than objectively observed) on native religion which could feed a nascent comparativism. Eighteenth-century gentleman scholars of religion, often loosely called deists, were using such material (incomplete as it was) to question the Christian claim to a unique revelation by finding a common, natural religion behind all positive religions, irrespective of particular revelation. Rationalists found evidence in the world's religions that the Christian revelation was not the axis on which the world turned —thereby challenging the intellectual and spiritual hegemony of the Church. More radically, David Hume used primitive religions as evidence that all religion had evolved from fear and superstition. And since the Age of Reason had grown out of superstition, it was also free to dispense with religion. Late eighteenth- and early nineteenth-century romanticism, whilst also critical of Judaeo-Christian dogmatism, did not cast aside the elemental religious impulse, but instead fired its imagination with the 'strange' religions of 'old' Europe and the East. Their sense of the mysterious found its way into Otto's concept of holiness—most obviously via Schleiermacher, for whom institutional and scriptural revelations were secondary to the immediate, private feeling of the divine.

Although romantic appreciation of the 'purity' of primal religion continued to influence scholarship (and is apparent in Otto's work), the twentieth-century development of the concept of holiness really began with the scientific study of religion. The science of religion has its roots in Darwinist evolutionary theory. In mid-nineteenth-century comparativist circles Darwinism had provided a method of uncovering the historical and spiritual laws governing the development of religion from the primal to Christianity; in short, a science of religions. Anthropologists and historians of religion were beginning to realize that the Christian tradition did not arise in a vacuum, but was part of a history of religious ideas in which certain elements recurred. The key to these common elements was the idea of the sacred or holy, which, common to the world's religions, could provide a valuable hermeneutical tool in the analysis of the origins and practice of primitive religion.[2] It took these studies and Otto's *Das Heilige* to awaken holiness from its moralist slumbers; and then only in some academic circles.

But the practice of the science of religion was not necessarily a way of undermining the Christian tradition; far from it. Like James Frazer and Edward Tylor, F. Max Müller contended that the very history of all human religion—a natural predisposition to search for the divine—is a process of general revelation, of which the life of Christ is the fulfilment.[3] And the Christian bias remained even when, during the last two decades of the nineteenth century, the new anthropological field-work (much facilitated by colonialism) replaced Müller's armchair linguistics and philology. Often conducted in the Pacific islands, field research was based on an assumption that religion is a unified, continuous, and evolving category in which a sense of the uncanny evolves into a belief in supernatural beings or gods. Deeply influenced by Darwinism, anthropologists looked at how the rites and customs of primitive peoples were a witness to the unfolding history of religion (as indeed was European folklore). The moralism and anti-sacramentalism of European Protestantism naturally fed the comfortable assumption that rational Protestant culture itself represented the final stage of religion's evolution from magical rites.

Nevertheless, Christian apologetics were not an urgent motive of the history of religions. The need to understand the essential nature of religion as a whole was of more immediate interest. Otto was not the only writer to suppose that the origin of religion would be its explanation. He was not alone in assuming that on the basis of linear evolution, the earliest

[2] C. Welch, *Protestant Thought in the Nineteenth Century* (New Haven: Yale University Press, 1985), ii. 117 f.
[3] See P. Byrne, *Natural Religion and the Nature of Religion* (London: Routledge, 1989), 192–4; F. M. Müller, *Anthropological Religion* (London: Longman, 1892); *idem*, *Introduction to the Science of Religion* (London: Longman, 1893).

religious beliefs of humanity could be inferred from the remaining primitive practices (what Tylor called 'survivals') available to observation at the end of the nineteenth century.[4] Working upon this assumption, early anthropologists of religion such as Robert Ranulph Marett took what they considered to be the earliest use of the concept of sacredness to unlock the mysteries of primitive religion, thereby revealing the fundamental nature of religion itself. In 1902, in *The Threshold of Religion*, Marett saw the Melanesian quasimagical term *mana* as 'the raw material of religion'. This term evokes a religious response prior to faith or knowledge. It is a feeling of the supernatural power and mystery of certain objects, and is best translated by the English word 'awe'.[5] Marett recognized that *mana* and taboo (which Otto was to identify with the primitive numinous) are quite independent of the moral dimension.[6] The following quotation illustrates what inspired Otto to say that Marett had come 'within a hair's breadth' of what he himself felt to be the truth about the essence of holiness:[7]

Mana is selected by me for special emphasis merely because it comes nearer than any other available term to the bare designation of that positive emotional value which is the raw material of religion, and needs only to be moralized—to be identified with goodness—to become its essence.[8]

Marett finds the negative element of *mana* to be the taboo; the two together define the fundamentals of religion. The taboo shows that an object or person has been set apart from common use, and therefore implies interdiction or danger, since the taboo alerts one to its supernatural power or *mana*.[9]

But scientific methods of studying religion also informed reductionist accounts of the psychological and social functions of religion, among which were those of Wilhelm Wundt,

[4] See J. Daniélou, 'Phenomenology of Religions and Philosophy of Religion', in M. Eliade and J. Kitagawa (eds.), *The History of Religions: Essays in Methodology* (Chicago: University of Chicago Press, 1959), 67.
[5] R. R. Marett, *The Threshold of Religion* (London: Methuen, 1924), 13.
[6] Ibid. 112. [7] *IH* 15 n. 1. [8] Marett, *Threshold of Religion*, p. xxxi.
[9] Ibid. 119.

Freud, Weber, and Durkheim, who were, for different reasons, concerned with the nature, function, and origins of religion in the collective mind.[10] Their methodological atheism was to put a previously unknown distance between culture and theology, in that the experience of the holy could now become an object of secular research. By the turn of the nineteenth century, religion could be investigated empirically and historically as an element of human and cultural development. Freud, for example, was to argue in a paper published in 1919, 'Das Unheimliche', that the feeling of the uncanny was explicable as a re-awakening of repressed infantile neurosis when naïve childhood beliefs are revived during certain untoward experiences in adulthood.[11] Significantly, he did not refer to Otto, whose views on the subject must have been well known to the intelligentsia by that time. Otto, by contrast, had argued that the tingling dread, or 'primordial emotional disturbance', of the uncanny was the underivable impulse to which one could trace the origins of religion.[12]

The works of Freud, Wundt (whose *Elemente der Völkerpsychologie* was published between 1900 and 1920), and Durkheim, who was influenced by Wundt in his *Les Formes élementaires de la vie religieuse* of 1912, were all engaged in forms of scientific reductionism that Otto and Nathan Söderblom would contest.[13] Working independently of Söderblom, Otto objected to Wundt's theory that religion is derived rationally from the concept of the soul. For Otto, the essence of religion is *sui generis*: the numinous. With reductionism in mind, in 1904 Otto wrote the polemical *Naturalism and Religion* to demonstrate the inadequacy of science to explain

---

[10] The material is too copious to refer to in a single footnote, but see e.g. Freud's comments on the holy in *Moses and Monotheism* (London: Hogarth Press, 1964), 120 f.

[11] See L. Dawson, 'Otto and Freud on the Uncanny and Beyond', *JAAR* 57/2 (1989), 286 f.   [12] *IH* 14–16.

[13] For Otto's response to Wundt's theory, see *IH* 118; Otto's article, 'The Sensus Numinis as the Historical Basis of Religion', *Hibbert Journal*, 30 (1931–2), 287, 420, 429; *RO* 61 f., 64; *ROR* 9. For Söderblom's response to Durkheim's theory that the sacred is merely an objectification of societal power over and against that of the individual, see his article 'Holiness: General and Primitive', 732; B. Meland, *The Realities of Faith* (New York: Oxford University Press, 1962), 340.

spiritual experience. Likewise, in 1913 Söderblom rejected the naturalistic reductionism in Durkheim's theory that the sacred is an objectification and idealization of the power of the community over and against the individual. That Otto and Söderblom stressed the non-human source of an individual's immediate and self-authenticating experience of holiness clearly differentiated their work from that of the sociology of the sacred.[14]

Söderblom's application of anthropological findings to the concept of holiness is particularly relevant to the present study. Söderblom brought the Western sense of the holy into explicit comparison with ethnographic data on *mana* and taboo. In this he accepted and made use of the work of empiricists. But while the empiricist refuses to speculate on the transcendental meanings of religious phenomena, Söderblom 'peers beyond those findings to their ultimate significance'.[15] He finds the origin of the concept of holiness —and hence religion—to lie in the subjective mental reaction of astonishment and terror. And objectively, the origin of religion lies in the cause of that elemental religious experience: the power—called variously, *mana, orenda, wakenda,* as the culture prescribes—which is resident in certain objects.[16] Söderblom argues that in primitive religion the taboo is simply an interdiction; an alarm bell to signify danger. Originally, the taboo did not even differentiate between cleanliness or purity and uncleanness or pollution, as illustrated by Plutarch's uncertainty as to whether the Jews worshipped or abhorred the pig.[17] Yet crucially, Söderblom, unlike other writers on holiness of the time, is not embarrassed by the conceptual origins of Christian holiness. On the contrary, the primitive concept of holiness has profound significance in tracing the connections of one religion to another. Believing that a religious person is one for whom something is holy,[18] Söderblom's declaration that it is more essential to have a concept of holiness than one of God, that there is no genuine

---

[14] Sharpe, *Nathan Söderblom,* 171.   [15] Ibid. p. xxi.
[16] Söderblom, 'Holiness: General and Primitive', 732.   [17] Ibid. 736.
[18] See Sharpe, *Nathan Söderblom,* 155.

religion without a distinction between the sacred and the profane,[19] can be seen as a turning-point in the rediscovery of the holy.[20]

Söderblom wants to restore the properly transcendental quality of holiness by reminding theologians that the origin of the Christian concept of holiness is in *quadosh*: that which is set apart from normal life. He regrets the Protestant attempt to abolish the externality of this distinction in favour of an interior perspective which tries to bring life in its totality under the auspices of the holy by a moral or spiritual reformation. He fears that it will lead to the secularization of religion.[21] Like Otto, Söderblom welcomes the ethical evolution of holiness, but at the same time wishes to retain at least the vestiges of its essential non-rationality or mystery—vestiges which Otto's *Das Heilige* attempts to uncover and restore.

The comparativism of both Söderblom and Otto qualified them as forerunners of the phenomenology of religion: they attempted to organize, observe, and empathize with all religious consciousness, and so isolate the essence of religion. But as Eric Sharpe has pointed out of Söderblom[22] (and it is equally true of Otto), neither used the phenomenological method as it would be used in the inter-war years, particularly in Holland and Scandinavia. Although most phenomenologists of religion, from Chantepie de la Saussaye (1848–1920) to C. Jouco Bleeker (1898–1983), were also Christian theologians,[23] Dutch scholars like W. Brede Kristensen and Bleeker did attempt to study religion without making value-judgements or imposing evolutionary unilinear schemes. Their methodology separated the practice of speculative theology from the science and history of religions. That this is so may be seen in Kristensen's disapproval of Otto's attempt to practice both at once.[24]

---

[19] Söderblom, 'Holiness: General and Primitive', 731.
[20] See Y. Brilioth's biographical introduction to Söderblom's *The Living God* (London: Oxford University Press, 1933), p. xix, where he states that Söderblom's theory of 1913 'anticipates' Otto's work on holiness.
[21] Söderblom, 'Holiness: General and Primitive', 737.
[22] Sharpe, *Nathan Söderblom*, p. xx.
[23] Sharpe, *Comparative Religion*, 237.
[24] W. B. Kristensen, *The Meaning of Religion* (The Hague: M. Nijhoff, 1960),

The Ethicization of Ritual Sacramentalism

It will be noticeable that most attention is given here to Protestant scholarship on holiness and to developments within the concept in Protestant thought. There are two reasons for this. First, Protestantism is Otto's own tradition. And second, Protestant theology works with a basically ethical concept of holiness: an analysis which Otto's arguments would assume and in many ways reject. The history of religions had uncovered tensions in the relationship between numinous power and the moral power of the holy, tensions which would, as we will see, create some of Otto's greatest difficulties as he tried to hold the two together in his own concept of holiness. It is only to be expected that the concept of holiness has developed within both the history of religions and theology. If holiness is held to be both the essence of all religion and, at the same time, the only logically appropriate definition and ontological qualification of any concept of God, it will be indispensable to both disciplines in their most generalized and inclusive forms.

At the turn of the century it became common, principally in liberal Protestant circles, to assume that the 'primitive' sacramental sacerdotal holiness of the Hebrews had been superseded by an ethical concept of holiness championed by the prophets and Jesus, who sought to liberate the holy from ancient Semitic superstition. This view of modern religion as continuous with its ancient pre-moral forms has a long history: holiness in Protestant theology has usually referred to God's moral goodness, and its emphasis on inner experience of God has meant that it has tended 'to think of holiness almost exclusively in personal and inward terms'.[25] As late as 1953, the Methodist scholar Joseph Baines Atkinson wrote, 'To the mind of the average person today

16–18. See also Bastow, 'Otto and Numinous Experience', 168–70; N. Smart, 'Truth and Religions', in J. Hick (ed.), *Truth and Dialogue* (London: Sheldon Press, 1974), 55.

[25] A. Allchin, 'Holiness in the Anglican Tradition', in M. Chavchavadze (ed.), *Man's Concern with Holiness*, 41. See also *COH* 56–60.

the essence of holiness is goodness.'[26] And this probably still holds true today, especially in evangelical Christian communities where holiness is a process of sanctification by moral purity of heart.

Ethnographic data had confirmed nineteenth-century Protestant moralist prejudice. In *The Christian Doctrine of Justification and Reconciliation*, Albrecht Ritschl proposed that divine holiness be dropped from Christian theology on the grounds that its interests were sufficiently accounted for by the idea of divine love. Ritschl contends that holiness is irrelevant for Christians, since its Old Testament meaning is obsolete and its meaning in the New Testament obscure. Moreover, he is offended by the results of Old Testament scholarship which show God's holiness to be far from equivalent to moral perfection, and therefore incompatible with the morality of divine love revealed by Christ.[27] To Protestants of the late nineteenth century, cultic holiness appeared too disreputable a conceptual relic to summarize the moral and spiritual perfection of the divine nature.

The results of ethnographic investigation had confirmed Christian prejudices, but had also offered reassurances that Christianity was the fulfilment of the evolution of holiness across two testaments. Biblical criticism of the Old Testament concept of holiness, as having been informed by primitive Semitic religious practices, could differentiate Christianity from Hebrew superstition. And the belief that the prophets themselves had challenged a cultic-magical concept of holiness in turn sustained the notion that theism had been evolving from the biblical period to its fulfilment in the Protestant Church.

The 'received' turn-of-the-century account of the transition of holiness from superstition to morality reconstructs the Hebrew concept of holiness as falling short of its Protestant counterpart. The former is territorial, nationalistic, intermittent in appearance, mediated by a priestly hierarchy, centred

---

[26] J. B. Atkinson, *The Beauty of Holiness* (London: Epworth Press, 1953), 21.

[27] A. Ritschl, *The Christian Doctrine of Justification and Reconciliation* (Edinburgh: T. & T. Clark, 1900), 274. Cf. Mackintosh's reply to Ritschl in *Christian Apprehension of God*, 155.

and concentrated in the temple cult, and separated from the experience of ordinary believers.[28] And in common with other primitive religions, holiness in Hebrew observance is cast as a quasi-physical positive quality of things derived from close contact with supernatural power, so that any confrontation with holiness would require prudence (rather than faith) in the face of the perceived perils of its sacred power.

Similarly, though much later, Johannes Pedersen argues that in the Hebrew mind, holiness cannot be seen as in a simple opposition to evil: 'In holiness psychic strength is so intensified that it rises above the contrasts of good and evil prevalent among men. The profane is equivalent to what is normal, what belongs to daily life.'[29] Other writers corroborate that holiness evokes not moral respect, but a form of fear: 'that which is holy is also dreadful and terrible.'[30] The power of holiness is generally symbolized by fire, earthquakes, smoke, and thunder. In a pre-scientific world, mighty natural phenomena parallel the way holiness 'surpasses what is *known* to ordinary human beings, hence they cannot control its laws, and do not know whether it will serve to strengthen or destroy them'.[31] The taboo is seen as an impersonal force activated against, for example, the cultic misdemeanours of King Azariah, Nadab, and Abihu and the impetuous behaviour towards the Ark for which Uzzah paid so dearly. Overall, these cases can be interpreted not so much as sin as carelessness: a failure to take the appropriate precautions against sacred power.[32]

In 1889 W. Robertson Smith confirmed for Christian apologists that ancient Hebrew religion was little more than superstition. He placed the earliest traditions of the Old

---

[28] See H. Wheeler Robinson, *The Religious Ideas of the Old Testament* (London: Duckworth, 1913), 130–3.

[29] J. Pedersen, *Israel III–IV* (London: Oxford University Press, 1940), 271.

[30] Ringgren, *Prophetical Conception of Holiness*, 10.

[31] See *COH* 31 f. For a full analysis of the fear of the holy, see ibid. 27–50.

[32] See Ringgren, *Prophetical Conception of Holiness*, 10. None the less, as H. Schwarz suggests of the Hebrew concept of holiness in *The Search for God* (London: SPCK, 1975), 190, 'while the essential aspect of holiness is that of power, it is power in the service of the God who uses all things to make his kingdom triumph . . . Holiness is always and particularly connected with the God of the covenant.'

Testament in their historical context in primitive Semitic religion, arguing that the rules of holiness in ancient Semitic religion have little to do with morality or purity of life.[33] The restrictions involved when dealing with sacred objects seemed formally identical to the rules of avoiding pollution or the unclean. Although the northern Semites had, he found, distinguished between the holy and the unclean, and so made 'a real advance above savagery', even in some 'advanced societies' there remained no clear distinction between them.[34]

The influential articles of R. H. Coats and O. C. Whitehouse are typical of the early twentieth-century Protestant concept of holiness. Whitehouse, like Smith, finds that 'the conception of holiness, when traced to its historic origins among Semitic peoples, is stripped of all the ethical qualities with which our Christian modern consciousness has invested it'.[35] Whitehouse believes that the destruction of the Temple accelerated the downfall of the ancient cultic, sacramental concept of holiness, with its affinities to primitive, magical taboo. It was replaced by the prophetic internalization of sacrificial law as seen, among other prophetic books, in Jeremiah's attempt to displace the 'externalities of ceremonial religion'.[36] And as Whitehouse puts it, this 'Umwertung aller Werte' can be traced through to Jesus's distinction between moral and ritual defilement in Mark 7: 15–23. The elevated morality of Jesus and the prophets had spurned the ancient Hebrew idea of holiness as a superstitious taboo and the punctilious legal codification of that taboo in Pharisaical Judaism.[37]

R. H. Coats's account of the Christian concept of holiness is typical of that prevalent until the publication of *The Idea of the Holy* and, in lay circles, well beyond it. He contends that despite vestigial Hebrew connotations in the Christian

---

[33] W. R. Smith, *The Religion of the Semites* (London: A. & C. Black, 1927), 140 f.
[34] Ibid. 153 f.
[35] O. C. Whitehouse, 'Holiness: Semitic', in Hastings (ed.), *Encyclopaedia of Religion and Ethics*, vi. 751.
[36] Ibid. 758.
[37] For a contemporary example of this tendency see Duquoc and Floristàn, *Models of Holiness*, pp. ix f. Jewish models of holiness are described with contempt, not for any disreputable numinous element, but for perpetuating the legalistic righteousness that Jesus is held to have condemned.

concept of holiness, these are now given 'inward spiritual sig-
nification' in light of the spiritual transformation of baptism.[38]
He offers an apology for Protestantism by arguing that the
Catholic concept of holiness, which he refers to with disdain
as 'a stream of forces in the sacraments' offering 'an infused
and almost quantitative grace' is 'corrected' by the Reformers'
democratized, fiduciary concept of holiness based upon the
religious experience of faith.[39]

Coats traces a shift from the sense of holiness expressed
by Judaic, reified, technical ceremonial acts to the Christian
quest for perfection: for goodness in will and deed without
ritual ostentation. Holiness is transferred to personal, moral
likeness to God—a God who is no longer a dangerous tribal
deity, but a loving father to guilty children.[40] As in Hebrews
12: 7–10, holiness comes to be seen as perfect moral sonship.
Above all, for Protestant theology, the Incarnation represented the self-abasement of the holy. The *evangelion* was that
the holy was now generally available to faith regardless of
cultic/legal status (or the monastic hierarchy of Catholicism)
and in a spirit of joy rather than dread. Indeed, the sacrifice
of Christ's body is held to abolish the sacrificial system of
the sanctification of things, rather than souls, offered to God
(1 Cor. 1: 30, Heb. 10: 14).[41] Although Coats makes some
faint concession to what could retrospectively be termed the
numinous by recognizing that the 'New Testament distin-
guishes holiness as something larger than morality', he also
anticipates what was to be the central plank of the criticism
of Otto's concept of holiness, and contends that Christianity
'knows of no divorce between holiness and virtue'. The distinction between holiness and virtue is, for Coats, quantitative, not qualitative.[42]

It will be apparent that Otto's stress on the terrifying,

---

[38] R. H. Coats, 'Holiness: New Testament and Christian', in Hastings (ed.),
Encyclopaedia of Religion and Ethics, vi. 743.　　　　　　　　　[39] Ibid. 747.
[40] See also A. D. Martin, *The Holiness of Jesus* (London: Allen & Unwin, 1934),
31, 324.
[41] Coats, 'Holiness: NT and Christian', 744. For a contemporary Catholic account
of the nature of Jesus's holiness, see Duquoc and Floristàn, *Models of Holiness*,
3–12.　　　　　　　　　[42] Coats, 'Holiness: NT and Christian', 745.

non-rational numinousness of the holy is out of key with the writings about holiness of other Christian theologians in the twentieth century. Although apparently confident that Christianity is the most refined, and therefore the best, of all religions, Otto undermines his claim by saying, in effect, that holiness at its most 'religious' in Christianity is as *unheimlich* a quality as it was at the time of the cult. More recently, however, writers have denied that the 'primitive' concept of holiness was ever sub-moral or sub-personal. Baines Atkinson, for example, disagrees with those claiming that holiness is devoid of morality until Isaiah. Morality may not, he says, have been dominant in primitive Hebrew religion; but the taboo may contain at least the germ of morality in its imposition of discipline and a sense of duty. Similarly, the primitive idea of the contagiousness of holiness need not be seen as superstitious but as a revelation of God's desire to share or communicate his holiness to his people.[43]

Clearly, holiness cannot be understood ethically without some degree of personalist predication of will to God. But O. R. Jones finds theistic personalism to be present in the very earliest Hebrew tradition. Consequently, fear of the holy is not that of an impersonal force like electricity, but rather the proper fear at the sense of the localized presence of Yahweh in the Holy of Holies or the Ark.[44] If this is so, the fate of the cultically careless (of which Uzzah is the classic example) can be interpreted less as merely breaking a taboo, than personalistically as the means by which the deity might reinforce the command to fear and respect his holiness.[45]

Whether or not an ethical, personalist element was present in the concept of holiness from its inception cannot be decided here. It can, however, be shown that the ethical and the 'primitive' concepts of holiness are at least continuous with one another, and can be seen contiguously in biblical texts. So it can be argued that 'obsolete' taboos were not straightforwardly *replaced* by a morally innovative concept of

[43] Atkinson, *Beauty of Holiness*, 22–8.   [44] *COH* 49 f.
[45] 2 Sam. 6: 6–8; Lev. 10: 1–2; 2 Chron. 26: 19–20. See also Robinson, *Religious Ideas of the Old Testament*, 131.

holiness, as was claimed at the turn of the century by writers such as Robertson Smith and Whitehouse. Rather, as Otto was to argue in the tenth and eleventh chapters of *The Idea of the Holy*, there was a gradual moral refinement of the concept of holiness, although the origins of the concept remain in evidence—whether vestigially in the forms of religion or in the emotional disturbances of religious experience.

H. R. Mackintosh, like Otto, finds the numinous *alone* to be an inadequate basis for a religion, and requires some degree of moralization. None the less, he detects a balance in the prophetic and New Testament texts suggesting that the element of awe and otherness did not disappear.[46] Mackintosh presents God as a 'living conjunction of the absolute good and the sacrosanct'.[47] Nearly two decades later, Helmer Ringgren rejected any sharp distinction between cult and ethics. He interprets prophecy as hostile not to the cult as such, but to certain misuses of it. Ringgren insists that with the prophets the idea of God becomes more ethical; not so the idea of holiness, which for some time to come remains separate from moralization: 'It seems likely that the notion of holiness retained so much of the old character of "*tremendum*" that it could not immediately be wholly transferred into the ethical sphere.'[48]

According to Ringgren, the mechanical conception of holiness can be traced in the later strands of the Old Testament, where holiness is still, for example in Ezekiel 44: 19, a 'powerful fluidum of some kind'. None the less, this conception is not idolatrous: here the holy has a divine source, and therefore belongs within the sphere of divine activity and power.[49] This is an important point. Even at the most crudely materialist states of its conception, holiness is never an inherent quality of a thing in itself; its power consists only in its relation to, or extension of, divine power and activity.[50]

---

[46] Mackintosh, *Christian Apprehension of God*, 150–3. Cf. Flesseman, 'Old Testament Ethics', 221.   [47] Mackintosh, *Christian Apprehension of God*, 156.

[48] Ringgren, *Prophetical Concept of Holiness*, 24. Fison, *Blessing of the Holy Spirit*, 50, also makes this point.   [49] Ringgren, *Prophetical Concept of Holiness*, 14.

[50] See e.g. Exod. 3: 5, 30: 25; Lev. 20: 3, 23: 20; 1 Kgs. 8: 4; Pss. 20: 6, 51: 11, 89: 7, 98: 1; Isa. 63: 10 f., 35: 8, 52: 1; Jer. 1: 5.

As Philip Jenson has argued of holiness in Priestly theology, holy things are not holy by themselves, but as appointed by God 'to create and sustain an ordered life and worship which will be consistent with the character of the God of Israel'.[51] As a means of cosmic ordering, cultic holiness has at least an equivalent 'spirituality' to that of the more obviously ethical prophetic concepts of holiness. Even in Judaism today, numinous power and moral righteousness are, as Flesseman recognizes, reflected in Torah, whose laws are both moral and ritual. Indeed, the numinous guarantees the ethical: 'Israel's ethics received their compelling force precisely through their dependence on the terrible and sublime holiness of God.'[52]

Scholars disagree over which testament an ethical concept of holiness emerged from. Yet even in the New Testament, a 'holy one' designates those who have undergone baptism and thereby entered the divine sphere, 'irrespective of their ethical qualifications'.[53] It seems unlikely that there was a permanent exchange of one concept of holiness as a form of *mana* for another as an ethical requirement. Söderblom writes that in the life of the Church, ' "holy" never became a merely ethical word, but chiefly suggests divine, supernatural power'. And he goes further: 'According to the history of religion itself, the conception of tabu results . . . in the idea of the supernatural.'[54] It is the sense of the supernatural, then, which spans the history of the concept of holiness, and hence religion as a whole.[55] Publishing between 1930 and 1950, writers on holiness such as J. E. Fison, A. D. Martin, and M. D. R. Willink were to follow his judgement that the ethical dimension gradually permeated holiness without ever eliminating the numinous.

The entire book of Isaiah is a case in point. Isaiah is a

---

[51] P. Jenson, *Graded Holiness: A Key to the Priestly Conception of the World* (Sheffield: JSOT Press, 1992), 215 f.

[52] Flesseman, 'Old Testament Ethics', 221.

[53] Ringgren, *Prophetical Conception of Holiness*, 30. See also ibid. 22 f.

[54] Söderblom, 'Holiness: General and Primitive', 740 f.

[55] See H. Söderblom, *The Nature of Revelation* (London: Oxford University Press, 1933), 2, where he writes that the human soul cannot survive on morality alone, and attacks Höffding's reduction of religion to mere faith in the persistence of values.

principal source of Otto's inspiration for the concept of the pre-moral numinous. Yet, as Otto recognizes, Isaiah also illustrates the consummation of the historical penetration of the older, numinous basis of holiness by the newer rational moral concept. For Isaiah assures his readers that God will display his holiness by his righteousness: 'But the Lord of hosts is exalted in justice, and the Holy God shows himself holy in righteousness.'[56] It is true that under the influence of prophetic criticism the numinous otherness of divine power evolves into righteousness and goodness, expressing the demand of righteousness through law and justice rather than cult. Isaiah 1: 16, 'Wash yourselves; make yourselves clean; remove the evil of your doings from before my eyes; cease to do evil', shows the conflation of holiness and morality in an ancient culture where morality and the regulations of ritual are not clearly distinguished. As Söderblom recognizes, growing ethical awareness entails that the holy can no longer mean only the forbidden, but also the commanded. Yet the older taboo sense of holiness as awe-inspiring and powerful still remains in the sense of the supernatural activity of divine being.[57] Moreover, there are numerous Gospel pericopae which demonstrate that the ancient concept of holiness was never neatly superseded by a new, moralized concept. Mark 6: 56 is an obvious example of the older concept of holiness as a power that can heal or destroy: 'And wherever he came in villages, cities, or the country, they laid the sick in the market-place, and besought him that they might touch even the fringe of his garment; and as many as touched it were made well.'

If Söderblom is right, this rational and non-rational duality in the concept arises from the fact that 'in the tabu-interdicts, what we call moral rules and ritual or "superstitious" commandments are intermingled without any attempt at differentiation'.[58] As will be seen, it is also Otto's contention that the Hebrew and Christian concepts of holiness are continuous with one another in biblical theism.

---

[56] Isa. 5: 16. See *IH* 75 f.
[57] Söderblom, 'Holiness: General and Primitive', 737–8.   [58] Ibid. 739 f.

It may be that the etymological root of the Hebrew equivalent of holiness, *quadosh* contains within it the seeds of the dual meaning of holiness. *Quadosh* means separated or set aside for divine use.[59] As such it may be seen as denoting less a quality of things—that is, their substantial purity or pollution—than their relation or connection to Yahweh. As Jones points out, holiness is no mere synonym for separation: 'things, places and people have been regarded as "separate" *because* they were holy, but the converse was not true.' It is only in their relation to God as his property that objects became holy and thereby separated from other objects.[60] If holy things are separated from profane things because they have been set aside for divine use, then the distinction can emerge between holiness and profanity whereby holiness is determined first by divine will rather than by the material properties of the object itself. The object becomes holy in its appointment by God. This represents a considerable religio-conceptual advance on the earliest view of holiness as some sort of contagion or dangerous force of energy. Söderblom calls this new distinction between substantial holiness and the holiness of a divine ethical will 'the momentous step in the evolution of holiness'.[61]

In this way, holiness becomes dependent on the personality of God rather than on the cultic manipulation of supernatural power. Once holiness is historicized as the product of a divine will understood as incontrovertibly good, the penetration of the ethical element in the concept of holiness becomes logically inevitable. This may be seen in the change of Israel from a people whose holiness cordoned them off from other nations by their rituals and (attempts at) genetic purity, as in Leviticus 20: 26, to the prophetic vision of Israel as holy in its vocation as called to be God's messenger to the nations. Even in the early Old Testament traditions, the ever closer association of holiness with divine will and

---

[59] Ringgren, *Prophetical Conception of Holiness*, 6, finds that the idea of withdrawal or separation is not always very prominent in the texts.

[60] *COH* 107. See also A. Kreider, *Journey towards Holiness* (Basingstoke: Marshall, Morgan & Scott, 1986), 35 f.

[61] Söderblom, 'Holiness: General and Primitive', 740.

personality, expressed in command and covenant, withdraws holiness from the sphere of taboo and relocates it in the sphere of duty and obedience to God, which is, arguably, the birth of ethics.

Acknowledging that primitive and recent concepts of holiness share more than might be expected, John G. Davies suggests that the 'true Church' should incorporate a combination of the numinous element of the Old Testament concept of holiness that has been preserved in Catholicism and the moralist concept of holiness espoused by Protestantism.[62] Undoubtedly, Protestantism has subsumed holiness into Christian ethics, and attempted to banish its ritual, magical associations. Tillich offers, in his own idiom, a standard account of the ancient struggle between ritual and ethical concepts of holiness. He acknowledges that when holy objects lose symbolic power as pointers to the holy and become established as holy in themselves, their holiness becomes 'anti-divine' or demonic. It is only the idea of justice that is the criterion for judging whether an object has become an idol and appropriated the honour due to God alone. It was the prophets who attacked holiness in the name of justice, just as the Reformers denounced a system which had appropriated holiness to itself in the furtherance of its own power. Yet Tillich, like Otto, recognizes that the triumph was ambiguous, since:

The degree to which the anti-demonic struggle was successful historically, the meaning of holiness was transformed. The holy became the righteous, the morally good, usually with ascetic connotations. The divine command to be holy as God is holy was interpreted as a requirement of moral perfection. And since moral perfection is an ideal and not a reality, the notion of actual holiness disappeared both inside and outside the religious sphere. The fact that there are no 'saints' in the classical sense on Protestant soil supported this development in the modern world.[63]

This, then, is the beginning of secularism: 'Moral law replaces the *tremendum* and *fascinosum* of holiness. The holy

---

[62] J. G. Davies, 'The Concept of Holiness', *London Quarterly & Holborn Review*, 185 (1960), 39. [63] Tillich, *Systematic Theology*, i. 216–17.

loses its depth, its mystery, its numinous character.'[64] The prophetical conception of the holy, espoused again by Protestantism, destroys the 'magical' immanence of the holy in sacramental objects once 'laden with divine power' but now, like the rest of nature, profane. Sacramental reality, the 'primitive unity between the holy and the real', is dissolved in the replacement of the holy by the moral demand.[65] And it is against the background of the Protestant, rationalist secularization of holiness that Otto's defiant contribution to the concept is launched.

[64] Ibid. 217. Tillich's debt to Otto here is clear.
[65] Tillich, *Protestant Era*, 120–2.

3

Otto's Contribution to the Concept of Holiness

Enough has been said to set Otto's work on holiness in context. It is now time to outline the main thesis of *The Idea of the Holy* in rather more detail than was given in the introduction to the present study. I shall be brief, because outlines of his work are common, and the three central areas of debate relevant to Otto's work (the nature and person of God, the place of morality in the category of holiness, and the role of religious experience) are dealt with in some detail in the next three chapters of this book.[1] After summarizing Otto's position, I shall seek to account for the immense popular appeal of the book in Germany after the First World War, and then assess the originality of Otto's position in the light of the main influences upon it. Finally, I shall show how, despite scholarly neglect of his work, Otto has influenced several theologians. As the focus of the present study is theological, Otto's influence upon historians and phenomenologists of religion (such as Eliade and Van der Leeuw) will not be discussed here.

Since Schleiermacher, German theology had been preoccupied with the quest for the essence of religion. Otto joined this quest in so far as he wanted to apprehend intuitively the distinctively *religious* element in what is classed as religious experience, distilled from all the moral and rational elements that have (quite properly) penetrated and become associated with that category of experience. Like Schleiermacher, Otto

---

[1] In order to avoid repetition this summary will not offer page references except where there is direct quotation. All significant references will be provided in subsequent chapters.

argues that the essential nature of religion is not thought about God, but a feeling; and the object of that feeling he calls, not 'God', but 'the Holy'. Otto then defines the holy as 'a category of interpretation and valuation peculiar to the sphere of religion'.[2]

Otto contends that religious knowledge and teaching cannot be subsumed into philosophy as a picturesque branch of ethics, but belong to the hidden depths of the spirit. By dividing the object of religion, the holy, into two elements that had previously been fused, the moral/rational and the non-rational, Otto avoids the usual identification of holiness with the divine perfection of moral goodness. The non-rational element, the numinous, stands for that essential aspect of the divine which transcends, and therefore eludes, rational comprehension: it has a purely religious meaning.[3] Otto insists that the pure essence of religion, present from the very beginning of its evolution, is entirely independent of ordinary human categories of value and experience. But in order to isolate the mysterious, awesome, fascinating, and overwhelming essence of the holy for analysis without the moral and rational elements it has accrued, Otto coined the word 'numinous' from the Latin *numen*, a deity or localized power.

The numinous moment, then, is for Otto the essence of religion as a human system: it is not a supernatural person, 'God', but a set and class of emotions evoked by a sense of the transcendent power and value of the divine. Numinous experience lacks the conceptual definition which might predicate a divine person called 'God' as its intentional object. So Otto does not describe religion as a system based on ideas and experiences of *God*, or, indeed, on holiness. Holiness is, like 'God', a *concept* compounded of a purely religious element (the numinous) and the moral accretion which 'fills

---

[2] *IH* 5.
[3] This is perhaps the most contentious of Otto's claims. See e.g. L. Hodgson's critique of Otto's discussion of the non-rational in religion: *The Place of Reason in Christian Apologetic* (Oxford: Blackwell, 1925), 7–12, 15. For a defence of Otto against Hodgson's critique, see J. M. Moore, *Theories of Religious Experience with Specific Reference to James, Otto and Bergson* (New York: Round Table Press, 1938), 110.

out' the meaning and significance of the ineffable numinous, but, in Western religion particularly, is in danger of engulfing it altogether.

'The numinous', confusingly, refers not only to the divine object but also to the state of mind its presence excites. This state of mind is the quality of religious experience as an irreducible, *sui generis* state of consciousness, correlated to the numinous value of the transcendent reality that is the object of religious experience.[4] However, as a theological realist, Otto goes beyond the psychology of religion. His work is based on faith that the numinous is no mere projection, but an objective datum of experience belonging to a 'wholly other' metaphysical reality whose presence can alone give rise to a numinous state of mind.[5]

The numinous 'cannot, strictly speaking, be taught, it can only be evoked, awakened in the mind; as everything that comes "of the spirit" must be awakened'.[6] Otto does so by the use of the ideogrammatic formulation *mysterium tremendum et fascinans*. Religion begins, then, with the arousal of numinous awareness by the sense of the uncanny at the feeling of a wholly other (and hence mysterious) presence, which is *tremendum* in its awe-inspiring power. The ideogram of *majestas* (majesty) unites the *tremendum* and the *fascinosum* in a twofold reaction in which a person is entranced and overwhelmed by this power (the *fascinosum* or Dionysiac element), yet at the same time feels repelled or horrified.

The numinous is the 'innermost essence' of all positive religious experience, distinguishing genuine religion from the daemonic dread that can be traced from the 'primitive' cult to the theology informing his own Lutheran faith. As such, pre-religious phenomena (such as animism, the worship of *mana*, fear of taboos and the unclean, magic, and so on) as well as the cerebral austerities of the most sophisticated forms of Western religion, are explicable alike by their relation to the basic religious element: the *sensus numinis*. For Otto, the Christian religion, as an expression of the sense of the holy, evolves (like other religions) in culture and

---

[4] *IH* 7.   [5] *IH* 11.   [6] *IH* 7.

ideation from the feeling of awe and mystery. He traces an unbroken line running from Luther back to the *quadosh* of the Old Testament and becoming diffused into 'the elements of religious awe in the history of religion in general'.[7] *The Idea of the Holy* was therefore relevant to both comparative religion and biblical criticism.

Otto also argues for the historical evolution of the numinous consciousness.[8] He postulates a cognitive process whereby numinous experience is refined and disentangled from superstition and interpreted by increasingly spiritualized analogies and subtle cerebrations. This sense that religion might clarify or reform its faith over time is not necessarily controversial. As F. E. England remarks, this kind of evolution would be no different from 'the process of gradual discrimination by which our everyday apprehension is made more luminous'.[9] No abstruse formal a priori categorical elements need be postulated, only discriminative mental processes which, correlative to intellectual progress or decadence, gradually refine or, as is logically possible, barbarize numinous consciousness.

The numinous is *sui generis*, of incommensurable value; that is, it is 'wholly other' to any other value such as beauty, goodness, or rationality. For Otto, numinous experience alone yields what is common to all piety: a feeling of the annihilation of personal significance and identity when confronted by something of non-natural value, of not merely a better, but entirely 'other' order from that of the creature. This sensation Otto calls 'creature-feeling'. Sin and God's wrath at sin are not, then, moral concepts, but a peculiarly religious experience of profanity in the presence of the holy. Otto finds that although the numinous is the essential 'moment' of the holy, it has, in biblical theology, become steeped or saturated with rational elements, principally ethical in character. Yet these rational elements, far from disfiguring holiness, actually provide a criterion for the ranking of religions in terms of their acceptability 'for all civilised humanity'. Without the

---

[7] *IH* 100.   [8] *IH* 124–5; also Otto, 'Sensus Numinis', 230, 423; *RO* 78–82.
[9] *The Validity of Religious Experience* (London: Ivor Nicholson, 1937), 218.

rational, religion develops into 'a mere rank growth of mysticality'; but with a surfeit of rationalism, religion withers and dies.[10]

The Idea of the Holy is not, then, a complete statement of Otto's theory of religion. Indeed, its liberal romanticism serves to emphasize 'the non-rational aspect of religious experience in a way which is easily misunderstood unless seen against a background of his other works'.[11] Otto stresses that the non-rational essence of religion may be its profoundest and most basic moment, but never its totality. Indeed, many commentators seem oblivious of Otto's concern that religion's rational and non-rational elements should not fall out of balance, leading to the extremes of either desiccated rationalism or religious fanaticism.[12] So it is the balance between the rational and the non-rational elements in any given religion that determines its spiritual maturity and rank. Otto claims that he has 'honestly and without prejudice' judged the union of the rational and non-rational elements in Christianity to represent the supreme example of the spiritual life: a harmonious balance of mystical depth and lucid thought.[13]

The union of the rational and non-rational elements of holiness in Christianity is not fortuitous. The necessary inner union of these elements has an a priori character whereby numinous feeling is progressively rationalized by moral and cultural factors. Otto likens numinous consciousness, which is not an ordinary sense perception, to Kant's 'pure concepts of the understanding', finding by introspection that the numinous is a priori by virtue of its issuing from 'the deepest foundation of cognitive apprehension that the soul possesses'. The fact of numinous consciousness points to 'a hidden substantive source, from which the religious ideas and feelings are formed, which lies in the mind independently of sense-experience'.[14] And again by critical introspection, Otto unearths a universal predisposition of the human soul to receive and judge true religion.

---

[10] *IH* 141 f.   [11] Moore, *Theories of Religious Experience*, 79.
[12] See Wach, *Types of Religious Experience*, 221.   [13] *IH* 142.
[14] *IH* 113 f.

Otto's work can only be understood if it is recognized that he considered all theoretical discussion of God and religion to be entirely redundant unless it is underpinned by, and derived from, religious experience. Hence roughly three-quarters of *The Idea of the Holy* is devoted to a non-doctrinal, empirical account of how the non-rational sense of the numinous is manifested in aesthetic experience, worship, the Old and New Testaments, Luther, and primitive religion. This is not, as it may seem, merely a case of holding a view a priori and then selecting examples to corroborate it.[15] It is a deliberate epistemological statement: like Kant, Otto recognizes that reason operating on sense-data cannot yield objective knowledge of transcendent, metaphysical realities. The reality of transcendental experience cannot be demonstrated philosophically; first-hand religious experience alone authenticates this reality, hence the notorious injunction for those unable to recall intrinsically religious feelings not to bother to read the book.[16] The numinous is a form of self-awareness evoked by the presence of a power of non-natural value; as such, it can be recognized only empathetically through the evocation of certain emotions excited by the *numen praesens*.

In sum, *The Idea of the Holy* can be seen as the product of three interwoven theses: philosophical, phenomenological, and theological.[17] Following Fries, Otto is philosophically convinced that humans can and do have knowledge of absolute or non-natural metaphysical reality. This is not a conceptual or rational knowledge, but rather a feeling or inexpressible apprehension. Reflection on this feeling can be conducted only by intuitive analogies to the feeling content. Therefore what is said about the holy is symbolic rather than literal.

The phenomenological thesis in *The Idea of the Holy* asserts that all religions are grounded not in theory or system, but on a universal, basically uniform numinous experience, historically and culturally variously expressed. Lastly, Otto's

---

[15] Bastow accuses Otto of doing this in his article 'Otto and Numinous Experience', 169. [16] *IH* 8.

[17] Welch, *Protestant Thought*, 121, accounts for the close interconnections of Otto's theses.

theological thesis asserts that the more fully a religion bases itself on numinous experience, the more profoundly it partakes of the essential nature of religion. Religion can begin only where there is immediate communion with the divine in the direct individual witness of the soul to the revelation of the will and presence of the divine in the *sensus numinis*. The codified, rationalized, historicized revelation of law and scripture, wherein humanity is given the means to atonement and salvation, is a development from the *sensus numinis*: it is not its inception.

Influences on Otto's Concept of Holiness

The best known of Otto's works were written in the latter half of his life: Otto was nearly 50 when *The Idea of the Holy* was first published. Although it was his only book to gain international renown in popular and academic circles, it was by no means a terminus for Otto's creative examination of the *sensus numinis*.[18]

Consequently, ideas that have become associated with Otto are themselves a product of manifold influences and dependencies. As Willard Oxtoby found, Otto's 'critical heritage is too vast to be set forth in detail', and this applies as much to the present book as it did to his article. Suffice it to say that Otto's work 'was a product of modern European culture, seeking an up to date but sympathetic expression of religion in terms of what that culture had at its disposal'.[19]

The formative influences upon Otto's work may be summarized as follows.[20] First impressed by Luther, Ritschlianism, and Kantian philosophy, Otto next came under the influence of Schleiermacher and then neo-Friesianism. He was not primarily interested in pure philosophical theory, and was influenced as much by Troeltsch's empirical approach

---

[18] Streetman, 'Some Later Thoughts', 371, claims that many essays written after *IH*, particularly the more esoteric studies of oriental religion, were not published in English because they were unlikely to be commercially successful during the Depression.   [19] Oxtoby, 'Holy, Idea of the', 432.
[20] This summary of Otto's intellectual affiliations is indebted to *ROR* 5–8.

to philosophy as by Fries. As can be seen in *The Idea of the Holy*, Otto shared Troeltsch's pluralistic world-view and his concern for the autonomy of religious consciousness. He also accepted the premiss of Troeltsch's religio-historical school: that the task of theology is the psychological analysis of the religious consciousness, though he did not make Troeltsch's connections between history, culture, and theology. Almond and Davidson have both offered clear and extensive surveys of the theological and philosophical provenance of Otto's work.[21] There is therefore no need to duplicate their findings here, where interest is focused on Otto's contribution to the concept of holiness, not on the wider issue of his participation in the debate on the autonomy of religion, as discussed by Troeltsch.

Otto's name is principally associated with that of Schleiermacher.[22] And since the latter made a greater contribution to *The Idea of the Holy* than any other writer, and Otto's relation to Schleiermacher is most pertinent to the development of the concept of holiness, I will examine only this relation in detail. Schleiermacher established the idea that the most distinctive aspect of religious experience is a particular feeling. In his earlier work Schleiermacher delineated religious feeling pantheistically as a sense of belonging to the divine in all things: 'The sum total of religion is to feel that, in the highest unity, all that moves us in feeling is one.'[23] Although, like Otto, Schleiermacher ranks Christianity as the highest religion, other positive religions are various and changing cultural responses to the essential religious feeling, and so should be appreciated on their own terms.[24] Of course, later in life, Schleiermacher chose to depict religious feeling less inclusively as a 'feeling of absolute dependence' on the Christian God. But where he made the deepest impression

---

[21] See *RO* 26–54; *ROR* 5–48.

[22] For the most important details of that relation, see *IH* 9 f., 20, 108, 145–50, 154 f.; 'How Schleiermacher Rediscovered the Sensus Numinis', in *RE* 68–77; *RO* 14 f., 32, 71–3; C. A. Campbell, *On Selfhood and Godhood* (London: Allen & Unwin, 1957), 219; J. Macquarrie, *Twentieth-Century Religious Thought* (London: SCM Press, 1981), 215.

[23] F. D. E. Schleiermacher, *On Religion* (New York: Harper & Row, 1958), 49 f.

[24] Ibid. 217.

on Otto was in building his epistemology and psychology of religion on the idea that immediate feeling is of another order,[25] something deeper and 'truer' than rational cognition or knowledge. Before Otto and Söderblom, Schleiermacher had already proclaimed that religion must always precede theology, and can be conducted without theology; not even the idea of God is a prerequisite for religion, only that the deity should be present to a person in feeling.

Otto concurs with the primary role of feeling in religion advanced by Schleiermacher, but goes on to refine its role and status. Otto argues that the religious feeling of dependence, or, as he prefers, self-abasement, is unique; it is born of the faculty of divination—a particular capacity to recognize the manifestation of the holy as an a priori category. The *sensus numinis* is, then, intrinsically and qualitatively different from natural or ordinary feelings of dependence; it is not merely a quantitative intensification of feelings of dependence of the sort a child may feel about a parent. Religion describes the primarily ineffable emotional response to the relation between a person and the divine: 'the emotion of a creature, abased and overwhelmed by its own nothingness in contrast to that which is supreme above all creatures'.[26] But Schleiermacher treats the religious feeling of dependence as if it were a form of *self*-consciousness, where the sense of one's dependence is accounted for by a causal inference to the fact of God. Otto, however, reverses the order: 'Rather, the "creature-feeling" is itself a first subjective concomitant and effect of another feeling-element, which casts it like a shadow, but which in itself indubitably has immediate and primary reference to an object outside the self.' The numinous is experienced as objective and outside the self.[27]

Otto's greatest advance on Schleiermacher was to establish Schleiermacher's feeling of the infinite in the finite, within a structure of purely religious value and experience. After all, as Davidson remarks, Schleiermacher's attempt to derive

---

[25] Ibid. 40, 43, 52, 54, 61, 87. Also H. R. Mackintosh (ed.), *The Christian Faith* (Edinburgh: T. & T. Clark, 1928), 76–8, 194–201.   [26] *IH* 10.
[27] *IH* 10 f.

religious knowledge directly from religious feeling had left the deep convictions of religious faith in uncertainty and requiring 'more ultimate formulation in terms of its unique value'. Otto carried out this task of the deeper substantiation of the epistemic claims of religious experience by his 'Ritschlian' description of religious consciousness primarily in terms of value rather than feeling. In Davidson's view this achieved 'a desirable reconstruction of Schleiermacher's position without sacrificing its original insights'.[28]

Otto was not the first to bring holiness to the attention of twentieth-century philosophical theology, though, interestingly, there is no reference in any of Otto's writings to the first writer to do so: the neo-Kantian, W. Windelband. However, it is generally accepted that, philosophically, the twentieth-century concept of holiness originated in 1902 with Windelband's essay 'Das Heilige'. Windelband, disliking reductionism in the study of religion, followed Höffding in promoting the holy as an absolute value. The holy or sacred (the German language knows no distinction) is the metaphysical ground of all rational values as they are related by religion to the realm of 'the supra-sensuous [which] forms the essence of every religious affirmation'.[29] It is the reality of this supra-sensuous realm of value which validates all intramundane evaluations. Mystical intuition is dismissed as 'a thing of moods', yielding 'no firm and distinct results'.[30] Religious judgement is secondary, since it has no values of its own; it is merely the absolute ground which all values require to guarantee them. The content of logical, aesthetic, and ethical values exhausts all value, so that 'when we speak of a realm of religious values which may be comprised under the title of the "sacred", we mean that all these values may assume religious forms'.[31]

It may at once be seen that if Windelband had any influence on Otto, it was negative. Windelband held that religion was grounded in rational value, relating all rational values to

---

[28] *ROR* 34. Davidson feels that *IH* is more dependent on this Ritschlian principle than Otto liked to admit.

[29] Windelband, *Introduction to Philosophy*, 332.   [30] Ibid. 329.

[31] Ibid. 324 f.

supra-mundane reality. This effectively denies religion any autonomy as a *sui generis* experience or realm of value. Certainly, Otto also sees the holy non-reductively as a category of value relating to a supra-sensuous realm of reality. But for Otto, the peculiar experience of numinous value guarantees the autonomy of religion. Religion arises from its own non-rational source in the mind and in the 'wholly other' reality of the sphere of the holy.

The Originality of Otto's Contribution to the Concept of Holiness

Apart from filling a lexical gap in the analysis of religion with his word 'numinous' for the non-rational element of religious experience,[32] it seems that there is little in Otto that is entirely original. Otto may only have popularized the word 'numinous'. Andrew Lang, the early anthropologist of religion, observed that historical research into the origins of religion points not to emergent belief in gods, but to 'an unanalysable *senus numinis*'. Yet, as Eric Sharpe asks (rhetorically), 'how many scholars, one wonders, writing about Rudolf Otto, have observed this passage in Lang?'[33]

Schleiermacher and Fries had already established the intuitive affectivity of the religious consciousness as against rationalism as a means to theological truth. Troeltsch's theory of the autonomy of religion and the religious a priori anticipates Otto's position, and Windelband had made an important connection between holiness and value. Söderblom had been exploring the use of the term 'holy' in the history of religions, whether simultaneously with or before Otto.[34] Frazer, Robertson Smith, Ives Curtis, and Marett had already made extensive studies of primitive religion and the sacred. Marett and Söderblom had recognized the independence of the sacred from morality. Indeed, John Oman was aware

---

[32] Eliade, *Quest*, 23, notes that the *mysterium tremendum et fascinans* has become 'part of our language'.

[33] A. Lang, *The Making of Religion* (2nd edn. 1900), 46, cited in Sharpe, *Comparative Religion*, 61.   [34] See *RO* 60.

that Old Testament scholars had recognized the non-moral quality of *quadosh* long before Otto.[35] In respect of his originality, Otto can, then, be regarded as a writer of eclectic interests whose significance lies in his 'highly distinctive' synthesis of at least half a century of German theology.[36] Otto's work on the evolution of primitive religion provided, in A. D. Martin's view, 'more of a new emphasis than a discovery'.[37] In sum, as David Bastow points out, none of the central theses of *The Idea of the Holy* 'can be taken as having been established by Otto'.[38]

W. B. Kristensen recognizes that the most important contribution of *The Idea of the Holy* is its analysis of the concept of holiness, though he does not find it a 'particularly original one'. Kristensen denies the originality of *The Idea of the Holy* not in terms of the history of ideas, but from within the logic of the category of holiness itself:

This book has been considered extremely important and Otto has been called 'the discoverer of the Holy.' But it would be just as true to say that he is the discoverer of the divine, or of religion, and this is simply absurd. People have been too impressed by the title *Das Heilige*.[39]

But this is unfair. Otto made no pretence of having discovered the category of the holy; in *The Idea of the Holy* he wished only to enquire 'into the non-rational factor in the idea of the divine and its relation to the rational'. Otto realizes, therefore, that the holy is no more or less than the divine, or what can be apprehended of it, and so could not be his discovery. And as anyone even glancing at *The Idea of the Holy* must recognize, Otto is attempting to *rescue*, not discover, a neglected but essential element of holiness by an analysis of the emotions associated with the reception of its manifestation.

There are, then, a number of ways in which Otto's work represents a significant, even original, contribution to the

[35] J. Oman, *The Natural and the Supernatural* (London: Cambridge University Press, 1931), appendix A, 'The Holy', 474.   [36] *ROR* 48.

[37] Martin, *Holiness of Jesus*, 7.

[38] Bastow, 'Otto and Numinous Experience', 176.

[39] Kristensen, *Meaning of Religion*, 16. See also ibid. 355–6.

history of the concept of holiness. First, it is Otto's phenomenological presentation of the holy, locating it independently of ethics as the object and essence of religion, that
makes him particularly significant for the development of
the concept. The relation of holiness and morality will be
discussed in a later chapter. Suffice it to say here that Otto's
originality lies in his use of holiness neither as some sort of
quasi-substantial quality of objects nor as an ethical value,
but in its numinous moment, as itself defining a religious
experience. With Otto, holiness becomes a moment of spiritual encounter with a transcendent value.

Second, Otto makes a significant methodological contribution to *Religionswissenschaft*. Writers such as W. James,
W. Wundt, and R. R. Marett had sought to investigate—
and in some sense 'solve'—the mystery of religion by empirical analysis. Otto, by contrast, used empirical analysis to
show that there is something in religion which can be called
an experience of holiness. This cannot be investigated by
normal empirical methods: it is not an object in the world,
and therefore cannot be known under the normal categories
of rationality. Rather, the experience of holiness reveals a
unique category of value and state of mind, as a response to
the apprehension of that value, that must be recognized in
the fullest sense of the word by its investigator. So Otto
continues to base his concept of holiness on empirical evidence, but relinquishes the scientific objectivity that normally
accompanies its analysis. Indeed, Otto offered a distinctive
application of phenomenological data produced by the early
science of religion and by study of the Eastern religions to
the experience of the divine described by biblical theism.[40]

Third, on the evidence of the history of religions, he argued
that the essence of religion is non-rational, thereby exclud-
ing morality from the primary and ultimate moments of the
divine–human relationship. Even if Otto was not the first to
recognize this, he was the first to publicize the connection

[40] See Eliade, *Quest*, 23. Here Eliade finds Otto to have 'tacitly' claimed the role
of a mediator between '*revelatio generalis* and *revelatio specialis*, between Indo-Aryan
and Semitic religious thought, between Eastern and Western types of mysticism'.

between holiness and the non-rational and to sustain this insight throughout his work. And it is an insight with weighty implications for one of the central questions of philosophy of religion: namely, the proper relation of morality and religious obedience to divine command. So, above all, Otto's concept of holiness has implications for the concept of God, the metaphysical status of theological statements, and the proper spiritual posture of human creatures in addressing God. Perhaps his greatest contribution to theology lies in the way in which he tried to clear the path to religious experience of the long-accumulated debris of intellectual history; to weed the conceptual undergrowth from the sense of the divine and give that sense light and air. Whilst one must be critically alert to the epistemological problems arising from claims to immediate experience, Otto wants to take his readers back to their first religious experience, to a point of openness to the numinous which, as the beginning of religion in general, is also a new beginning for personal spirituality in particular.

The Popular Enthusiasm for Das Heilige

Das Heilige was published in 1917; twenty-five editions were printed before 1936, and the thirtieth appeared in 1958. Heinz Zahrnt claims that 'it is probably the most widely read theological work in German of the twentieth century'.[41] Joachim Wach, to whom Otto was something of a mentor, applauds The Idea of the Holy as 'one of the profoundest analyses which have ever been made to indicate the objective character, the meaning of religion'.[42] As Willard Oxtoby remarks, The Idea of the Holy is 'a landmark among theories of religion'. Furthermore, it is 'a mark of its greatness' that 'it takes account of the cumulative critical and scientific tradition of modern Europe and claims a place of respect

---

[41] H. Zahrnt, *The Question of God: Protestant Theology in the Twentieth Century* (London: Collins, 1969), 48. Kristensen, *Meaning of Religion*, 15, makes the same remark. See also *ROR* 3.   [42] Wach, *Types of Religious Experience*, 217.

for religious experience and religious thought in a modern age'.[43] But Otto was also read by his non-academic contemporaries, perhaps because, compared to the average theological or philosophical text, past or present, *The Idea of the Holy* is unusually exhilarating to read. Written with an invigorating passion, it must have seemed, to those who had hoped for it, a liberation from nineteenth-century moralism and *petit bourgeois* values.

Certainly Otto's aesthetic temper is romantic. His travels and his ideas share the romantic fondness for strange, terrifying, and remote places and experiences. He was a solitary, often unhappy man, for whom intense emotion was more spiritually compelling than pious moralizing and the more prosaic forms of worship.[44] As Eliade remarked of *The Idea of the Holy*, 'because of the great popularity of the book there is a tendency to regard [Otto] as an "emotionalist"'. It was perhaps the excitable tone of the book that resulted in its making 'a more enduring impact on the Western, especially German, cultivated public than on historians of religion proper or theologians'.[45]

If, as has been shown, little in *The Idea of the Holy* was entirely original, then it seems odd that *Das Heilige* should have caused the sensation it did. It may be that this single, compact volume simply became accessible and appealing to the educated public in a way that more arid and extended scholarship could not. The Catholic theologian F. K. Feigel offers a credible, if pejorative, explanation of the excitement created by *Das Heilige*.[46] It was first published when Germany was in the final throes of the First World War and facing imminent defeat. The war had left Germany psychically exhausted and bereft of its hitherto complacent sense of civilized order and values. Feigel feels that the German people were vulnerable and spiritually exposed. German youth were particularly disorientated. For them, culture was in crisis, because it had come to doubt its own past and future. Moral

---

[43] Oxtoby, 'Holy, Idea of the', 432.   [44] e.g. *IH* 5 f., 28 f., 65–9, 210–14.
[45] Eliade, *Quest*, 23.
[46] In F. K. Feigel, *Das Heilige: Kritische Abhandlung über Rudolf Otto's Gleichnamiges Buch* (Haarlem: De Erven F. Bohn, 1929).

and intellectual values were being undermined in the realization that rationality and progress were a fiction; that in
the unconscious and at the heart of civilization there was a
dark void. *Das Heilige*, however, made that void seem attractive, necessary to the search for truth, even glamorous.
Feigel believed that the rich oriental colouring of *Das Heilige*
had merely enchanted its readers by its mystical exoticism
without offering any substantial theology. Clearly concerned
that spiritual disorientation was compounded by Otto rather
than alleviated, Feigel felt that, traumatized by war, Germans
were inevitably drawn to the non-rational and ahistorical
lure of an opiate mysticism.[47]

But Otto's theological intentions, and the experiences that
gave rise to them, cannot be seen as identical with the contingent spiritual needs of his readers.[48] How and why *Das
Heilige* was received as it was is not necessarily an accurate
gauge of its actual meaning and content. Bearing this in
mind, and extending Feigel's suggestion, one might speculate that in the moral disorientation of war, God's capacity
to guarantee morality and rationality had been put into question. Otto's mysterious, powerful, fearful 'numen' might then
have seemed a more appropriate object of worship than the
God of the nineteenth-century bourgeoisie—a God who was
to be discredited yet more profoundly by the events of the
Holocaust.

Feigel, in fact, regards *Das Heilige* as a theological failure:
'Otto searched for the divine but he found only the human.'[49]
And he was not alone: many of Otto's Protestant contemporaries felt that Otto had simply uncovered the atavistic,
unreasoning elements of the human psyche without any convincing promotion of the rational achievements of theology

---

[47] Ibid. 3, 5. Cf. J. Oman's review of *IH*, *Journal of Religious Studies*, 25 (1924),
275, where he says that the book is 'an important document of the effect of the
War in Germany', and attributes its success to 'economic distress and political
despair'.

[48] The relationship of biographical and theological determinants in *IH* is discussed by W. Haubold, *Die Bedeutung der Religionsgeschichte für die Theologie Rudolf
Ottos* (Leipzig: Leopold Klotz, 1940), 19–21. See also Almond's discussion of the
impact of Otto's travels on the development of his theology, *RO* 12–15, 17–19.

[49] Feigel, *Das Heilige*, 123.

and morally obedient relations with God. But as James Webb has pointed out, in Germany during the 1920s (just as in England today) a spiritual hunger was already feeding a market for questing, heterodox spirituality: 'for what was wonderful and beyond the veil'. During the same period in which *Das Heilige* was so popular, the haunting novels of Hermann Hesse—saturated with *Ahndung*—were also much in vogue.[50] And scholarship, as much as Germany's political catastrophes, may have helped to loosen the hold of parochial theology. Although resisted by orthodox theology, early comparativists like Müller, Loisy, Söderblom, and Otto himself had contributed to the beginnings of inclusivism and tolerance of other faiths by pointing to a common bid for transcendence in all religious consciousness.[51]

But the timing of *The Idea of the Holy* was crucial. George Steiner has argued that in early twentieth-century Germany there was a fatal eruption of the desire to rid society of the claim, challenge, and burden of the eternal moral demand of biblical monotheism, and for men to appropriate that power for themselves.[52] If Steiner is correct, then Otto's model of a powerful, pre-moral numinous deity could not have come upon Germany at a more propitious time.

Indeed, it seems to me that, rather than Otto's concept of holiness itself, the popular appeal of the numinous in Germany during the 1920s owes a good deal to its being an *unwitting* preview of the Nazis' divorce of moral values from the exercise of power. Of course, the popular distortions of Nietzsche were a more obvious contributor to this process. But the spirit, rather than the content, of demonic neo-pagan Nazism that was to grip Germany only sixteen years after the publication of *Das Heilige* is, I think, continuous with the spirit of much of the book. This is especially marked when the contents of *Das Heilige* are sundered, as they often

---

[50] J. Webb, *The Occult Establishment*, ii: *The Age of the Irrational* (Glasgow: Richard Drew, 1981), 27.

[51] See Friedrich Heiler's remarks to this effect (he was a disciple of Söderblom and Otto) in Sharpe, *Comparative Religion*, 272.

[52] See G. Steiner, 'A Season in Hell', in *In Bluebeard's Castle: Some Notes Towards the Re-definition of Culture* (London: Faber & Faber, 1971), 36–42.

are to this day, from Otto's less controversial rationalist provisos.

That the non-rational energies of the book were commandeered during the period of the Third Reich is particularly unfortunate. The concept of *das Heilige* was subject to gross political distortion during this era. The Holy, the Party, and the Nation became one and the same, so that 'Rudolf Otto's reputation suffered at the hands of those who believed in ideologies such as this'.[53] Whilst Otto never legitimized the occult, he quite properly acknowledged that magic and religion cannot always be clearly differentiated. Yet in his perceived, and authoritative, admission of the magical and irrational into religion, Otto may have helped to legitimize the widespread devotion to the occult in the inter-war years in Germany, in which high-ranking members of the Nazi party (including Hitler himself) could be numbered.

Moreover, in *The Idea of the Holy* Otto comes close to glorifying the numinous energy and *tremendum* of what he calls 'men of vehement and overpowering personality'. He quotes Goethe's celebration of Napoleon and other men in whom the 'daemonic' character could be divined as being 'in its most *dreadful* form when it stands out dominatingly in some *man* ... an incredible force goes forth from them and they exercise an incredible power over all creatures, any, perhaps even over the elements. And who can say how far such influence may not extend?'[54] These are inspiring words for the Hitlers of this world. Whilst in a note at the bottom of the page Otto reminds the reader that such men are numinous, not holy, he has none the less allowed that the power of the sacred can be manifest in highly autocratic forms of political leadership.

It is no coincidence that several scholars have sensed the numinosity of great evil. Otto does so himself when he acknowledges that 'the "fearful" and horrible, and even at times the revolting and the loathsome' are analogous to and expressive of the *tremendum*.[55] When Tom Driver visited the site where the atomic bomb was dropped on Hiroshima, he

---

[53] Sharpe, *Comparative Religion*, 173 f. n. 6.   [54] *IH* 152.   [55] *IH* 62.

was reminded of how Otto had said that the holy is experienced as both fearful and fascinating, that 'holiness is not always goodness'. He goes on: 'I had the feeling at Hiroshima that the place was holy not in spite of but because something unspeakably bad had happened there.'[56] I experienced something similar when I visited Babi Yar, where, in September 1941, 33,771 Jews were murdered by Nazi and Ukrainian *Einsatzkommandos* in two days.

Of course, there is a sense in which discussion of the relation of holiness and horror parodies Otto's argument by neglecting his injunction that, despite its non-rational essence, religion is best served when penetrated by rationality. It mistakes Otto's defence of the 'not-yet rational' for promotion of the irrational. So if *The Idea of the Holy* contributed to these enormities by playing on some of the fevered imaginations of the time, that doubtless owes less to Otto's intentions than to the *sensus numinis* itself: a primal emotion which pre-dates and can subdue Western moral sensibilities. None the less, it must be said that a strictly logical reading of some passages in *The Idea of the Holy* would imply that if divine will is unknowable because inconceivable, and revelation is a human rationalization of the *numen praesens*, then the religious imperative of obedience to divine commands becomes problematic. When awe overwhelms reverence, all that seems to remain is Kierkegaardian 'fear and trembling': submission to the intoxicating terror of absolute divine might. It is, I think, a fair reading of *The Idea of the Holy* to suppose that the idea of a good and rational Father-God is merely a symbol or outer casing for a reality whose innermost being is a numinous *energicum*; a pre-Judaic power.

But, to repeat, a text, its author's intentions, and its readers' interpretations are not identical. That this is true of *The Idea of the Holy* may be shown by a glance at Otto's own experience in Germany during the 1930s. Otto did entertain a fleeting hope that the Nazi Christian movement might

[56] T. Driver, *The Magic of Ritual* (San Francisco: HarperCollins, 1991), 41 f. Cf. M. Lodahl on the *tremendum* of the Holocaust in *Shekhinah/Spirit: Divine Presence in Jewish and Christian Religion* (New York: Paulist Press, 1992), 127.

rejuvenate German Protestantism.[57] But when a form of neo-paganism triumphed politically, Otto appears to have become increasingly distressed by Nazism. He retired from Marburg before it became compulsory to join the Nazi party in order to retain one's academic post, so that particular crisis of conscience would not have arisen. However, it is possible that his depression subsequent to the Nazi authorities' refusal to allow him to adopt the son of a close Jewish friend who had, in fear and despair, committed suicide could have contributed to his own attempted suicide in 1937.[58]

Only Eric Sharpe reports that in Otto's last years 'his internationalism caused him to fall foul of the Nazi government in Germany'.[59] However, I have found no evidence or reports of any form of confrontation between Otto and the Nazi authorities. *Das Heilige* was not on any of the extensive lists of books banned under a Nazi dictatorship which had itself a marked preference for numinous sensation. None the less, Otto cannot be called a Nazi or accused of holding pro-Fascist sentiments any more than Nietzsche, and certainly less than Heidegger or Eliade. In fact, Otto was, despite the evangelical prejudices of his childhood,[60] a cultural cosmopolitan, rejoicing in both Christian and non-Christian religious expression alike. He would, I am sure, have regretted the sneering anti-Semitic remark made by H. Frick in an oration at his funeral in 1937. Frick found great comic irony in the fact that Otto, a Marburg professor, should have awoken to the true import of the holy in a 'wretched little synagogue'.[61]

In the Introduction I discussed the neglect of Otto in

[57] See Harvey's preface to *IH*, p. xi. For a summary of the relation of the Protestant Church to Nazism between 1933 and 1937, see e.g. W. Shirer, *The Rise and Fall of the Third Reich* (New York: Simon & Schuster, 1960), 234–40.

[58] See Almond, 'Rudolf Otto: Life and Work', 320 f. Almond provides strong cumulative evidence that Otto attempted to take his own life by throwing himself from a 60-foot tower at Staufenberg, near Marburg.

[59] E. Sharpe, 'Six Major Figures in Religious Studies', in R. P. Beaver *et al.* (eds.), *The World's Religions* (Tring, Herts: Lion Publishing, 1982), 16.

[60] *RO* 10. Otto is quoted as saying: 'I couldn't read any history calmly unless I was convinced beforehand that the people in it were also devout and not "catholic", or Jews or heathens.'

[61] *Rudolf Otto: Zum Gedächtnis* (Leipzig: L. Klotz Verlag, 1937), 5.

contemporary scholarship. This neglect can be traced back to Otto's own lifetime and the immediate post-war period. The obscure epistemological provenance of *The Idea of the Holy* in the writings of the neo-Kantian philosopher J. Fries was almost bound to alienate British theologians of the period. One cannot help thinking that H. W. Garrod's disparaging remarks are typical of many British writers of the first half of the century, when referring to German scholarship: 'In philosophy [Otto] belongs to the school of what may be called "puffy" Idealism. He delights to edify, and he exercises this irritating and not difficult art in quite masterly fashion.'[62] After two World Wars with Germany it is hardly surprising that all but the last generation of English-speaking scholars would give Otto's work a rather cool reception.

More generally, the traditional Protestant wariness of the holy should not be forgotten. Despite Otto's critical role in the defence of the autonomy of religion against twentieth-century secularism, the holy—let alone the numinous—is still considered suspect in some Protestant quarters. This may owe something to its threefold association with the betrayal of Christian supremacy by comparativism, with the asceticism and sacramentalism of Catholicism, and with primitive religion.[63] W. R. Inge, in 1925, remarked that 'the concept of holiness has not had an edifying history', and alerted Christians to the dangers of Otto's theory of religion. Despite allowing that the numinous is indeed 'an essential element of religion', he finds that the impression left by Otto in *The Idea of the Holy* is deficient in the sense of divine love, and over-weighted with that of fear. Apprehensive of the spiritual and psychological imbalance resulting from a preponderance of feeling at the expense of love, truth, and value, he warns that 'the stimulation of violent emotions may leave permanent traces on the mind. . . . The undifferentiated inchoate religious sense is thus intensified and fixed, to the great and lasting injury of the spiritual life.' Inge admits that awe is

[62] H. W. Garrod, review of *Naturalism and Religion*, by Rudolf Otto, *Hibbert Journal*, 42 (1943), 698.
[63] See Coats, 'Holiness: New Testament and Christian', 750.

common to all religion, but fears that 'the impression made by Otto's book may lead to this feature being somewhat over-emphasized'.[64] Even Willink, who was generally appreciative of Otto's concept of holiness, feared that confrontations with the holy could be psychologically damaging.[65] Similarly, B. H. Streeter considered that Otto's influence on the Christian theology of the 1920s and early 1930s is 'by no means wholly for the good'. According to Streeter, Otto is guilty of dragging religion down to the level of vague mysteries, 'half emergent from the dark demonic murk of primeval shudderings'.[66] And in 1953, Baines Atkinson regretted that

to extol the message of holiness is not to be indifferent to the suspicion the word arouses among many good Christian people. In some quarters it is literally drenched with odium. It is really amazing that a word, which is certainly one of the greatest in Scripture, should be so suspect.[67]

In 1925 Otto was referred to less as an academic than as an 'apologist and converting preacher',[68] though not, per-haps, an entirely successful one. But despite Otto's 'rather chilly reception in the ranks of orthodox theology', Charles Campbell, in deeming him 'by a wide margin, the most illu-minating religious thinker of modern times', fears that this judgement might seem strange or 'shocking' to British theo-logians reared in a tradition valuing common sense and 'a deep-rooted suspicion' of the mysterious and supra-rational. After all, as Campbell notes, British theologians, unlike their Continental colleagues, 'like to pride themselves on keep-ing both feet firmly on the ground—which seems a rather unpromising way of reaching Heaven!'[69]

Lastly, it may be to the detriment of his reputation that

---

[64] In his Conclusion to J. Needham (ed.), *Science, Religion and Reality* (London: Sheldon Press, 1925), 378.   [65] Willink, *Holy and the Living God*, 225.

[66] B. H. Streeter, *The Buddha and the Christ* (London: Macmillan, 1932), Appen-dix II, 'The Idea of the Holy', 325.   [67] Atkinson, *Beauty of Holiness*, 14.

[68] Hodgson, *Place of Reason*, 16.

[69] Campbell, *On Selfhood and Godhood*, 327, 341. Macquarrie, *Twentieth-Century Religious Thought*, 214, largely agrees with C. A. Campbell, his former teacher, in this estimation of Otto, adding that 'Otto is in his own right a religious thinker of the first importance'. Despite the undeniable suspicion with which *The Idea of the*

Otto's work has become loosely associated with the more esoteric elements of religion which I referred to earlier in this chapter. This association may stem from the inspiration he gained from his travels (Otto was the first German scholar of religion to participate in the life of a Japanese Zen monastery) and from his reputation as a mystic[70] and as an Indologist. Now, at the end of the twentieth century, the technical theological term 'numinous' has passed into the educated vocabulary, but often with occult connotations: in one of Umberto Eco's recent novels the narrator remarks, 'but the fact is that it doesn't take long for the experience of the Numinous to unhinge the mind.'[71] The popular meaning of 'numinous', although related to Otto's original definition and use of the word, has become debased as an adjective describing the quality of subconscious forces or archetypes.[72] Otto had, however, intended the word 'numinous' to be a way of naming the essential character, value, and reality of that divine presence through a primary form of religious experience. Numinous experience was not, for Otto, an end in itself. He considered religions in which the numinous overwhelms the rational to be immature or incomplete without the rational elements that complete the numinous as the holy. (However, it must be conceded that, if taken out of context, certain passages in *The Idea of the Holy* with a markedly romantic aesthetic could contribute to this loss of lexical precision.[73]) The cumulative effect of these mild abuses of Otto's concept of holiness may have put his work beyond the pale of biblical religion.

Holy was regarded, the Archbishop of Canterbury wrote in a letter dated 30 May 1937 to W. R. Matthews, the Dean of St Paul's who was to attend Otto's funeral, that Otto had made a 'profound' impression on British readers and a 'remarkable' contribution to theology. This letter was published in the *Gedächtnisfeier* of 1938.

[70] J. Wach wrote of him: 'Neither before nor since my meeting with Otto have I known a person who impressed me more genuinely as a true mystic. There was something about him of the solitude into which an intimate communion with the Divine has frequently led those who were favoured in this way' (*Types of Religious Experience*, 211).

[71] U. Eco, *Foucault's Pendulum* (London: Secker & Warburg, 1989), 6.

[72] The numinous is used in this way in C. G. Jung and M.-L. von Franz (eds.), *Man and his Symbols* (London: Aldus Books, 1979), 79, 94 f., 99, 101.

[73] e.g. *IH* 68, 119, 126–8.

The Idea of the Holy has had little subsequent influence on theology. Although Philip Almond believes that the theistic (rather than the mystical) implications of Otto have been 'overemphasised',[74] it is not clear to me by whom. It is true that in the late 1920s and early 1930s several British theologians, such as Willink, Mackintosh, and Martin, ignored Inge's warnings and risked their spiritual equanimity to use Otto's topical study of holiness to renew a proper religious emphasis on mystery or awe.[75] But no theologian working with a biblical model of sin, revelation, and salvation has used Otto's concept of the holy as an overall structural dynamic whereby this model of divine–human relations might be creatively employed.[76] Both Paul Tillich and John Macquarrie have accommodated and utilized Otto's insights into the holy in their own existential concerns, but not as a starting-point or foundation for their work. Both use Otto's work less for its theological insight than to draw upon its phenomenology of holiness to show that the holy is the mystery of the power and depth of being, and that Otto's notion of 'creature-feeling' may be understood as the root of existential anxiety.[77]

However, the assimilation of the Ottonian concept of holiness into existentialist philosophies is foreign to Otto's thought. At the end of his life, Otto utterly derided the equation of the 'Holy' and 'Being'.[78] He did not consider 'being' holy in itself. For Otto (at his most sweepingly dualistic) a human being is defined by creatureliness, which is, by its nature, profane. Certainly, Otto consistently denies that the creature can achieve holiness by moral endeavour. But neither can a human being achieve holiness through existential decisions or merely by becoming 'open' to the sacrality of his or her being.

---

[74] Almond, *Mystical Experience*, 92.

[75] See respectively Willink, *Holy and Living God*, 19 f.; Mackintosh, *Christian Apprehension of God*, 149; Martin, *Holiness of Jesus*, 7.

[76] In the penultimate sentence of his postscript to *RO*, and as an afterthought, Almond writes: 'The feeling of truth and the objectivity of religious experience philosophically underpin a theology of revelation and grace.' However, the latter does not determine Almond's interest in Otto.

[77] See Macquarrie, *Principles of Christian Theology*, 78 f., 87, 127, 192 f.; *idem, In Search of Deity* (London: SCM Press, 1984), 246 f.   [78] *KGSM* 51.

Over the course of this chapter it has become clear that Otto's development of the concept of holiness is perhaps less linear than circular. He drew the twentieth-century concept of holiness back round to a romantic eighteenth-century vision of holiness. In the eighteenth century, Schleiermacher treated the holy as an aesthetic intuition of the infinite in the finite. In the nineteenth century, if any interest was shown at all, that interest was moral. By the twentieth century, with Otto, holiness is once again an aesthetic experience, but with the addition of two new elements. The first is axiological, drawing upon the work of philosophical theologians interested in the relation of religion and value, and the second is phenomenological. Otto's concept of holiness is moulded by the study of primitive religion, which seems to provide evidence that the numinous was the original moment of the holy, and thereby the basis on which a given religion develops. Perhaps it is in his sustained synthesis of axiological and phenomenological insights, correlated with his account of what it is like to experience the God of the Bible, that Otto has made the greatest contribution to the Western understanding of holiness in the last 200 years.

4

Holiness and Divine Personality

In 1923 Otto published an essay which, had it not been published as the fifth appendix to the present edition of *The Idea of the Holy*,[1] would have remained an even more obscure part of the Ottonian corpus than it is today. This short essay, 'Das Überpersonliche im Numinosum', translated as 'The Supra-personal in the Numinous', represents Otto's only sustained philosophical enquiry into the question of divine personality. It may seem disproportionate, then, to devote a whole chapter to one of his lesser interests. But there are two good reasons for doing so. First, despite its evident importance in the elucidation of Otto's understanding of the numinous and of God, there has been no detailed scholarly notice of the essay, and this lack of exegesis needs redressing by a detailed consideration of the text. Second, if Otto's concept of holiness is to have any developed utility and relevance for theism today, the relationship between the numinous element of holiness and the divine person needs to be made explicit. After all, holiness appears to run counter to the modern theological possibility of God's passibility.[2] Divine holiness summons images of divine sovereignty and unavailability. But these awesome images of God offer little to those suffering under political systems which have legitimated their own authority by imaging God's personality in the idiom of dictatorship. Indeed, it is, to use John Gammie's words, 'precisely because the biblical doctrine of holiness in

---

[1] *IH*, Appendix V, 197–203; first published as 'Das Überpersönliche im Numinosum', in *Aufsätze das Numinose betreffend* (Stuttgart: Verlag F. A. Perthes, 1923), 42–51. Further references to this Appendix will be listed simply under *IH*.
[2] See 'Editor's Foreword', in J. Gammie, *Holiness in Israel* (Minneapolis: Fortress Press, 1989), pp. ix f.

the past fed a repressive paternalism and sexism',[3] that the second half of this chapter has been written. There I will examine John Armstrong's condemnation of the concept of holiness as a personal quality of the God of biblical theism in *The Idea of the Holy and the Humane Response*.[4] Armstrong's theory is of particular interest as it is a passionate rejection of the Ottonian idea of holiness in which the numinous power of deity is given a personalistic form.

The word 'holy' has been put to work both as an ontological definition of the *mysterium* of the Godhead and as the defining quality of the divine personality.[5] In Jewish and Christian theology God is, above all other gods, worthy of worship because he alone is holy. Indeed, it has been suggested that the logical kinship of the words 'holiness' and 'God' entails that to know the meaning of the word 'holiness' requires knowing what sort of entity God is. And just as the word 'Socratiness' might be coined to define the essential character of the particular person Socrates, so too may 'holiness' be understood as defining what is meant by a divine person—that is, what sort of an extraordinary 'person' the name 'God' refers to.[6] But monotheism might properly object to the use of holiness as a form of personal identification tag as being vestigially henotheistic. It seems preferable to understand holiness not as a qualifier to the word 'personality' but as the essence of divine being, making the meaning of the word 'holy' dependent on the meaning of the word 'God'. Thus Bilaniuk: 'The holiness of God is the deepest mystery of the very being of . . . God. It is the highest thing one could possibly utter about God . . . in reality the holiness of God is supremely simple, identical with his infinite essence.'[7]

If, then, God's holiness is not like the personal holiness of, say, the elder Zossima in Dostoyevsky's *The Brothers Karamazov*, because Zossima's holiness is not his ontological

---

[3] Gammie, *Holiness in Israel*, 5.   [4] (London: Allen & Unwin, 1981).

[5] Tillich addresses this dual function of holiness in *Biblical Religion and the Search for Ultimate Reality* (London: Nisbet, 1955), esp. 21–5, 79–85.

[6] *COH* 144–5.

[7] P. Bilaniuk, 'The Ultimate Reality and Meaning Expressed in Eastern Christian Icons', *Ultimate Reality and Meaning*, 5 (1982), 309.

definition (it does not make him God), then, as something distinct from a personal characteristic, holiness becomes an ineffable mystery.[8] If God's holiness is not something we can say *about* God, but is a purely formal definition, it becomes incomprehensible as something ontologically 'wholly other' to humanity. This is Otto's point of departure. Otto wants to say that there is something in holiness which transcends the finite qualities of personal existence, whether human or divine. If the totality of God is holiness itself, holiness cannot be *both* personal predicate *and* definiton: 'God, eternal concrete spirit does not *have* holiness, as one has predicates, but he is "holiness itself".'[9] So holiness is attributed to God as his defining attribute, to show that he is God and not merely a supernatural person.

None the less, Otto's reluctance to predicate personality of the numen is problematic if we want to put his concept of holiness to work in the biblical tradition in which God is experienced and imaged as a divine person. H. H. Farmer, who was contemporary with Otto, warned against a model of the divine wherein the numinal and personal elements of God are out of balance. If ontological and axiological 'otherness' are overemphasized (as he felt Otto to have done), then the sense of God as person is diminished, and 'may even vanish altogether in vaguely numinous or mystical states of mind'.[10] Of course, as John Hick has pointed out, the God of Israel is not quite personally identical across the Hebrew scriptures: over a period of a thousand years the perception of the Ultimate as a savage tribal deity mellows to that of a universal father.[11] Even so, Jewish and Christian religion is historically driven by the assumption that God is more or less personally continuous over time, so that revelation constitutes the coherent story of a relationship.

If Otto wants to say that holiness, as the completion of the numinous, is a relational category, in that it is how humans experience the divine presence on earth, he must also accept

---

[8] See Davidson, *Theology of the Old Testament*, 151.   [9] *IRG* 134.
[10] H. H. Farmer, *Revelation and Religion* (London: Nisbet, 1954), 60.
[11] J. Hick, 'Is God Personal?', in F. Sontag and M. D. Bryant (eds.), *God: The Contemporary Discussion* (New York: Rose of Sharon Press, 1982), 176 f.

that divine presence is willed and therefore rational—what we would call personal. And since theistic religion not only experiences God as a super-person but also attributes consciousness and will to the very being of God, Otto has to come to terms with the necessary relationship of holiness and personality. In theism, God is not just a tingling private intuition, but also a political reality; a Lord of history who appoints and sets apart the people, times, and places which will reveal him. So the theological utility of Otto's concept of holiness stands or falls on his ability to hold together private numinous experience of a numinous Godhead with the collective reception of God's historical self-revelation. Whether he can do so convincingly will become clear in the following discussion. If he cannot, that may owe less to the failings of his own work than to a lack of coherence in theistic personalism itself. For by defining God as 'holiness itself', theism seems to withdraw the relation of persons to deity from the analogy of private relationship; the inaccessible *mysterium* of the Godhead is established. If holiness is the ontological definition of Godhead rather than the summary quality of divine personality, then whether the personal and the ontological can be satisfactorily reunited in the one category of holiness is open to question.

There is a sense in which Otto's evaluation of human personality sets up an immediate conflict with his idea of the holy as being of transcendent value. Otto takes a pre-emptively naturalistic, flawed, contingent, and finite view of personality, and then quite properly finds it incompatible with the extraordinary value, modality, and ontic status of holiness. Yet salvation is, after all, the story of a historical relationship between humankind and God. As Ninian Smart puts it, 'salvation is nothing other than the sharing in the holiness of the object of man's worship.'[12] Holiness is both medium and *telos* of that salvific relationship. The divine command to become holy as God is holy means that holiness should have some affinity to the personal as the 'voice' of divine will and as the transformation of human behaviour.

[12] N. Smart, *Philosophers and Religious Truth* (London: SCM Press, 1964), III.

For Otto, however, the contention of biblical theology that humankind is made in the image of God is not extended to the personality, but to the spirit alone. His dualism created obstacles in advance for the affirmation of divine holiness having personal, hence rational, characteristics. Had Otto taken an ideal rather than phenomenological model of personality, where divine personality would have been the prototype of human personality, he might have side-stepped the categorical antinomy of holiness and positive personality. However, Otto does not adopt this manœuvre because his epistemology precludes inferential, rational knowledge of the being of God. And since I have chosen to clarify his position, I will conduct my discussion on the terms set by Otto himself.

Otto's Account of the Supra-personal in the Numinous

Otto's work reflects a peculiarly bleak estimation of humanity. Humanity's numinous disvalue, or profanity, is at the heart of his theology, and informs his phenomenology of religion. The human personality is not a source of wonder or religious exhilaration to Otto. His austere settings for numinous awakening are markedly unpeopled, characterized by stillness, emptiness, silence, and oncoming darkness.[13] This sense of the individual's spiritual alienation from communal life may have been fostered by his estrangement from many of his colleagues at Marburg, his recurrent depression, and his— later regretted—remoteness from his students. (Given his ascetic appearance, abstracted and reserved manner, uncertain health, esoteric scholarship, and Prussian moral rectitude, it was surely predictable that these students would give him the punning nickname '*Der Heilige*'.[14]) If intellectual development and biographical circumstance are mutually informing, then the anthropomorphic model of God and salvation as a social *telos* are unlikely to have appealed to Otto. In common with

[13] *IH* 65–70.
[14] See Almond, 'Rudolf Otto: Life and Work', 3–25; P. R. McKenzie, 'Introduction to the Man', in Turner, *Rudolf Otto*.

much of the mystical tradition, Otto found holiness in the dissolution of the personal rather than its fulfilment.

It is now generally accepted that personality develops as a product of interaction with other people within various networks of relationships.[15] As Otto clearly subscribes to the modern naturalistic concept of personality, it is unthinkable that the God of classical theism, let alone the Numen, should be dependent on any sort of social life or subject to processes of development within itself. And since personality is not ascribed to the ultimate reality of many of the non-theistic religions which Otto studied, the personal would have been more dispensable for him than for an exclusivist Protestant theologian. Moreover, it is not only his work in the history of religions which would have convinced Otto that holiness as an object of religious consciousness is supra-personal. Otto's wariness of personalism may also owe something to his dependence on the work of the early Schleiermacher, who felt that the personal in God is merely an idea: 'Yet the true nature of religion is neither this idea nor any other, but immediate consciousness of the Deity as he is found in ourselves and in the world.'[16]

In his treatment of non-Christian religions it looks as if Otto's argument is non-normative and primarily phenomenological. Typically generous in the scope of his analysis, he claims that all gods are more than personal, in that in their 'ancient character as "*numina*" they burst the bonds of the personal and theistic'.[17] Some forms of Christian mysticism have also allowed the assimilation of human and divine in numinous experience.[18] And biblical religion uses reverential circumlocution such as '*Ruach*' (OT) and 'Light'

---

[15] See Hick, 'Is God Personal?', 172.   [16] Schleiermacher, *On Religion*, 101.
[17] *IH* 199.
[18] *IH* 199, 200. See C. Franks Davies, *The Evidential Force of Religious Experience* (Oxford: Clarendon Press, 1989), 53–4. She finds that not all numinous experience is typical of personalist theism. Personalism may seem crude in association with the numinous, but that does not mean that the numen is impersonal in the sense of being a mere unconscious principle. None the less, numinous experience tends to lead less to conventional worship than to 'the sense of annihilation of the self in the sole reality of the numen'. Ninian Smart, however, is well known for his opinion that the numinous presupposes a duality of human and divine agency,

and 'Life' (NT) as 'the complete realisation of what was all the while potential in the character of Yahweh in His essence as a numen'.[19]

But Otto's ontological account of the Godhead also goes beyond the phenomenological. Rather than using philosophical terminology like 'essence' and 'being', he evokes the inner being of God with his own term, the 'numinous'. The numinous conveys the eternal, objective being of God 'prior' to revelation, creation, and human conceptualization. Even before God becomes holiness itself (that is, a complex of rational, moral, and numinous elements in the history of our idea of God), he is the Numen.[20] The ground of God's being is the numinous. His personality, however, belongs to his *holiness*—that is, the 'numinous completely permeated and saturated with elements signifying rationality, purpose, *personality*, morality'.[21] These 'rational' attributes of God do not, according to Otto, exhaust our experience of deity or the being of deity itself:

they in fact imply a non-rational or supra-rational Subject of which they are predicates. They are 'essential' (and not merely 'accidental') attributes of that subject, but they are also, it is important to notice, *synthetic* essential attributes. That is to say, we have to predicate them of a subject which they qualify, but which in its deeper essence is not, nor indeed can be, comprehended in them; which rather requires comprehension of a quite different kind.[22]

The non-rational essence of divine holiness is the numinous, which is apprehended as mysteriously dreadful, awesome, and mesmerizing, as possessing an energy analogous to absolute power (the *tremendum* and *majestas*).[23] This is a power

---

which mysticism tries to abolish. See e.g. his *Philosophers and Religious Truth*, 131; *idem, Dimensions of the Sacred: An Anatomy of the World's Beliefs* (London: HarperCollins, 1996), 95, 175–6.

[19] *IH* 201.

[20] In *IH* 197, 199, Otto uses 'The Numen' instead of 'numen' to signify the absolute Deity.   [21] *IH* 109; emphasis added.

[22] *IH* 2.

[23] *IH* 62. See also Zahrnt, *Question of God*, 49; Macquarrie, *In Search of Deity*, 246, where he notes that the 'anthropomorphic expression, "the wrath of God", seems to symbolise most vividly the non-rational, non-personal depth of deity'.

that cannot be contained by the personal element of the completed category of the holy. Indeed, if Otto's balance of the rational and non-rational elements in the idea of God described on the first two pages of *The Idea of the Holy* is neglected, then it would seem as if the presence of the numen would kindle an enthralled, horrified fascination with a deity of uncertain personality allied to unlimited non-rational power—hardly a revelation of God. Phenomenologically, the basic apprehension of deity by numinous consciousness seems to Otto to be of a non-rational and non-personal divine entity.[24] Otto contends that the primary experience of holiness as the numinous is non-rational, and thus supra-personal, for two reasons: first, because in the history of religion the numinous temporally precedes the rationalization of the divine; and second, because the numinous evokes non-rational/conceptual sensations such as 'dizzy intoxication', dread, 'stupor', and a sense of the weird or strange.[25]

An experience of numinous presence such as, in Otto's example, Jacob's at Bethel has an awesome, mysterious power that resists 'distinctly anthropomorphic' words such as 'Being', 'Person', 'Thou', and 'He'. He finds these 'strangely alien and repugnant to the very import of the experience'.[26] An 'I/Thou' relationship with God of the type made famous by Martin Buber is utterly rejected by Otto as being absurdly importunate and deficient in reverence. If the seraphim of Isaiah 6 would not venture such an address, then, *a fortiori*, creatures must be screened off from direct personal confrontation with divine holiness lest they be annihilated.[27] The foundational element of holiness is found to repel the personal. The experienced *energicum* and *tremendum* seem to forbid address of the numen as, in any sense, a fellow person: a futility analogous to building a structure of twigs in a hurricane.

The title of this essay, 'The Supra-personal in the Numinous',

---

[24] Cf. Tillich, *Biblical Religion*, 23, where he comments that all that has ever become a medium of the divine mystery—i.e. the holy—has in the course of religion received 'a personal face'. See also *idem*, *Systematic Theology*, i. 223.

[25] See e.g. *IH* 16, 26, 31.   [26] *IH* 198.   [27] *IH* 202; cf. *IH* 99, 105.

leaves uncertain in both English and German the degree of personality predicated of the numen. It implies a part of the numinous that is something other than personal. But Otto cannot logically remove the consciousness that is a pre-condition of personality from the numen altogether, since that would make its 'presence', presumably willed, inexplicable. Again leaving faintly ambiguous whether or not the numen may be termed an agent of consciousness, and therefore in some sense a person, Otto complains that 'it is a defect in our devotional poetry that it hardly knows any other image for the eternal mystery of the Godhead than those drawn from social intercourse'.[28] The 'personalism' on which basis most ordered worship is conducted tends to exclude the numinous. In attempting to accommodate the numen in its own historical narrative, theistic worship has to render the numen in more definitely representational, anthropomorphic forms, and as a consequence suffers a loss of religious depth.[29]

But if the argument for the supra-personality of the numinous is accepted, with personality predicated only of the completed semi-conceptualized 'holy', there is a crucial difficulty. The problem for theology is how, if personality is not essential and primary to God, it can ever become anything but a secondary appendage, placing a question mark over the integrity of divine will, and making all creative intervention in history discontinuous with his essential nature.

Otto's Attempted Solution

Although it may at times appear so, Otto does not try to argue that 'in fact' God is simply a numen, theology being a speculative tarnish that the pure religious experience of the numinous will wipe away. He argues that God is both personal and, more essentially, supra-personal. He does so on the grounds that dogmatic assertions of divine personality

[28] *IH* 203.   [29] *IH* 198.

are constructions that can neither exhaust nor do justice to the non-rational essence of their subject. A failure to respect the inconceivable nature of God gives the idea of God a 'one-sidedly intellectualistic and rationalistic interpretation'. Personality, as a rational predication, sets up an antinomy with the non-rational elements in the idea of the divine produced by numinous experience. To the subject of numinous consciousness, the 'wholly other' aspect of the numen is felt to resist 'every analogy, every attempted comparison, and every determination'.[30]

It is not always clear whether what Otto finds predicated of God in the history of religions is also what he thinks should be theologically predicated of God himself. But this lack of a clear transition between the history of religions and theology is a function of Otto's philosophical agnosticism, expressed theologically in the notion of God as 'wholly other', something 'whose kind and character are incommensurable with our own, and before which we therefore recoil in a wonder that strikes us chill and numb'.[31]

For Otto, 'God' is a title, a conceptual construct beneath which, and still discernible in authentic religious experience, is the 'real' divine, the unnamed absolute Deity or Numen; a hidden but intuited presence behind the shuttered façade of the history of theology, itself constructed and buttressed by the finite understanding. Crucial to this interpretation is the statement:

the non-rational which we were looking for in the idea of the divine was found in the numinous, and in our recognition of this we came to see that before God becomes for us rationality, absolute reason, a personality, a moral will, He is the wholly non-rational other, the being of sheer mystery and marvel.[32]

[30] IH 197. In Our Knowledge of God (London: Oxford University Press, 1939), 228 f., J. Baillie argues that God cannot be both the ground of his being, yet also 'wholly other' than himself. He finds Otto's use of the term, and as followed by Barth, Brunner, and Heim, to be clouded in confusion. It is unclear whether it refers to numerical identity or distinction, or qualitative resemblance. And though the former may be so, the latter cannot be, since humanity is made in the image of God. [31] IH 28.
[32] IH Appendix IV, '"Spirit" and "Soul" as Numinous Entities', 193.

This may account for his reluctance to 'name' the Numen, to circumscribe and reduce the abyss to the particular, the identified and differentiated.[33] The name 'God' covers a pretentious ignorance, but also has 'a strange power of hiding God'.[34]

However, it must be stressed that this by no means *excludes* some sort of personal consciousness from the divine; it simply prohibits *literal* predications of the known category of personality to a 'wholly other' object. Otto's conviction of God as 'wholly other' must, as Almond points out, entail important consequences for the relation of God to the world.[35] Clearly, 'wholly otherness' must imply that the divine is suprapersonal, if 'personal' refers to anything of the same kind as human personality. Almond uses Otto's statement in the *Religious Essays* to establish the point that any analysis of that part of the religious consciousness apprehending the numen as *mysterium* entails the Kantian limits on the scope of religious knowledge. Thus Otto: 'the divine transcends not only time and place, not only measure and number, but all categories of the reason as well. It leaves subsisting only that transcendent basic relationship which is not amenable to any category.'[36]

Where Otto diverges from Kant and follows Fries is in his replacement of the Kantian conviction that the object of religion is unknowable with the conviction that while the ability to *think* about the divine is highly circumscribed, the ability to experience it is not. Positive rational predications of the 'wholly other' are therefore precluded or have, at most, only a limited claim to truth. The transcendent relation of God to the world is primarily felt or intuited by *Ahndung*. And the status of any personalistic description of the numinous must be considered a 'schematization' of numinous emotion —necessary to religion, but secondary nevertheless.[37]

But it is significant that Otto's designation of God as 'wholly other' is not just a theory about the divine, but a religious experience: a mental reaction of 'stupor' or dumb amazement indicating the numinous object to be something

---

[33] See *IH* 2, where language is held to necessarily rationalize a divine object.
[34] *IH* 221, Appendix VI, 'The *Mysterium Tremendum* in Robertson and Watts'. (Otto quotes F. W. Robertson here.)   [35] *RO* 69 f.
[36] *RE* 87.   [37] See *IH* 47–9.

'wholly other'. It is important to recognize that Otto's concept of holiness as the first object of religious experience entails that a person cannot experience God as person until her or his numinous experience has been schematized and assimilated into the dogmatics of faith.[38] It is not reason but the *Seelengrund* (because of its spiritual, and therefore ontological, affinity to divinity) that apprehends the numinous. And since the *Seelengrund* is a non-rational faculty, it will not apprehend a rational object, but only the non-rational numen as it awakens religious emotions.

However, Otto's position is ambiguous. He wants to say that the numinous cannot be a person in the familiar sense of that word, since it is manifested and experienced non-rationally as something 'wholly other'. Yet, as in much of his other work, Otto's position is clouded by his idiosyncratic use of the word 'rational'. There are two possible interpretations of his intended meaning. First, he may want to say that the rational factor in holiness to which personality must belong is simply that side of the divine to which we may apply ideogrammatic symbols such as 'love' and 'mercy'. It is that part of the experience of the Holy to which relatively precise analogical formulations may be applied. We could call this formulation A. Or second, B, a more normal interpretation of 'rational' would find God's personality indissolubly linked to rationality because, analytically, rationality must be predicated of personality. So in predicating, for example, will, freedom, and love of God, one is saying that his personality is a necessary pre-condition of his nature as rational. However, in A, divine personality belongs to the rational and symbolic construct 'God', which suggests that the divine personality is merely ornamental to the basic ultimate reality of the numen.

Charles Campbell calls Otto's semi-agnostic approach to God 'supra-rational theism'.[39] Here the being of God can only be described symbolically. That language becomes symbolic

---

[38] It is as such that Otto can speak of God, e.g. in *FN* 8, as 'die höchste Person'.

[39] Campbell, *On Selfhood and Godhood,* 341. That Otto assigned to theology 'the function of formulating not conceptual truths, but mere conceptual ideograms' explains, for Campbell, Otto's 'rather chilly reception in the ranks of orthodox theology'.

does not indicate the reduction of truth, but is simply an acknowledgement that the symbols refer to a form of being and reality incommensurable with the finite being of human persons. In accordance with this classification of Ottonian theism, Campbell interprets Otto as having adopted the position I have called A, and concludes that, unpalatable as it might be to Christian theology, the non-rational element of divine holiness is 'fundamental and ultimate' in ways that the rational element is not.[40]

It is arguable that personality is simple: it is the totality of what it is to be an individual. Persons are rational, conscious agents who are irreducible to parts of themselves. But Otto's use of the word 'person' does not, and cannot, refer to the totality of the divine entity. Yet a personality that is not fully integral or rational may fail to be consistent, logical, just, and infallible—the sort of qualities normally expected of the Judaeo-Christian God. Perhaps because Otto's 'God' can be seen as a conflation of several models of God (biblical, oriental, Platonic, and 'primitive') his own presentation is blurred. It is religiously suggestive, but perhaps conveys little more than a vision of swirling darkness and fire, of unimaginable glory. The inherent rationality of goodness, the essence of divine personality, seems to be relegated to the contingent. At times, Otto clearly wants to say that God is numen before he is schematized as God. This accounts for God being deemed both supra-rational, yet also the bearer of rational attributes. The complexities of Otto's reasoning seem to frustrate hope of a neat dichotomy whereby personality could be attributed to the conceptualized rational 'façade' of the God of revelatory experience, and supra-personality could belong to the numinous, unfathomable Godhead. In fact, despite regretting the fixity of representation that the numen suffers in mythology, thereby losing something of its original wealth of meaning, he perpetuates a weak personalism by the following remark:

The numen has, no doubt, in itself personal features, which some-how enable the worshipper to refer to it by a pronoun as 'he' or

---

[40] Ibid. 340.

'she'. But while the limits of the personal are at this stage still fluid, they cannot (any more than in the case of the definite figure of the 'God') quite comprise the full import of the inapprehensible and unnameable, which presses out beyond them.[41]

This is unsatisfactory. It is ambiguous whether he is referring to the historical evolution of the idea of God (in which case he should omit the phrase 'in itself') or, alternatively, to the 'private' actuality of the numen, which then turns out to be rather less 'wholly other' than the reader has been led to believe. And the meaning of the casually inserted 'fluid' limits of the personal defeats comprehension. Mystification is further compounded by Otto's occasional suggestion that the numen may itself be subject to an internal rational evolution independent of human ideation.[42] For the sake of brevity and clarity, this 'curious doctrine', as Campbell calls it,[43] of the internal evolution of deity itself can be set aside. It is worthy of mention only to demonstrate the tortuous, indecisive quality of Otto's thinking here.

Without wishing to imply that all its problems can be dealt with conclusively, I would like to offer an interpretation of Otto's intentions here, based on the two disciplines which shaped his concept of holiness: theology supported by the phenomenology of religion.

Theology: The Ontological Solution

The paradox of God being both personal and suprapersonal is not peculiar to Otto's theology. Arguably, the attribution of personality to God was not a prerequisite of orthodoxy until the sixteenth century, when anti-Trinitarians used it as a means of denying that God was three Persons. Historically, an affirmation of the personality *in* God has been common to Christian theology since the third century; *persona* was first used to describe the three names of the Trinity, expressing the fullness of the Godhead, but only much later

---

[41] *IH* 198.   [42] *IH* 110.   [43] Campbell, *On Selfhood and Godhood*, 341.

was it used of the Godhead as a whole. And even where theologians of the biblical tradition have predicated personal attributes to God, this is distinct from describing God *as* a person. It is therefore clear that Otto's hesitation to predicate personality of the divine is not without historical precedent. It is not, after all, controversial to say that representations of divine personality will be symbolic rather than direct, and that God is personal and more. No theology can pretend to re-create the actuality—the inner being of the divine subject— any more than a human biography can re-create the private subjectivity of a public personality. Of course, what is usually intended by 'divine personality' is the affirmation that human persons and God can enter into some sort of reciprocal relation. Whilst it may seem implausible or even paradoxical that God is both rational super-person and numinous supra-person, perhaps this is no more so than the traditional Trinitarian model of God, full of the mysterious coming and going of divine traffic.

It has been stressed that holiness can be nothing less than the ontological definition of God. It is holiness that exhausts the being of God, not personality.[44] And since the totality of God, all that could be said about God, cannot be said, holiness does indeed belong to the *tenebrae aeternae*, to that which lies infinitely beyond knowledge. As holy being, the undifferentiated abyss of divinity does not belong to history. As such it is supra-conceptual. But this numinous abyss of God's being, speaking mythologically, also holds within itself the historical possibilities that are the subject of revelation.[45]

However properly agnostic theology might be about holiness as the quality that summarizes the ontological distinction of the Godhead, biblical religion is organized around a special form of personal relationship with God that will render the faithful holy themselves. Justice, mercy, righteousness, and love are personal attributes of God on which humans

---

[44] Cf. P. Tillich, *The Courage to Be* (London: Nisbet, 1952), 176.

[45] Cf. Macquarrie's account in *In Search of Deity*, 174 f., of the dialectical opposition in God between his primordial unity and the fullness of his being: the one and the many. He looks at the idea that 'holy being' comprises a number of modes: primordial, expressive, and unitive.

model themselves in the attempt to be holy as God is holy. Furthermore, linguistically at least, worship and prayer in the biblical traditions assume a rational, personal divine subject who is responsive to human devotion. The dynamics of the salvific relation must be underwritten by the rationality of conceptual symbols such as 'divine will' and 'divine love'. Without the functions of a purposive, rational personality, the holiness of God is empty of salvific power and love. Without an intelligent will, God's desire for the human *summum bonum* (reconciliation with himself) becomes incomprehensible. Otto acknowledges all this by what Campbell calls his 'supra-rational theism'. Given, then, that the inner being of God can only be described in symbolic language, it is to be expected that, in the closing remarks of Appendix V, Otto would resolve the antinomy of personality and numinous through an analogy:

Assuredly God *is* for us 'Thou' and a Person. But this personal character is that side of his nature which is turned manward—it is like a 'Cape of Good Hope', jutting out from a mountain range which, as it recedes, is lost to view in the *'tenebrae aeternae'*—only to be expressed by the suspension of speech and the inspiration of sacred song.[46]

In itself, the theological implication of this image must be correct: God is experienced and known only in what he chooses to reveal of himself. But Otto goes further than that. The image can be interpreted as meaning that the public aspect of God, what can be experienced or seen, is personal, while the private, more introverted Godhead is non-personal: a nameless numen.[47] If this is so, then the God-ness of God, his holiness, is merely masked, but not penetrated, by his personhood: a *persona* in the archaic sense of the word. But the motive for assuming the costume of 'God' would then seem inexplicable, since motive belongs to will, which belongs to

---

[46] *IH* 203.

[47] See E. Underhill's reference to this image in *Man and the Supernatural* (London: Methuen, 1927), 116. Underhill finds the image of divine personality as a 'Cape of Good Hope' instructive as a means of evoking how 'the Ultimate' reveals itself in humanly comprehensible terms.

actual persons. The use of mythical imagery suggests that the person assuming the mask is a kind of person who is not readily comprehensible without anthropomorphic aids to comprehension. If that is so, Otto may then share the conventional position that God is a person but not a human person (assuming it makes sense to talk of non-human persons).

Perhaps I have taken the image too literally—straining it until it collapses into absurdity. Otto does not, after all, offer a precise philosophical analysis of the supra-personal in the numinous. He assembles and authenticates his argument with selected corroborations from religious literature, none of which exemplifies Patristic precision. There remain, however, certain ambiguities in Otto's position. The sentence 'God *is* for us "Thou" and a Person' in the first line of the quotation above might refer to two separate divine states. First, 'for us' may mean that the human construct called 'God' is fashioned by reason and faith into a person. This would entail that if one remains a realist at all, God is not 'really' personal, but a 'substance', *x*, possibly quite alien to the personal—in which case it is not only the numinous that is supra-personal but the totality of the divine, since the numinous is the 'private' and 'real' totality of God. Alternatively—and I think preferably—the sentence may be illuminated by Otto's own interpretation of his image by religious ontology.[48]

I interpret Otto as follows. His dualistic anthropology of persons as transcendental souls with historical bodies mirrors his theology of God as both numinous and personal. In the duality of the Godhead there is no 'flesh', but an unknown 'wholly other' type of person of whom a unique form of consciousness can be predicated, but any discussion of which can only be symbolic and dimly intuited by numinous experience completed by faith. The human soul, in Otto's phrase, 'lies beneath' the personal ('all that we can know or name in ourselves at all'), and is hence 'impenetrable to any concept'. However, the soul can be symbolically conceived in numinous self-feeling 'by one who has experience

[48] *IH* 203.

of the deeper life'. By analogy, the same might be true of the numinous essence of God.[49]

On this model, analogous to saying that sub-personal sub-conscious forces determine and are sometimes manifest in the human totality, Otto finds the supra-personal *energicum*, the hidden depth, the abyss of the God of revelation, to be continuous with the revealed totality of God as rational personality. Indeed, unless Otto predicates some mysterious form of rationality to the Godhead, he loses biblical theology altogether. After all, holiness belongs to the salvific purpose of God, entailing that a personal and instrumental model of holiness is to be preferred to an emanatory one, in which holiness is simply the quality of divine being made manifest, much like his radiant glory. If holiness does belong to the personal purposes of the divine, then it must issue from the divine reason. But there is nothing to suggest that, in keeping with Otto's emphases, divine reason should not itself remain a *mysterium*, 'wholly other' to human reason. No one can know the mind of God, but that does not mean he has not got one.

On this interpretation, the original, primordial being of God is non-rational. The divine may be pictured as two circles, the smaller fitting inside the larger (numinous Godhead and rational God, respectively). Here God's nature as numen is encompassed by the totality of his personal Godness. This is comparable to the traditional dualistic anthropology of a person's first and final reality being their soul, even though their full hypostasis is as a person: a material body, a rational consciousness, and a soul. Otto's idea of God is di-polar, rather than dichotomous: the holy is the unity of poles, the numinous 'completely permeated and saturated with elements signifying rationality, purpose, personality, morality'.[50] This model of God as personal but not exhausted by his personality seems to elucidate the complex relation of the holy, the numinous, and the divine personality in a

---

[49] One could also use a Jungian model of the relationship of an alien, symbolic, archetypal pre-conscious unconscious to the rational, interactive personality. See L. Bregman, *The Rediscovery of Inner Experience* (Chicago: Nelson Hall, 1982), 6, 29 f.   [50] *IH* 109.

way that is least offensive to biblical theology, and is already familiar to mysticism.

Phenomenology: The Dialectical Solution

Otto resolves the problem of the relation of holiness and divine personality both theologically and phenomenologically. Theologically, as we have seen, he uses a model of God in which holiness is the wholeness of divine being: God is holiness itself, which includes personal attributes, but is also primarily and essentially numinous. And he ties this speculative argument to evidence from the history of religious experience, so that the two arguments are mutually informing.

In *The Idea of the Holy* Otto offers apologetic both for mystical, apophatic religion and for dogmatic Christianity, when, even-handedly, he applauds the New Testament for its humanizing conception of the fatherhood of God.[51] On the opening page of his book Otto claims that theological accounts of deity as (analogically) rational and personal give content to faith and make '*belief* possible in contrast to mere *feeling*'. For Otto, it is the conceptual characterization and knowledge of God as Father and Lord that makes Christianity pre-eminent among religions. The highest conception of God includes both the frightful and non-rational and the transcendent grace and goodness of the rational/personal God of Christianity.[52] Consequently, I would hold, with Almond, that this earnest attempt at balance can be explained by Otto's sense of the dialectical relationship of personality and the numinous element of the holy in the life of religion.[53]

The Idea of the Holy may be understood, then, as a 'dialectical corrective'. Otto's subject is the *idea* of the divine, and he urges that the rational and non-rational aspects of a given idea of the divine are to be kept in balance in order to motivate and justify faith and praxis. This conception of God is a corrective in the sense that, as the nineteenth century had neglected or denied the non-rational *mysterium tremendum*

---

[51] *IH* 82.   [52] See *IH* 1, 56, 142, 172 f.   [53] See *RO* 127–9.

in the idea of the holy, Otto is concerned to revitalize it, not merely as legitimate, but as essential.

In his essay, 'Mystische und gläubige Frömmigkeit', Otto argues that there is a dialectical relation between the strongly numinous element of supra-personal mysticism and the rational personalism of biblical theism.[54] The two are united in the depths of the numinous itself and in human religious sensibility.[55] According to Otto, when any act of devotion is performed with particularly heightened emotion, it will merge into a mystical perception of God as supra-personal, where, in union with the numinous object, the worshipper's sense of time and self collapse.[56]

The two antinomous elements of religious perception are resolved by Otto in the two ways that religion has of apprehending God: that of mysticism, in which there is (broadly speaking) a dissolution of personal categories, and that of biblical faith, where the personal qualities of God's love, loyalty, justice, and so forth have a salvific function. He writes:

each of the two, the personal and the mystical, belongs to the other . . . They are not different forms of religion, still less different stages in religion, the one higher and better than the other, but two essentially united poles of a single fundamental mental attitude, the religious attitude.[57]

Hence the non-rational aspect of the divine may, as the numinous, be experienced as impersonal or supra-personal; but because the divine also has a rational character, it may be known as personal Lord and Father.[58] This is hardly an original insight. Amongst others, Ninian Smart, Conrad Hyers, S. Radhakrishnan, and Winston King have argued

[54] Literally, 'Mystical and Believing Piety', in *Aufsätze das Numinose betreffend*, 71–107.
[55] Ibid. 71. See also ibid. 77; *MEW* 216; *IH* 198, 201, 203; *RO* 127–9.
[56] Otto, *Aufsätze*, 75. However, according to Söderblom, *Living God*, 261, Otto defines mysticism as personal fellowship with God, as opposed to traditional piety. Much hangs on one's definition of mysticism.   [57] *IH* 202.
[58] Otto hints at this solution in *IH* 199, with his parallel illustration from the Hindu concept of God as Bráhma / bráhman (personal / supra-personal). Otto's awareness of the peculiar logic of the mystical paradox can also be seen in *MEW* 64.

that personal and impersonal symbols for the divine—and for the human relation to the divine—coexist in all the major religious traditions.[59]

Even so, despite the equivalent value of the rational aspect of the idea of God to the non-rational aspect (suggested by his favoured metaphor of woven fabric), his corrective tendency gives the rational a lesser status. Otto's own religious temper, betrayed by the passion of his language, clearly veers towards, for want of a less contested word, the 'mystical'.[60] And it is doubtful that what Otto calls the 'superiority' of the rational element in religion ('superior' is only a relative term) can be of greater value than what is 'most profoundly religious': its non-rational, numinous element.[61]

But as a dialectical corrective, Otto's position represents a renewal of reverent emphasis. As an affirmation of the transcendent mystery of the Godhead, Appendix V precludes the reduction of God to an anthropomorphic and patriarchal projection. Even with the best intentions, if divinity is made ontologically continuous with humanity, divine holiness comes within the sphere of knowledge, within human grasp and therefore, most importantly, within the sphere of human control. With Scripture, Otto affirms that the human vision 'cannot bear the perpetual sight of holiness without an occasional screen'.[62] If the familiarities of personalism are spiritually presumptuous, then the text of Appendix V can be read as a reminder in devotional etiquette.

In sum, Otto's concept of holiness requires a divine ontology that includes the pole of rational (that is, conscious) personality, symbolically characterized by 'will' and 'love', and the pole of the non-rational numinous essence or abyss of the Godhead, characterized through the experience of its awesome power as the *mysterium tremendum et fascinans*. Whilst this model of God cannot be 'thought out', it is vindicated phenomenologically. Otto's phenomenology of the

---

[59] See I. G. Barbour, *Myths, Models and Paradigms* (London: SCM Press, 1974), ch. 5.

[60] See Almond, *Mystical Experience*, 56 f., for the way in which the word 'mystical' can be applied to numinous experience.　　　　　[61] *IH* 1–4.

[62] *IH* 202.

holy as a union of rational and non-rational experiences is paralleled in the dialectical relationship in theism between the non-rational (what Otto calls 'mystical' experience of the divine as supra-personal, and therefore non-rational) and the rational faith in, and collective devotion to, the personal God revealed in history.

Holiness and Divine Will in History

In this second part of the chapter I would like to relate my discussion of the personal aspect of divine holiness to an argument about the politics of the holy that is particularly forcefully expressed in John Armstrong's *The Idea of the Holy and the Humane Response*.[63] Armstrong's argument is an important counter to the idea that holiness necessarily, and by definition, represents what is perfectly desirable about the divine personality. Indeed, as Armstrong is aware, if holiness is a relational category, it may also become a political category, and thus subject to enquiry into its socio-political effects. Any examination of holiness in the late twentieth century must take into account the emancipatory criticism of religion, whether feminist, Black, or ecological, which, singly and together, have raised awareness of the often oppressive politics of theology and religion. Religion is inherently political, because the holy is a distinctive means to power. Gerardus Van der Leeuw's *Religion in Essence and Manifestation* is probably the best-known exposition of the claim that power is the hermeneutical key to the sacred, and F. J. Leenhardt has also argued that the priestly caste maintained its exclusive privileges by telling the Hebrew laity that holiness was dangerous to any but specially appointed personnel.[64] But in recent years religious feminist scholarship has mounted perhaps the most trenchant criticism of the ways in which mediatory persons (traditionally men) have controlled other

[63] Hereafter, since this is the only work by Armstrong referred to, page references will be given in parentheses in the text.

[64] F. J. Leenhardt, *La Notion de sainté dans l'Ancien Testament: étude de la racine QDhSh* (Paris: Libraire Fischbacher, 1929), 228.

people's (usually women's) access to God—and therefore to spiritual and political power—by defining what is holy and what is profane and by conducting ritual and dispensing privilege accordingly.

And it is not only feminist criticism that has exposed the derivation of religio-political authority from theological language and has shown how religious pictures of cosmic ordering can legitimate secular law and authority. That being so, emancipatory theologians might well be as concerned as Armstrong is with the way in which holiness has, in the Old Testament particularly, consisted in the potent combination of divine otherness and might. Don Cupitt is not alone in thinking that the 'prophetic, numinous experience of God as *other*, as a holy and sovereign will that calls, commands, and puts words into our mouths', is 'no longer an authentic religious possibility'.[65] Whilst Otto would have resisted the use or threat of holiness as a mere instrument of socio-religious power-broking, it is none the less important to look at ways in which the holy has been so deployed. A late twentieth-century critic of Otto must consider Armstrong's rejection of the grandeur and abstraction of holiness as creating a divine personality inimical to compassion, to 'proper distress' at the suffering of the world. Armstrong sees holiness as an insufficiently criticized tool of oppressive religious ideologies which seek to inhibit the process of laicization that would distribute religious power and authority more evenly (75, 166).

Although Otto's work uses the language of theological dogmatics as a system of ideograms, for Armstrong, the analogical characterization of the numinous as awesomely majestic has, none the less, led to a renewed emphasis on the rumbling, smoking, sovereignty of God's personality, rather than his mercy and concern. It is certainly true that in Otto, holiness, as the defining property of divine personality, is darkly transcendent, and sets the stage for monarchical monotheism at its most impressive. In Otto's analysis of creature-feeling, the holiness of the divine person tends to define the

[65] D. Cupitt, *Taking Leave of God* (London: SCM Press, 1980), 31.

human personality as abject, if not crushed.[66] Armstrong contends that the history of the idea of the holy as a *tremendum* leads to a literally unbalanced divine personality, a distorted idea of the Holy One, God. The awful isolation of his transcendence and otherness, his limitless authority exercised in lonely totalitarian power, his monopolization of value—all seem to sever any possibility of intimacy with creation.

Armstrong traces the idea of holiness as what he calls 'absolute centralised power' to the historical requirement of the Hebrew people in the advent of Mosaic Yahwism to find 'psychic strength and potency to yield the necessary martial prowess for the gaining of land and political status'. In their 'self-aggrandising ambition' the Hebrews required a 'powerful smiting God' to fulfil their 'territorial obsession' (12). It was political insecurity which led to the 'rabid jealousy for [God's] incomparable glory' and honour (13). Armstrong claims that it is unbridled dreams of dominion that lead directly to the desire for a holy god: a stable, necessarily preeminent locus and source of power such as that described in Psalm 72: 8–11 (13).[67]

By 'monogamous' relations with their protector, or Lord, the Hebrews appeased and appropriated Yahweh's holy power by tribal association and minutely specified sacralist cult. By holy imperialism, men guaranteed their safety and their domination of territories held in the name of Yahweh, in the certainty that they were doing the unalterable will of the Lord. Armstrong finds the consequence of this kind of sacralization morally disturbing; the holy war is interpreted as the 'raging will to annihilate the unholy, as an intolerable exception and threat to the pure ascendancy of holiness' (31; see also 74, 94).

Armstrong (in common with feminist and ecological theology, much of which was to be written later, in the 1980s and 1990s) mourns the loss of what he calls the 'organic idea of

---

[66] See *IH* 20.

[67] Armstrong fails to note that the verses immediately preceding and following these describe this power less as dominion, but more as informing moral virtue and fostering responsibility to the natural bounty of divine creation.

blessing'. This is a primary biblical tradition which he traces in teaching found in such books as Jonah and Hosea, and resurfacing in a final efflorescence in the Gospel teaching of the fatherhood of God (32, 124). In the pre-sacralist strand of Old Testament writing, God is conceived as 'present and closely accompanying', through the nurture of his creation. Armstrong argues that the divine was once characterized by harmonious immanence rather than towering transcendence. More farmer than holy emperor, the divine was once a guide and protector, blessing creation with fruitfulness and the multiplication of humans and animals (5, 16).

However, politically based sacralism is held by Armstrong to have destroyed the natural harmony in the divine–human relation. The new concept of holiness literally disintegrated the divine personality, and allowed the exploitation of divine holiness as the means and will to power. God now ruled creation from the transcendence of a heavenly throne, 'controlling the forms and forces of nature but present in none' (17). Monarchical monotheism enthroned God as a Lord appointing priestly generals to extend the territory subject to his victorious power (3, 73).[68] According to Armstrong, the disintegration of the old organic relation between God and humankind by holiness is exemplified in some 200 biblical references in which the metaphors for holiness are drawn from the mountains, 'mostly with ecstatic or numinous overtones' directing the mind to 'what is uncompromisingly high and far above and apart from nature, in other words the holy God' (50, 7–8). Armstrong insists that the concept of holiness inexorably creates a supernatural divine realm in transcendent opposition to the natural world which, as the profane, represents the dwindling and final extinction of natural immanent value.[69]

---

[68] Cf. Grossman, 'Holiness', 391 f., which supports Armstrong's argument. Grossman writes that in Rabbinic usage the Holy One of Israel 'expresses his power as a man of war by his holiness, the determinator that defeats all the facts of the world'. The political has religio-metaphysical meaning: 'Holy war is the semantic war of holiness upon the world of pagan and secular reference . . . holiness makes war against culture—the making or imagining of anything that is not itself.'

[69] See *IH* 29.

In a sense, Armstrong is arguing that, with the attribution of holiness, God's personality receives a potent instrument of power. It is as if—despite the metaphor of 'farmer', prior to the predication of holiness of God—Armstrong wants to say that God is not really a personality at all, but an immanent, regenerative power in the phenomenal natural world. So, for Armstrong, it was only in Israel's severance of God from the world that he acquired the firm outlines of a personality defined by transcendence; by a commanding, purposive will, and, I would add, an exclusively male personality. And it was as Creator, giving the 'most dramatic and conclusive exhibition of centralised power that can readily be imagined' (18), that God came to rule history by holiness. Any offence against holiness constituted 'sin'. This is described by Armstrong with an Ottonian turn of phrase as 'utter inadequacy before the transcendent majesty of divine holiness' (22). Although humanity was commanded to imitate divine holiness (so furthering its expansionist drive), that holiness became as removed from the possibility of personal rapport as the lion by which God's glory was symbolized (44).

Giving his argument a Nietzschean flavour, Armstrong denies that the cult of holiness promotes strength in its practitioners. The Holy One is in fact 'partial to the suffering, miserable and weak but only in so far as they wait for his mercy . . . He raises the lowly at the mighty's expense' (60). The divine personality shows its power by reversing human fortune (as can be seen in prophetic and apocalyptic eschatology) and promoting numinous awe by crushing and humiliating the strong who might have threatened the power of the holy. Consequently, the understanding of human holiness has been distorted in such a way that righteousness has become a function of obeisance to holiness, and morality identified with merely prudential appeasement of the holy (93).[70] Armstrong's study ends with a brief examination of

---

[70] See *IH* 101 f. Otto explicitly rejects the 'repulsive doctrine' that God is *ex lex* (outside the law), which turns him into a 'capricious despot' with a 'fortuitous will'. Otto accounts for what is surely Armstrong's error, by noting that the doctrine arises only when a religion allows too great an emphasis on the numinous and neglects 'the absoluteness of moral values'.

the perpetuation of holy inhumanity in the medieval Church, in which he finds the bishops to have inherited their sacerdotal power from the Hebrew tradition. Greek philosophy fused with the cultic will to power to create indifference to the suffering of the world, for 'to belong to this world was to desert the highest ideals' (114, 116, 117).

An Ottonian Response to Armstrong

The central question posed by Armstrong's argument must be whether the logic of holiness, as the *mysterium tremendum* of unlimited power, does in fact disfigure our model of divine personality that theism requires to be defined by its goodness. But before that can be answered, we need to examine Armstrong's argument a little further. Perhaps the greatest problem with his psycho-social critique is that he treats God's holiness not as an ontological definition, but as a projected quality of personality and a weapon of spiritual terrorism. In effect, he mistakes the projection of characteristically patriarchal pseudo-holy values on to God for the holy itself, which is manifest in divine love and justice. Armstrong has equated a politically motivated model of the divine personality with holiness itself, making the holy demonic by the identification of an infinite divine power with finite political power.[71] Indeed, against Armstrong, it must be stressed that Otto's imagery for the object of numinous experience is not final or absolute. Otto's monarchical imagery for numinous power is no more than a set of symbolic expressions evoking absolute value, and, as such, is replaceable by images that better reflect the religio-political sensibility of the time.

Holiness is a category of relation. And the personal is one possible (though probably the highest) mediator for reconciling human and divine being in the commonality of holiness. (As Grossman observes of Judaism, 'holiness is an aspect of the divine nature appropriation of which is commanded by God.'[72]) But God's will to relation is not identical with

---

[71] Tillich, *Systematic Theology*, i. 223 f.   [72] Grossman, 'Holiness', 396.

human relationality, and our model of God must reflect this. If, as Tillich claims, the symbol overtakes the reality, and gods become 'idealised men', they are robbed of divine ultimacy:

They [the gods] have no numinous power. The *fascinosum* and *tremendum* are gone. Therefore religion imagines divine personalities whose qualities disrupt and transcend their personal form in every respect. They are subpersonal or transpersonal personalities, a paradoxical combination of words which mirrors the tension between the concrete and the ultimate in . . . every type of the idea of God.[73]

Moreover, the Ottonian phenomenology of the numinous, in which Armstrong seems to share, forms a peculiar category of value that the latter ignores. In his conviction that as *fascinans* the numinous is an absolutely desirable but 'wholly other' good, Otto would strongly resist Armstrong's essentially moral and rational argument against a particular corruption of holiness. Theologically, Armstrong has distorted the holiness of the divine personality by giving disproportionate emphasis to power at the expense of grace. It is a mark of God's love that creation be sanctified so that he can draw near. Humanity is sanctified by obedience to God, and that which is blessed is very close to that which is holy.[74] Theism understands human holiness as the coincidence of human will with the will of God. Certainly, geo-political and spiritual imperialism have driven wars that have been waged in the name of the holy. Be that as it may, Armstrong has confused the contingent symbolic representation of the holy with the ineffable reality of holiness. Yet, as Tillich notes, 'if a segment of reality is used as a symbol for God, the realm of reality from which it is taken is, so to speak, elevated into the realm of the holy. It is no longer secular. It is theonomous.'[75]

As a feminist I have strong objections to monarchical imagery for God, because it sanctifies hierarchical, exploitative, and alienated social relations. Yet, contrary to Armstrong, I would argue that the Ottonian language of monarchical monotheism at least represents analogically the ontological

[73] Tillich, *Systematic Theology*, i. 223.   [74] Grossman, 'Holiness', 390.
[75] Tillich, *Systematic Theology*, i. 241.

and metaphysical ultimacy of holiness, with its intrinsic power to sublate all patriarchal value. Otto (who, ironically, was pilloried by the Barthians at Marburg for his liberalism) certainly likened numinous experience to that of being in the presence of majesty. But, as Otto notes, the 'majesty' of the numen is an analogy, and therefore contingent on a given society's (hierarchical) idea of definitive power. In *The Idea of the Holy* he remarks that spiritual visions are often given form by 'clothing' them in the images of glory supplied by the period.[76]

However ineptly, monarchical language does indicate that God's power belongs to a non-ordinary, ultimate dimension. In Hosea 11: 9, God says, referring to his mercy, 'I am God and not man, the Holy One in your midst.' Whilst fearsome models of God have stood guard for violent social structures, it is also arguable that the otherness of the Numen precedes its patriarchal mediation as tyrannical deity, and, manifest as a God of justice, constitutes what is worthy of worship. As *mysterium tremendum*, he is one whose mysteriousness is resistant to any attempt to project our political purposes on to his will. His 'overpoweringness' is of a wholly other value that pronounces dreadful judgement upon the demonic values that drive military and economic imperialism and hubris. And as *fascinans*, the Numen is an object of the religious longing for the holy which drives the religiopolitical transformations that are premissed on the conviction that precisely *as* holy, all created things are, and must be treated as, ends in themselves.

Holiness, then, prophetically negates the world's (patriarchal) values within its own axiological incommensurability. In this sense, the 'wholly otherness' of the holy can represent a righteous refusal of worldly powers, not their cultivation. For Otto, human hubris stands under the judgement of the revelation of holiness as a value 'wholly other' to those of the world. Holiness is not God making war on the world, but a gracious revelation. And if sin is understood as the abuse or pollution of God's holy human and non-human creation,

[76] *IH* 225.

then wrath is incurred not simply because the irrational controlling will of God has been defied, but because hubris has impugned the value of the holy.[77] Submission to the value of holiness is not so much a dismissal of creaturely value as a reproof of human arrogance by reminding it of the profanity of its arrogant misuse of all other created things. This does not diminish the value of the creature; on the contrary, it is an assertion of the absolute and inviolable value of the creature to God. Human holiness need not, then, be a ritually infused means to power for the subjection of other persons. It is properly the opposite: a recognition that as creature one has no right to commandeer other created things to the service of one's own interests. Holiness does not inevitably lead to the religio-political barbarism described by Armstrong. Arguably, the roots of barbarism are found in the uncontrolled ascendancy of personal will and the destruction of love, not in the realization of one's finitude and relative insignificance. The *fascinans* element of numinous experience is completed not as greed for political power, but as the yearning for communion with God and the gracious empowerment for love and prophetic witness such communion bestows.

Armstrong's analysis of holy power is too limited to place Otto's concept of holiness in jeopardy. Holy power may, as the numinous, evoke awe. But if, as I argue in my final chapter, that awe is mixed with numinous fear, that is because those who profane God's creation stand under judgement; they are accountable to the holy. Yet, in Jewish and Christian theology, the numinous is not only wrathful but also merciful and gracious. Holy power is constituted by its goodness. Certainly, the theonomous goodness of God is awesome, but in the eschatological mythologies only the deliberately evil are at risk. The 'wrath of God' is a picture by which theology affirms that God is just, that he takes evil seriously. Wrath and love are poles of divine holiness, where God's wrath is ultimately a function of his love for the innocent who have been wronged.

[77] See *ROR* 5.

In short, the idea of holiness should not be confused with political manipulation of the symbols of its ultimacy. A purely socio-political reading of biblical literature ignores the prophetic sense of the holy as an empowering liberation from alienated worldly power into the sphere of the theonomous good. Holiness is 'wholly other' to the unredeemed world of conflict and exploitation. Far from being a weapon of oppression, authentic holiness establishes the possibility of divine immanence, and therefore reunites humankind and God.

5

Holiness and Morality

It is possible to make a very sharp distinction between holiness and morality such that holiness is essentially non-moral because its practices and values refer to a non-ordinary dimension of reality, and morality refers simply to the good conduct of a given community.[1] But this implies an extremely minimal and relative account of morality. If one wants to say that morality is not just the observance of rules necessary for the government of a civilized society, but rather tells you something about the nature and will of God, then a dichotomy between moral and holy value is by no means self-evident.

Otto and the later commentary on his work have struggled to do justice to the two values of moral goodness and holiness, trying not to collapse the one into the other or to elevate the one at the expense of the other. But neither Otto nor his critics can be said to have been wholly successful in this regard. When, in 1947, G. E. Hughes asked whether the analysis of holy value must be conducted exclusively within the parameters of theological discourse, or whether it is also capable of analysis in non-theological, moral terms, he stalled at just the point at which his argument might have been expected to reach a conclusion, and he admitted that it is a question which he simply cannot answer.[2] Like Otto before him, there is a sense in which this question defeats him. As Philip Almond justly observes, 'Otto has not worked out anything like a complete account of the relationship between

---

[1] Grossman makes this distinction in 'Holiness', 390.
[2] G. E. Hughes, 'An Examination of the Argument from Theology to Ethics', *Philosophy*, 22 (1947), 12 f.; see also p. 15.

religion and ethics, and although the general thrust of his argument is plain, much about it is unclear.'[3] The present chapter makes no pretensions to a final resolution of the issue, but offers an account of Otto's progress through these philosophically treacherous waters and presents a theological defence of his final position within it.

Otto's Account of the Relation between Holiness and Morality in The Idea of the Holy

Although *The Idea of the Holy* is not the only text in which Otto presents his view of the relation between holiness and morality, it is the best known. Here Otto argues that holiness cannot be subsumed into the category of moral value, and on the fifth page of *The Idea of the Holy* asserts that it is instead 'a category of interpretation and valuation peculiar to the sphere of religion'. The book then devotes attention to analysis of the unique, irreducible feeling response elicited by the presence of the numinous, one which, in itself, is quite independent of ethical significance or intention. Yet part of the shudder of numinous experience is a judgement of appreciation: a sense that the numen is 'precious beyond all conceiving' and absolutely worthy to be praised.[4]

Max Scheler considers that 'splendid book', *The Idea of the Holy*, to have been 'written with the purpose of refuting the idea that the holy is no more than a blanket-conception covering "the good, the true and the beautiful"'.[5] This is certainly the case, but Otto also intends to show that religion is an autonomous category, and must be more than the sum of superannuated knowledge of the world that can be replaced by science, more than a form of metaphysics, and, above all, more than a guarantee and reward for supererogatory moral commitment. Indeed, in *The Idea of the Holy* a large part of Otto's purpose is to clearly distinguish morality from holiness in order to preserve and underline the transcendence

---

[3] *RO* 106. Boozer, in his review of *RO*, p. 44, feels that Almond's remark is unjustified, but does not elaborate on his objection.   [4] *IH* 52.
[5] Scheler, *On the Eternal in Man*, 315.

of the divine. He wants to say that the being of God cannot be exhausted or domesticated by known value. Knowledge of the divine cannot be achieved by the most outstanding rational achievements or earned by the most heroic moral endeavour.

The separation of religion and morality is relatively modern, and can be traced to the Enlightenment's attempt to found ethics on reason, freedom, and individual responsibility, rather than on the sacred authority of revelation and supernatural agency. Otto, following Schleiermacher, attempts to rebut the attack on religion that rationalist moral philosophy implies, by withdrawing religion altogether from the moral realm and locating it instead in the feeling of the awesome, mysterious, ineffable holy. Otto is by no means alone among German theologians in his attempt to establish the independence of religion from rationality. This is a Northern European tradition that can be traced from Luther, via Schleiermacher and Kierkegaard, to Barth.[6] And it could be argued that Otto belongs to a Lutheran tradition which reads St Paul as teaching that salvation is by faith in the free grace of God, not through works and law.

Much of Otto's thought on the relation of holiness to morality can be traced to his rejection of Kantian moral philosophy.[7] For Kant, holiness is the perfect accordance of the will with the moral law; it is goodness itself, such as 'no rational being of the sensible world is capable at any moment of its existence', and so requires the postulation of the immortality of the soul for its attainment.[8] The holy will stands under no imperatives, because the 'I will' is already in harmony with the law of autonomy, the moral law.[9] Indeed,

[6] See *ROR* 180; J. Pelikan, *Human Culture and the Holy* (SCM Press, 1959), 80 f.

[7] Diamond, in *Contemporary Philosophy*, 77, regards Otto's stress on the nonrational as a function of his historical situation, in which post-Kantian religion was equivalent to popular moral philosophy.

[8] T. K. Abbott (trans.), *Kant's Critique of Practical Reason* (London: Longmans Green & Co., 1898), 218; see also ibid. 58.

[9] See also H. J. Paton (trans. and ed.), *The Moral Law: Kant's Groundwork of the Metaphysic of Morals* (London: Hutchinson, 1948), paras. 39, 86. Otto refers to Kant's conception of the 'holy' will in *IH* 5.

God is holy simply on the grounds of the coincidence of his will with the moral law. By contrast, *The Idea of the Holy* largely ignores moral duty. *Contra* Kant, religion is absolutely not derived from moral obligation, but from the sense of divine presence which is analogous to, but in itself discontinuous with, other forms of experience. This is crucial to Otto's concept of holiness. In Kant, whatever can be known of God is a product of human knowledge of good and evil: God is known through the workings of the *practical reason* in the moral conscience, in the attuning of the will to the ethical a priori of the categorical imperative of duty. But for Otto, what can be known of God, the Holy, is a product of the *emotional* content of the religious life. Even Otto's method of alerting his readers to the numinous is non-rational: Otto has to stimulate a sense of it using techniques akin to those used in teaching courses in music or art appreciation.[10]

The Non-rational and the Holy

Since the relation of the non-rational and holiness has caused so much confusion, it might be helpful to borrow John Reeder's suggestion that Otto's concept of the holy is analogous to the concept of a father. Fatherhood embraces both social and moral roles, but also, most fundamentally, what Reeder calls 'biological' fatherhood. While both are essential to the meaning of the 'complex' concept, 'biological fatherhood' is the context and presupposition or foundation for the social role. Accordingly, both rational-moral and non-rational / non-moral are essential elements in the idea of the holy, but the latter is 'the logical basis for the yoking of the two'.[11]

The concept of holiness is described in *The Idea of the Holy* as a complex category of rational as well as non-rational elements, defined respectively as the moral element and the

---

[10] Diamond, *Contemporary Philosophy*, 77.
[11] J. P. Reeder, 'The Relation of the Moral and the Numinous in Otto's Notion of the Holy', in G. Outka and J. P. Reeder (eds.), *Religion and Morality* (New York: Anchor Press Doubleday, 1973), 263 f.

peculiarly religious numinous element, fused in permanent synthesis. After all, the distinction of religion from morality does not mean its isolation or alienation from morality. Religion is given form and content by reason and its values;[12] emotions alone do not constitute religion.[13] Concepts are required to 'translate' and articulate the numinous experience of divine self-manifestation into moral and religious legislation.

Böhme and Luther are reported in *The Idea of the Holy* to have spoken of God's awefulness as a wrathful will 'fundamentally independent of *moral* elevation or righteousness, and as indifferent toward good or evil action'.[14] But Otto urges that this should be interpreted only symbolically. It evokes the dreadful mystery of divine being; of a power which, because supra-conceptual, is not subject to human control. Otto recognizes, then, that theology's sense of the essential non-moral element in the holy can, and has, resulted in tipping the balance in the concept of divine holiness between the moral and the numinous too far to the latter side. This produces the 'repulsive doctrine that God is *exlex* (outside the law), that good is good because God wills it, instead of that God wills it because it is good, a doctrine that results in attributing to God an absolutely fortuitous will, which would in fact turn Him into a "capricious despot"'.[15] In this caricature of the numen, what is morally right is contingent on an arbitrary divine will and command, so that 'right' means only what happens to be commanded, and does not reflect divine moral intention. In his rejection of the doctrine of God as *exlex* Otto denies that the numinous 'side' of God is an irascible, amoral, and arbitrary will which determines the good and right by whim. Rather, the numinous element of the divine simply eludes conceptualization; it is 'that which lies altogether outside what can be thought, and is, alike in form, quality, and essence, the utterly and "wholly other"'.[16]

---

[12] *IH* 141.   [13] *IH* Foreword and p. 1.

[14] *IH* 107, also ibid. 6; Reeder, 'Relation', 261.

[15] *IH* 101. For a full discussion of this point see Reeder, 'Relation', 255–61.

[16] *IH* 141.

'Schematization' in The Idea of the Holy

As a duality of rational and non-rational elements, Otto's concept of holiness partitions holiness and morality. Yet recognizing that morality is a necessary, legitimate, and phenomenologically integral part of religion, Otto is compelled to find a way to reunite morality with holiness without diluting the supernatural quality of the latter. In the interest of a coherent account of religion, which is, after all, a human conceptual system, Otto wants to unite the purely emotional reaction to the *numen praesens* with the moral implications of the altered disposition and values subsequent to religious experience. The psychological transformation of the numinous experience into an experience of the holy, which properly includes a moral element, is achieved by what he calls 'schematization'.

Theologically, schematization is developed in order to tie together the rational and the non-rational side of the holy. The rational side of the holy is reflected in God's creation of the moral order and his demand that humanity be righteous; the non-rational side represents the depth of the divine which is the object of primary, non-moral numinous experience. The holy is a product of the schematization of numinous experience, the primary experience of the divine:

Now the relation of the rational to the non-rational element in the idea of the holy or sacred is just such a one of 'schematization', and the non-rational numinous fact, schematized by the rational concepts we have suggested above, yields us the complex category of 'holy' itself, richly charged and complete and in its fullest meaning.[17]

The word 'schematization' seems to bear little relation to Kantian schematism, a process in which the data of sense experience become intelligible by their subsumption under the rational categories of understanding, such as causality or substance.[18] Campbell is correct to say that 'what Otto means

---

[17] *IH* 45.   [18] See *COH* 127; *RO* 37; *ROR* 187; Reeder, 'Relation', 266–81.

by it in its religious context seems tolerably clear without reference to its highly technical application in the *Critique of Pure Reason*'.[19] Most writers have regarded Otto's use of the Kantian term as highly questionable.[20] Be that as it may, in Otto's own use of the term 'schematization', the foundational non-rational elements combine with the rational element to produce the phenomenon of religion in its fullest expression. By his theory of 'schematization', the non-rational sensations of numinous experience are made intelligible by their subsumption under the categories of rational understanding. In this way, Otto attempts to retain the absolute autonomy of religion as psychologically and logically differentiated from ordinary states of mind, while allowing their intimate relation.

In his analysis of the evolution of religious consciousness, Otto finds that religious and moral elements necessarily coexist in the developing religious consciousness:

The histories of religion recount indeed, as though it were something axiomatic, the gradual interpenetration of the two, the process by which 'the divine' is charged and filled out with ethical meaning. And this process is, in fact, *felt* as something axiomatic, something whose inner necessity we feel to be self-evident.[21]

Each aspect of the numinous experience is schematized by a corresponding moral or rational ideogram, operating by a psychological association of ideas. In its historical and psychological affinity or association with other values, the numinous feeling may, although actually *sui generis*, become conjoined to (as in the present case) the moral, by reason of its analogy to moral value as *augustum* and *fascinans*. Numinous experience and moral experience may, in their analogous relation, 'reciprocally excite or stimulate one another and cause one another to appear in the mind', and in doing so create a permanent inward connection: a *schema*.[22] As Campbell explains, this 'inward necessity' is not fortuitous. Rational concepts are applied to God by an a priori schematization of numinous experience because, despite their qualitative

[19] Campbell, *On Selfhood and Godhood*, 336.   [20] *ROR* 187.
[21] *IH* 136.   [22] *IH* 44, 46.

difference, an a priori connection is affirmed between these and the supra-rational object of religious experience. The basis of this a priori connection is the awareness of an analogy between the emotions evoked by the numinous object and the particular rational quality, here moral goodness, used to describe God.[23]

In Otto's analysis of the numinous experience as that of something *mysterium tremendum et fascinans*, each element of the numinous is immediately schematized by rational concepts, which eventually form a theology. The *tremendum* element of numinous experience is at once schematized by the concept of divine moral command, disobedience to which evokes the wrath of eschatological justice. Correspondingly, the *fascinans* element, schematized by the concepts of mercy and love, comes to be summarized in the concept of God's 'grace'. The mystery of divinity permeates all these elements: 'the moment *mysteriosum* is schematized by the *absoluteness* of all rational attributes applied to the Deity'.[24] Here, the mysterious lies outside thought as the 'wholly other', and this corresponds to the concept of the absolute as that which exceeds not our power of conception, but our power of comprehension. Therefore the rational side of the divine is absolutely good; but this is not the kind of goodness that can be comprehended—Otto therefore (confusingly) calls it 'non-rational'.

The objective value of the numinous is characterized as *augustum*: recognized as 'possessing in itself *objective* value that claims our homage'.[25] As such, it has close links with other values, whilst retaining its absolute 'otherness'. As Scheler remarks, no witness of goodness, truth, or beauty can of themselves 'produce the characteristic impression of *holiness*'.[26] The 'august' aspect of the numinous is schematized by the moral. But Otto will not allow the numinous to evaporate into the moral, as occurs when 'the holy' is identified in the Kantian manner with the 'perfectly good will'.[27] It is, after all, the subject whose mind makes the transition

---

[23] Campbell, *On Selfhood and Godhood*, 354.   [24] *IH* 140 f.   [25] *IH* 52.
[26] Scheler, *On the Eternal in Man*, 316.   [27] *IH* 49.

from the feeling of the numinous to the sense of the moral value of the holy; the actual numinous feeling does not transmute or change in quality.[28]

Few have been convinced by Otto's theory of schematization. R. F. Davidson notes that 'no aspect of Otto's thought has been more widely criticised, and none for that matter as generally misunderstood by British and American critics' than that of schematization. He himself finds Otto's idea of schematization 'much too obscure and poorly defined in his own mind to merit very serious consideration'.[29] To its critics, schematization seems to imply that the moral dimension of religion is an appendix to experience of the holy. This was not a popular suggestion. Roughly contemporary with Otto, J. Baillie's response to his work is interesting because it typifies the characteristic British embarrassment at the extravagance of Continental, romantic emotion in the first half of this century. Baillie wants to look for manifestations of the divine not in the 'guttural frenzies' of divination, but in the voice of conscience obedient to the claim and revelation of moral value. 'The footprints of Divinity' are not to be detected in numinous experience, which he describes as 'the occasional disturbances and obscurations of our human nature'. It is not in the sense of the holy that God is revealed, but in the brisk witness of moral personality in 'the fullest daylight of its reasonable and healthy exercise'.[30] Baillie has a profound mistrust of what he calls 'esoteric mystic visions', preferring instead 'the sentiments of a well-behaved soul'.[31] (And if one examines the lives of men like the aristocrat Benvenuto Cellini—a murderous profligate who lived in a daze of religious exaltation[32]—one might have some sympathy with Baillie's view.)

Almost all Otto's critics claim that his fundamental mistake lies in his uncompromising desire to preserve the full autonomy of religion. In his attempt to do so, Otto is considered

---

[28] *IH* 42.
[29] *ROR* 181, 192. Sharp criticism of schematization can also be found in *COH* 127; J. Baillie, *The Interpretation of Religion* (Edinburgh: T. & T. Clark, 1929), 250; Oman, review of *IH*, p. 285.   [30] Baillie, *Interpretation of Religion*, 461.
[31] Ibid. 124.   [32] See Spencer, 'Religion, Morality', 349.

by many to have left holiness and religion as a whole, morally and intellectually isolated and therefore deprived of their full meaning. At the same time, morality is demoted to mere social convention. Indeed, Otto seems to withdraw religion from the arena of intra-mundane value to such an extent that he makes a radical existential division between religion and morality, which no amount of ingenious artificial schematization can appear to reunite. The theological dilemma which Otto's conviction of the axiological otherness of the holy presents may be stated as follows: if holiness is not perceivable as a value, it is not worthy of worship. But if holiness *is* perceivable as a value, it is *not* other.[33] Yet Christianity, at least, does not worship a 'wholly other' God: the Incarnation is a mark of God's self-revelation as being in some sense ontologically compatible with the historical realm.

It may, in fact, be acceptable, and even useful, to argue that, psychologically, religion and rationality are distinguishable. But their separation in *The Idea of the Holy* makes it impossible to make any transition from the numinous intuition to the moral 'ought' which Otto himself sees as fully appropriate to religion.[34] Otto recognizes that by treating religion and morality as both equally a priori and *sui generis*—that is, independent in experience and origin—he has no logical grounds for postulating their necessary synthesis in the consciousness of the holy. In order to resolve the problem, he is 'forced to assume an obscure *a priori* knowledge of the necessity of this synthesis'. In consequence, as Oman acidly remarks, Otto separates holiness and morality theoretically, but 'in the interest of experience and common sense' concedes that they are related a priori.[35] A particularly incisive objection to schematization (which he calls 'ingenious nonsense') is made by B. H. Streeter, who argues that far from *completing* the religious qualifications of the subject, schematization seems, under Otto's own criteria at least, to reduce them:

---

[33] I owe this formulation of the dilemma to a comment made to me by Professor Keith Ward.

[34] C. A. Bennett, 'Religion and the Idea of the Holy', *Journal of Philosophy*, 3 (1926), 465. This remains one of the clearest and most succinct treatments of this issue.   [35] Oman, *Natural and Supernatural*, 63.

'It would seem to follow that the more completely a man becomes a Christian, the less there will be of the numinous in his experience of God—a remarkable phenomenon if the numinous is in any sense the *basis* of religion.'[36]

Whilst these criticisms are logically compelling, it may be that schematization complicates numinous experience unnecessarily. It is possible to interpret Otto as having in fact side-stepped the hazards of schematization in *The Idea of the Holy* by saying that the *augustum* element of the numinous is both 'wholly other' and known to religious feeling. I interpret Otto as saying that holy value can be known, as it were, by default. The feeling of unworth—of profanity in the presence of numinous value—reveals the content of this incomparable 'other' value almost by a *via negativa*. Numinous value is known as a deficiency in alienated or false human values, as what has been missing since 'the Fall'. Furthermore, it is not the case that if divine value cannot be assimilated to any natural value, then it cannot be recognized at all. G. E. Hughes contends with Otto that while religious experience recognizes divine worth as the holy, it cannot measure or grasp it. Indeed, 'it is just this conjunction of the ability to recognize God as possessing this worth or value, and the inability to measure it by any standard we can understand, which seems to be the source of religious awe.'[37]

Freiheit und Notwendigkeit: *Otto's Modified Position*

Otto's later contribution to the understanding of the relation between holiness and morality is, theologically, more promising than that of his theory of schematization. Yet, apart from Reeder, Almond, and to a lesser degree Davidson, Otto's critics seem oblivious of the fact that schematization is not Otto's only attempt to suggest a proper relation between holiness and morality. This was an inevitable result

[36] Streeter, *Buddha and Christ*, appendix II, 'The Idea of the Holy', 322 f.
[37] Hughes, 'Examination', 14. Cf. Bennett, 'Religion and the Idea of the Holy', 464.

of the fact that most of the commentary on Otto was written while *The Idea of the Holy* was still topical, and *Freiheit und Notwendigkeit* was published when Britain and Germany were once again at war.

In the last weeks of his life, profoundly depressed and ill —in his 'schweren Krankheitsstunden'[38]—Otto wrote *Freiheit und Notwendigkeit*: a 'conversation' with Nicolai Hartmann about the relation of autonomous ethical value to the theonomous divine value of holiness. Otto died three years before the essay was published. Had he lived to promote its argument, it might have corrected the commonly held assumption that he had irresponsibly jettisoned morality from the definition of religion and replaced it with what was at best morally equivocal: the *sensus numinis*.

In *Freiheit und Notwendigkeit* ('Freedom and Necessity') Otto proposes numinous value as the basis of moral obligation. As Almond puts it, here

the relationship between the Holy and the sphere of moral values is two-fold. The apprehension of the nonrational side of the divine (*das Heilige*) is coordinated with moral value, and the God who is both rational and nonrational (*der Heilige*) is the divine source and logical possibility of moral value.[39]

In order to reach this conclusion, Otto examines Hartmann's antinomy between 'the autonomy of the Good in and of itself and theonomy, that is, the establishment of all "laws" by God; the antinomy between "moral law and divine will"'.[40] I do not want to enter into the debate over Otto's treatment in *Freiheit und Notwendigkeit* of the relationship of autonomous morality and divine command. This has already been covered with great expertise by Almond and Reeder.[41] Since my interest lies primarily with holiness, and not with the perennial questions of moral philosophy, I will look instead at the ways in which Otto's revised position clarifies the role of his concept of holiness for theology.

In *Freiheit und Notwendigkeit* Otto finds that the feeling of

---

[38] T. Siegfried's 'Nachwort' to *FN* 19.   [39] *RO* 105.
[40] *FN* 8 (unless otherwise stated, translations are mine).
[41] *RO* 103–6; Reeder, 'Relation', 282–92.

the holy—that is, in this context, the numinous[42]—is itself a feeling of value (*Wertgefühl*), which, phenomenologically, can be argued to be what Goethe called an *Urphenomene*: a primal, universal experience which widens the claim of value 'far beyond the merely ethical sphere'.[43] The feeling of the holy, and its accompanying sense of profanity or sinfulness, cannot, then, be traced narrowly to the sense of the 'merely ethical'.[44] Holiness has to be something other and more, something that will always elude domestication by human conceptualization. To underline this conviction, Otto constantly appeals to a higher court of meaning and value: the intensely private certainties of the 'deeper feeling of value', contrasted with what he calls 'the legalities of the world'.[45]

None the less, mundane laws are far from empty of significance for ordinary moral conduct. Otto accepts the autonomous moral law as regulating and protecting the 'basic right of the other person'. Secular moral law is the basis of the moral imperative which governs ordinary conscience, whether one is religious or not.[46] Therefore at no stage does he dismiss the seriousness of objective obligations to others.

All objective ethical value, whether it is an extension of divine will or a human construction, is grounded in the value of the holy as the perfectly good essence of divinity. Otto expresses the conviction that all modes of moral value emerge from the numinous depth of the Godhead, with the image of the holy as a metaphorical sun whose beams are felt in the world as morality.[47] Holiness is the 'source and ground of possibility of all actual or possible values in the cosmos'.[48] All value originates in the 'eternal, original value' of the divine

---

[42] See Reeder, 'Relation', 283. Reeder assumes that Otto is referring to the numinous element of the holy, since he draws a contrast between holy value and ethical value. [43] *FN* 9–10.

[44] *FN* 10.   [45] Respectively *FN* 10, 16, 17, 18.

[46] See Otto's article, 'Wert, Würde und Recht', *Zeitschrift für Theologie und Kirche*, 12 (1931), 58; also *IH* 43; *FN* 12; *RO* 103.

[47] *FN* 15. Cf. Pelikan's account of Luther's concept of holy value in *Human Culture*, 95: 'The Good was not the Holy, and yet it was in the holy God that man was to seek goodness, for He was "the eternal Good, an eternal fountain spilling over with sheer goodness from which there flows everything that is good or is called good".' On p. 117 Pelikan himself adopts this very image to summarize his own understanding of the relation of holiness and morality.   [48] *FN* 11.

being. For it is the Creator alone who has the 'primary autonomy' in the creation of all value, so, as a result, 'the autonomy of the creature is subsumed in theonomy'.[49]

Otto makes no apologies for his restriction of the autonomy of moral goodness. It is firmly tethered to God's command, heard in the conscience, that humanity be holy because he is holy—that is, absolutely good. Otto's model of God, as the source and meaning of goodness, in effect, makes the full autonomy of human moral reasoning an impossibility. Communion with God is the means to holiness and, thereby, goodness. None the less, at no time does Otto deny human freedom to remain in a profane state if one so chooses. There is no developed concept of divine punishment or reward in Otto's work. Furthermore, the coherence of his phenomenology of numinous experience depends on spiritual and psychological freedom to recognize and desire holy value and distinguish between that and profane value.

Otto contends that God has created people as free agents: neither blind to value, nor programmed for blind obedience.[50] People can, then, be properly moral (in a loosely Kantian sense), and not merely blindly obedient to a despotic will. The intra-mundane values forged in historical experience allow the free recognition 'that what God commands is right in terms of "autonomous" value, and that this same divine reality as value is the "ground" of all values'.[51] The will becomes self-legislating by virtue of its free inner affirmation of the validity of the commandments.[52] Where moral goodness is a product of divine holiness, it cannot be regarded as arbitrary. For the *holiness* of God's will (that is, its goodness and power) determines a priori that his will is good; it is, by definition, to use Reeder's translation of the phrase, a 'self-founded value depth'.[53]

It can, of course, be argued that one cannot attribute a

---

[49] *FN* 15. Cf. *FN* 18, where Otto claims that the essence of all things imitates and issues from God's essence; *FN* 17–18, where he compares the relation of God to the world to that of an artist whose values are expressed in his work, and ties his own image into the tradition of 'Logos-theology'.   [50] *FN* 11.
[51] Reeder's paraphrase of *FN* 11, in 'Relation', 283.   [52] *FN* 11.
[53] *FN* 10 f., 14, 15, 17; Reeder, 'Relation', 284.

moral nature to divinity if the morally good is not determinable independently of the meaning of God.[54] But Otto is not arguing that God is simply a moral being. Rather, God's ontological composition has two elements: the rational/conceivable side of his holiness, conceptualized as divine moral goodness, and the numinous, non-rational/inconceivable side, which is a mystery but, as the essence of Godhead, must be the essence and source of his goodness.[55] This entails that numinous experience will be a supra-moral experience, recognizing the ineffable value of divinity to such a degree that the human concept of moral goodness is mystically sublated in the non-natural goodness of the divine. Yet gradually, as the original numinous experience is accommodated to everyday conditions of life and the teaching of religion, the sense of the numinous is 'translated' into the sense of the holy and one's proper duties towards it. Some of these duties will be ritual, others ethical, so that holiness and morality may come to overlap in the finite world. But this does not entail that the beginning and end of morality cannot, ultimately, be absorbed into the holy as its source and judge.

Otto stresses that the image of human value as a 'beam' from the radiant divine value is an ideogram: there can be no literal assertions of the relation of God to the world or of the rational to the non-rational. Instead, theology must be symbolic, with its images pointing towards something which is 'certain enough in our dark feelings'.[56] The *Urwert* makes an inherent demand, and this is symbolized by the concept of the 'will of God'.[57] Yet the good is not good simply because God wills it to be so, but because he created a world of value which reflects his own value as holiness itself. Therefore Otto sees human moral value not as a rival of divine

---

[54] See *RO* 74.

[55] Otto appears to be undecided as to which 'side' of God's holiness is the source of moral value. In *FN* 10–11 moral value originates in the union of both sides of the divine, but as Almond points out (*RO* 160 n. 67), the 1936 edition of *Das Heilige* states that the non-rational side of the divine is the source of moral value. However, these two statements do not seriously contradict one another, for the numinous, as the essence of the Godhead, has logical priority, and is therefore the ground of the union of the two 'sides' *and* the source of all value.

[56] *FN* 17.   [57] *FN* 18.

value, but as doing its work through the operations of the divinely created conscience.[58] So, finally, at the end of his life, in *Freiheit und Notwendigkeit* Otto has done what his critics had always recommended he do: relinquish any *radical* distinction between the numinous and the moral.

An Assessment of the Argument of Freiheit und Notwendigkeit

On the surface at least, it would appear that in *Freiheit und Notwendigkeit* Otto has simply beaten a retreat from his position twenty years previously in *The Idea of the Holy*. But I am not sure that this is the case. Admittedly, it would be surprising if Otto's ideas had not developed at all in this period, but it seems to me that *Freiheit und Notwendigkeit* cannot be regarded as a volte-face but more as the culmination of a shift in his thought about holiness during the last ten years of his life. In fact, sometime between 1924 and 1936, and included in the later German editions of *Das Heilige*, Otto hints at his final position in *Freiheit und Notwendigkeit*. In these later editions of *Das Heilige* Otto affirms that the *augustum* element of the numinous is the non-rational ground (*Urgrund*) from which all possible objective value springs.[59]

In *Freiheit und Notwendigkeit*, the intimate relation of holiness and morality entails that the numinous actually 'gives birth' to morality. But when Otto first wrote *Das Heilige*, and until at least 1924, he believed that there was only a necessary schematic correlation between them. However, as

---

[58] *FN* 15.
[59] *Das Heilige* (Munich: Biederstein Verlag, 1947), 63. 'Numinose Wert' is 'der irrationale Urgrund und Ursprung aller möglichen objectiven Werte überhaupt' (1936, p. 67). This key sentence does not appear in any English editions of *The Idea of the Holy*, as it was added by Otto after Harvey had translated *Das Heilige* and was overlooked in the preparation of new English editions. The English editions retain the sentence Otto wanted to remove from the text: 'Es ist der *numinose Wert*, dem auf Seiten der Kreatur ein numinoser *Unwert* entspricht' (*Das Heilige* (Stuttgart: Verlag F. A. Perthes, 1923), 62. Here, numinous value is opposed to, rather than continuous with, human value, a view Otto clearly wanted to retract. See also *RO* 102.

a general point, I would argue that this apparent discontinuity between *The Idea of the Holy* and *Freiheit und Notwendigkeit* can be accounted for by the difference in the issues they address. The former work can be understood as a phenomenological investigation of humanity's emotional reaction to numinous presence. The latter work is a theological investigation of the relation of the moral good to the holy as the essential property of the divine Creator. None the less, all that has actually been dropped from Otto's analysis is his previous a priori separation of religion and morality.

In softening the distinction between the good and the numinous in *Freiheit und Notwendigkeit*, Otto is prepared to sacrifice the full logical autonomy of moral value. That much has been established. But is it possible that in doing so he *also* relinquishes the full autonomy and otherness of religion which in his earlier life he had laboured to secure? In fact, it may be that Otto has to forfeit the full autonomy of religion in order to accept morality not just into the holy, but into the numinous itself. But the price might not be as high as it seems. For by retaining the primacy of numinous value in the being of God and religious experience, Otto has avoided turning religious value into a merely elevated mode of a natural, human value.

However, this text has not entirely satisfied its tiny band of commentators. Almond complains that in *Freiheit und Notwendigkeit*, Otto's grounding and subordination of moral value to numinous value is 'the least coherent part of his argument'. According to Almond, Otto is faced with a 'conceptual dilemma'. On the one hand, Otto needs to maintain that if the numinous is genuinely *augustum*, it must have a clear, phenomenological relation to mundane value. On the other hand, Otto cannot say that the non-rational numinous is the ground of rational mundane moral value, because the numinous is by definition non-moral. Almond finds Otto's resolution of this dilemma by grounding all mundane value 'in the *combined* nonrational and rational Holy' 'somewhat arbitrary'.[60] Similarly, according to Reeder, if the image of

---

[60] *RO* 106.

God as the 'ground' of all value is in fact 'a substantive conceptual analogy', then Otto has violated 'his own insistence that the numinous cannot be brought within our conceptual frame'.[61] Reeder's point is essentially a query about Otto's religious epistemology. However, both queries can be met in terms of a theological defence of Otto's image. For it seems to me that in making the numinous the ground and source of moral value, Otto has not betrayed his own conviction that the numen is an incommensurable *mysterium*. For whatever is the source of all value, of all goods, *must* in any case be an ineffable mystery.

There might seem to be a contradiction between Otto's statement in *The Idea of the Holy* that the holy 'is not originally a *moral* category at all'[62] and his position in *Freiheit und Notwendigkeit*. For in the latter work, the moral and the holy appear to belong to the same category by emerging from the same source: the numinous being of God. But if Otto says in *The Idea of the Holy* that the holy is not originally a moral category, he may simply mean that holiness precedes goodness in the Godhead: that the 'moral' element in the divine nature is encompassed and determined by the totality of its holiness. This image of the Godhead means that the divine nature cannot be conceptualized as can a perfect moral personality, but is a mystery which is known intuitively as absolutely good.

So even in *The Idea of the Holy*, Otto is *not* saying that the numinous is separate or opposed to the moral, but simply that in religious experience the moral judgement is preceded by the numinous judgement which sublates one's natural sense of goodness so that it is absorbed in that of the numinous as *augustum* and *fascinans*. The result is that one is left with a sense, perhaps expressed in the ecstatic hyperbole of religious emotion, that this is a 'wholly other' good. It may be that even as far back as *The Idea of the Holy*, the 'wholly' in the phrase 'wholly other' should not be taken literally, but merely as a rather emphatic way of expressing the theological particularity of holiness. Otto can then maintain his distinction

---

[61] Reeder, 'Relation', 290.   [62] *IH* 52.

133

between numinous and moral value, and still claim that the one is the 'ground and source' of the other.

Significantly for our understanding of how the concept of holiness has developed in the work of Otto, Reeder questions Otto's contention in *Freiheit und Notwendigkeit* that moral value is logically dependent on the numinous. Reeder feels that in this contention, Otto seems to destroy the distinction between them both.[63] But Reeder's objection can be answered if it can be shown that a thing can produce something else that is quite other than itself. After all, if God is logically continuous with the world as its creative cause, this does not mean that God *is* the world. On the contrary, the contention that God is transcendent and ontologically other to the world is quite compatible with the notion of his making it, just as if I draw a picture of a bowl of lemons and then say that I am neither a piece of paper nor a bowl of lemons.

In the same way moral goodness might be traced to the numinous essence of the Godhead. But this does not mean that the numinous can be conceptualized as a moral good, or that it can be exhausted by the concept of morality, any more than the 'I' of my private being, which is made up of rational and sub-rational elements, is exhausted by the sum of my moral acts. Of course, the ontological link between God and goodness is more intimate than that between persons and good or bad acts, but the principle remains the same: that something rational or conceivable issues from something non-rational or inconceivable, X, does not necessarily make X rational or conceivable.

There are, of course, philosophical difficulties with the theological contention that the supreme worth of holiness gives rise to all moral obligation.[64] As G. E. Hughes points out, our moral duties to X cannot derive solely and directly from X's moral goodness, since this would entail that we have no moral obligation to those who are not morally good— which is not the case.[65] Yet this does not, in my view, apply to the case of God's holiness. Only God has holy worth,

---

[63] Reeder, 'Relation', 288.   [64] Hughes, 'Examination', 15.
[65] Ibid. 16.

therefore humankind is ultimately obliged to worship God rather than worldly goods like territorial dominion or vast accumulations of capital. This lies at the very heart of mono-theistic biblical teaching. As a divine creation, humans participate in God's holy worth, and so must show love and respect towards that creation, which includes themselves.[66] In a religious context this love and respect become the practice of personal holiness. Hughes chooses this theological solution himself. He accepts that God's holiness means that his goodness surpasses that of all other objects to such a degree that its claim obliges not merely respect, but love or devotion.[67] Holiness, then, is the ground of human moral obligation. A religio-moral personality is the product of devotion to God. It results from the numinous apprehension of the value of the numen.

Otto's implicit rejection of the full logical and meta-physical autonomy of moral goodness may not impress some moral philosophers. But that he has based his link between holiness and morality on solid theological ground should become clearer in the latter part of this chapter. Suffice it to say here that worship (or the adoration of divine worth) is not an ordinary moral experience. Otto believes that the innermost experience of religion is mystical rather than moral: 'the soul seeks God with rage, seeking the eternal unchanging Godhead who was never concerned with any work.'[68] Religious obligations have a different quality from ordinary moral obligations. The latter have a purely intra-mundane application, whereas those of religion have a metaphysical and *sui generis* reference to the divine, and are therefore applicable within the world at the spiritual as well as at the historical and material level. And since the religious consider holiness to be a higher value than moral value, the holy can overrule the ethical only in the sense that it seeks the highest good of all: *shalom* in all of God's creation.

In *Freiheit und Notwendigkeit* Otto rejects Hartmann's op-position of self-subsistent metaphysical value over and against the sphere of divinity. Since mundane and ideal values and

---

[66] Cf. ibid. 17.   [67] Ibid. 17 f.   [68] *MEW* 196.

the human capacity to recognize them are equally derived from divine power in creation, they are both logically and metaphysically dependent on the Creator.[69] Although the possibility of good and evil can arise only historically as a choice, motivation, or development of the moral disposition, holiness precedes history as the essential power by which the historical possibility for *shalom* was created.

Theology and Holiness as a Spiritual Value

A more detailed theological defence of Otto's final subsumption of morality into holiness would now seem worthwhile. The argument presented in *Freiheit und Notwendigkeit* is, I think, a substantial improvement, in terms of theology, on that of *The Idea of the Holy*. Theologically, Otto could not be satisfied with the notion that goodness exists independently of God. All goodness must logically originate in the absolutely good will of God. If moral value is determined by divine will operating in accordance with the divine holy essence, which is, analytically, good, then morality cannot be tainted by voluntaristic arbitrariness. Logically, if God commands in accordance with his essence, he cannot require unwilling subjects to be wicked in his name or to sin against the good in order to be obedient to himself. Indeed, such a position would make nonsense of the theistic premiss that God is absolutely good, that a holy will is the very meaning of God. Furthermore, Otto's argument in *Freiheit und Notwendigkeit* is true to the traditional theistic insistence on the otherness and pre-eminence of God. It is an account of the good which is in accordance with the doctrine of divine aseity: that is, that divine self-sufficiency of being establishes God's primacy and independence over all other meaning and value.

In *Freiheit und Notwendigkeit* Otto has found a twofold strategy to confirm the absoluteness of the value of holiness and to exclude secular self-serving values that profane God's

---

[69] *FN* 15.

world. First, he denies the autonomy and claim of all natural value by saying that its origin is not rational, but originates in numinous being and authority. Second, he extends the meaning and reality of the numinous, both uniting it to the rational will of God and projecting numinous value out into the world, making every instance of moral obligation an obligation to the numinous itself. Nor does Otto lose the radical otherness of the numinous. Divinity remains transcendent as the *fons et origo* of value; it is untouched by secular concepts of value. The divine would lose transcendence only if its private actuality became available to human concepts, which is impossible, or if it became in any way logically dependent on finite concepts of value. Where finite value is a 'translation' of numinous value under the conditions of existence, its 'original text' remains untouched by that rational process. Numinous value remains non-rational—that is, ineffable and supra-conceptual, available only to feeling in religious experience.

To say that God's goodness is absolute does not, however, mean that it exhausts his holiness. On the contrary, God's holiness is the fusion of his goodness and his otherness. It is this which entails that divine goodness is not identical to human goodness, that his will is neither arbitrary or merely an amplified version of our own, but is a holy will. A holy will may then be defined as a will whose 'omnipotence' cannot, ultimately, be frustrated, and whose 'omniscience' entails that, correlated to his perfect love, divine will is perfectly orientated to the ultimate human good. And in its numinous otherness, holy will is both an awesome, mysterious potency and an object of trust.

Certainly Otto's thinking here is not foreign to the Jewish perception of the nature of moral value. Indeed, one of Moshe Meiselman's recent texts cites *The Idea of the Holy* as an authority for the fundamental conviction that as the source of absolute value, God, not reason, is the source of ethics. Echoing Otto's point in *Freiheit und Notwendigkeit*,[70] Meiselman argues that 'man acquires ultimate value only because

---

[70] *FN* 15.

on the sixth day of creation he was created in the image of God'.[71] So humanity is not, in itself, a source or arbiter of value, but only in its relation to God. This means that the first words of the *Shema*, 'Understand O Israel, the Lord is our God, the Lord is [the only] one', affirm that no other value coexists with God. Otto's final understanding of holiness as (theologically) the only logical source of morality is clearly acceptable to theists, for whom morality is generally derived from religion.

Accordingly, the following discussions of sin, the imperative of holiness, and salvation represent examples of the significance of Otto's work to theology. In treating these, I will draw heavily upon the insights of Jaroslav Pelikan's exhilarating book *Human Culture and the Holy*. The distinction between holiness and morality is, for Pelikan, the most profound implication of the Christian gospel: 'the madness of the Holy', which 'does not pretend to be easy or rational or normal'.[72] Pelikan (who, like Otto, is a student of Luther) realizes that no human value can have precedence over divine value when he speaks of the existential dread that follows the creature's attempt to pass a natural value-judgement on his Creator. To do so would domesticate the holy by blasphemously equating it with human value. Like Otto, Pelikan believes that God does not merely demand moral improvement, but 'lays His claim upon the total man. Nothing less will satisfy Him. A refusal to let Him rule over the total man is sin.'[73] It is not, then, violation of the moral law which alone profanes us, but the sin of refusing inclusion in God's holiness.

Pelikan cites three thinkers as his predecessors in the non-rational recognition of the holy as a non-natural value. He finds that, in emotional *extremis*, Dostoyevsky, Nietzsche, and Kierkegaard all distinguished the holy from the morally good. Their knowledge 'came in the clarity of mind and

---

[71] M. Meiselman, *Jewish Woman in Jewish Law* (New York: Ktav Publishing House, 1978), 6, 7.   [72] Pelikan, *Human Culture*, 83.

[73] Ibid. On p. 82 Pelikan goes so far as to suggest that 'moralism', the view that holiness is a part of goodness, which thereby uses moral achievement to gain equality with God, can become the 'mark of the Antichrist'.

singleness of heart that are the peculiar gift of the insane. Their insanity helped them to insights of which the normal and balanced mind is rarely capable.'[74] All three identified sin as a religious, rather than a moral, category, and knew that what determined sin was not 'relationship to a moral code but relationship to the Holy himself'. Pelikan concludes in truly Ottonian style: 'No distinction between right and wrong will avail me anything when I am faced by the awesome and fascinating presence of the Holy. Obedience to law and loyalty to social convention fall harmless to the ground before His glance.'[75] Although he makes only brief reference to Otto's work,[76] Pelikan does in fact offer a radical analysis of the relation of holiness and morality, which, being so close to that of Otto, gives further emphasis and clarity to Otto's position.

Otto believes that people are condemned by their profanity or 'numinous disvalue', rather than their moral guilt. This implies that, for him, sin is a barrier dividing God and humanity that is erected by more than immorality. Here sin is not moral guilt but godlessness, which leads to infringement of holy value, which includes but also transcends all that is *only* moral.[77] For Otto, the pronouncement that humankind is in sin is a religious judgement, not determined initially by the sinner's conduct but by his or her separation from holiness. Presumably (Otto is not explicit here) moral evil is, then, a part and result of sin: the estrangement from God that is the profanity of hubris.

The numinous evaluation has priority over the moral evaluation for Otto: 'that which is recognised as the Holy is not of this world, and as clarity of vision grows, its nature is seen in contrast to all mundane things.' In so far as a person perceives 'the essential nature of the Holy and its demands', he or she 'moves and lives in a sphere of existence entirely

---

[74] Ibid. p. ix. The reference to 'insanity' could be misleading here. Perhaps what Pelikan is referring to is not the absence of reason, but the suspension of normal, received, rationalist perception, liberating the subject for 'abnormally' heightened intuitions.　　　　　[75] Ibid. 79, 80.

[76] Ibid. 68, where he pays tribute to Otto's 'penetrating' distinction between holy and moral value.　　　　　[77] *RE* 1.

different from the merely "natural", and at the same time different also from the sphere of moral freedom'.[78] Thus sin becomes the refusal to enter the supernatural domain of the Holy.

Although Otto is more interested in the psychology of numinous consciousness than numinous praxis and devotes little space to holy living, the lives of the medieval saints can be read as an intriguing illustration of a holy life driven by the *sensus numinis*. There are, of course, many ways of reading the lives of these saints; I am only using them as an illustration of the difference between an ordinarily virtuous life and a holy life *par excellence*. The lives of the medieval saints can be read as exemplifying Otto's account of the numinous transvaluation of values in such a way as to underline and support his contention that sanctity can transcend—though not repudiate—ordinary morality. As is revealed by their ascetic practices, the medieval saints desired to live neither fully in nor out of the world. They inhabited a symbolic realm, a lonely frontier between heaven and earth where holiness is a bridge between the immanent and transcendent realms which can reunite God and humankind.[79] Saints are spiritually— and often physically—marginal. They inhabit the very edge of society, whether amongst the sick and poor or in closed religious communities. So even while alive, the saint is a symbolic embodiment of the trans-categorical nature of holiness, and as such can mediate between heaven and earth because she or he belongs properly to neither.[80]

---

[78] R. Otto, 'In the Sphere of the Holy', *Hibbert Journal*, 31 (1932), 415.

[79] For analyses of holiness as a 'border-territory' or 'frontier' in which normal values and practices are suspended, see M. Buber, 'The Heavenly Journey', in *The Legend of the Baal-Shem* (Edinburgh: T. & T. Clark, 1985), 79–81; R. Caillois, *Man and the Sacred* (Glencoe, Ill.: Free Press, 1959), 36; *COH* 111, Eliade, *Sacred and Profane*, 37; P. Evdokimov, 'Holiness in the Orthodox Tradition', in Chavchavadze (ed.), *Man's Concern*, 153, 160; Grossman, 'Holiness', 114, 115; M. Raphael, *Thealogy and Embodiment: The Post-Patriarchal Reconstruction of Female Sacrality* (Sheffield: Sheffield Academic Press, 1996), ch. 6; Van der Leeuw, *Religion in Essence*, 400, 680–2.

[80] I accept that this is a different interpretation of the holiness of medieval saints than that offered of female saints by E. McLaughlin, in 'Women, Power and the Pursuit of Holiness in Medieval Christianity', in R. Ruether and E. McLaughlin (eds.), *Women of Spirit: Female Leadership in the Jewish and Christian Traditions*

Richard Kieckhefer's study of the saints of the late medieval period depicts the 'agonizing struggle for holiness' as 'a strenuous and uncertain groping towards a goal not fully perceived let alone conceptualised'.[81] And in their recent study of fourteenth-century saints, Donald Weinstein and Rudolph Bell offer ample evidence that these holy lives were a focus more for numinous awe than moral approval. The *vitae* evoked a sense of mysterious, miraculous supernatural power: 'what interested the faithful was the holy life and above everything else in that life, evidence of supernatural power.'[82]

It could be said that the witness of the fourteenth-century saints is an unbalanced, violent quest for perfection.[83] The saintly *via dolorosa* may be seen as the path of a spiritual malaise, in that the consolation of grace, the resurrection, and the satisfactions of an easy conscience seem to be neglected or ignored. God's beneficent provision seems to be cast aside: Clare Gambacorta ate only refuse, Francis of Assisi mixed ashes with his food,[84] and Dorothy of Montgau is reputed to have been relieved at the loss of eight of her nine children as this released her for pilgrimage. Dorothy bears her husband's abuse with cheerful serenity, and when

(New York: Simon & Schuster, 1979). McLaughlin understands the holy vocation of female saints to have been manifest in their affective piety, learning, and the strength of their Christian obedience. So too in her book *Holy Feast, Holy Fast: The Religious Significance of Food to Medieval Women* (Berkeley: University of California Press, 1987), C. Walker Bynum has argued that the female saints of this period achieved holiness not through miraculous transcendence of their embodiment but through the relation of that embodiment to that of the incarnate Christ. In the present brief discussion I have found the extremes of personal holiness to be far more supernatural in character.

[81] R. Kieckhefer, *Unquiet Souls* (London: University of Chicago Press, 1984), 12, 10. Certainly, the numinosity of the saint could not easily be accommodated by the ecclesiastical criteria for canonization. See Evdokimov, 'Holiness in the Orthodox Tradition', 158.

[82] D. Weinstein and R. Bell, *Saints and Society* (Chicago: University of Chicago Press, 1982), 142. See also Caillois, *Man and the Sacred*, 48; Willink, *Holy and Living God*, 133; Söderblom, 'Holiness: General and Primitive', 740; *idem*, *Nature of Revelation*, 166 f.

[83] Although it is liberally sprinkled with generalizations, see William James's disquisition on the excessive virtues of the saints in *The Varieties of Religious Experience* (London: Fountain Books, 1977), 258–365, esp. 333–57.

[84] Kieckhefer, *Unquiet Souls*, 141.

bricked into the cathedral walls, she refuses blankets against the freezing winter night.[85]

From a numinous perspective, the marvellous faith of the saints is not a moral virtue to be accommodated in rational or moral categories.[86] In the cult of saints, devoted petitioners are less dazzled by the moral righteousness of the saints than by the numinous power of their abnormal suffering for the sake of faith.[87] It is the numinous impression, then, with its accompanying sense of supernatural power, that may account for the accretion of the fantastic and miraculous around the life and death of a saint.[88] The legends of the medieval saints record their spectacular triumphs over the limitations of temporal existence and the laws of nature. Otto himself notes that genuine holy men create a spontaneous impression of the numinous, of 'a being of wonder and mystery, who somehow or other is felt to belong to the higher order of things, to the side of the numen itself'.[89]

But leaving aside the heroic extremes of numinous behaviour, it needs to be said that moral evil is a sin against the holy. Although, in *India's Religion of Grace and Christianity Compared and Contrasted* Otto recognizes that God 'as a *holy* being must be angry' at sinful and idolatrous 'life and conduct which attack profoundly the sphere of holiness itself, i.e. the holy sphere of ultimate values',[90] he would have done well to stress this more firmly. To abuse the divine creation is a sign of profound personal profanity, for, as Pelikan notes, the holiness of life is derivative, possessed of an 'invested holiness'. Murder, for example, becomes a sin: it is to 'lay profane hands upon that which, by the creation of the Holy

---

[85] Ibid. 53.

[86] The numinosity of the late medieval saint spills over from the merely formal criteria for canonization used by the Church, namely doctrinal purity, heroic virtue, and miraculous intercession after death. See Weinstein and Bell, *Saints and Society*, 141–7.

[87] Evdokimov, 'Holiness in the Orthodox Tradition', 152, remarks that the saints 'shock' a 'forgetful world' by putting themselves entirely at 'the disposal of the Transcendent'.

[88] For an analysis of the numinous power of saints' graves, see P. Brown, *The Cult of Saints* (London: SCM Press, 1981), 106.   [89] *IH* 158.

[90] *IRG* 107.

One, was holy and set aside for His purposes'. Reverence for God entails reverence for all his works. As my concluding chapter will argue, this is a timely lesson in an age of what Pelikan called, more than thirty years ago, the 'blasphemy' of ecological desecration, wherein 'the sense of the holiness of the earth'[91] seems dangerously atrophied. Profanity is manifest not only in one's personal moral status. Immoral acts such as crimes against the environment are also religious crimes against the sanctity of God's creation, and are (literally) polluting. The 'primitive' idea of holiness and profanity as contagious has new truth for today. Holy living entails, therefore, proper reverence for the things God has made. In this sense morality, as an expression of reverence, may become sacramental, and may further the resacralization of the earth: God's creation demands a special respect that can be expressed in one's religious duties towards it, such as conservation and the absolute refusal to steal, poison, or destroy creation for selfish ends. So although a religious obedience to God may be manifest in acts that 'look' like moral acts, that further the socio-historical good, they differ in at least one important respect: that of motivation. The motive of a religio-moral act is obedient, but chosen, self-dedication to the 'Holy Imperative' as expressed in forms of covenant and sacrifice.

Whilst hubris and profanity imitate the *tremendum* of divine power, it is only an *ersatz* form of God's creative power to call objects into existence. But as creator, God has, like an artist, certain rights over the creation on which he labours.[92] The demand that humanity be holy as he is holy is a demand that we accomplish his design of humans as images of himself; this is the purpose of creation. And despite the biblical narrative of the Fall, biblical theism does not countenance the final frustration of his ultimately beneficent divine power: in God and his saints holiness is 'a consecration of power

---

[91] Pelikan, *Human Culture*, III, 112.
[92] See B. Brody's discussion of the implications of God's ownership of the universe in 'Morality and Religion Reconsidered', in P. Helm (ed.), *Divine Commands and Morality* (Oxford: Oxford University Press, 1981), 141–53.

in the service of love'.[93] The dynamic of holiness, as a means to salvific reunion, is dependent on humanity's obedience to God's command to be holy as he is, whilst also remaining human. As the rabbi of Kotzk once put it: 'Ye shall be holy unto me, but as men, ye shall be humanly holy unto me.'[94]

Arguably, all religion is based on the need for humans to transcend their limitations—to get closer to the divine. But it is regrettable that Otto (who in other ways relied heavily on the prophets) should have had such an introverted idea of salvation, where social justice is not the pre-condition of holiness. Otto's concept of salvation as the final *telos* of holiness is a *sui generis* religious good.[95] It is a state independent of human conception or achievement of any value: that is, it is definitely transcendental, though not post-mortem. Yet individual holiness might justly be found a social irrelevance if it cannot take on a collective form. But the relationship of Ottonian holiness to morality has a wider collective implication than Otto's rather narrow view might have been aware of. His anxiety that holiness not be rationalized away by utility endangered the transformatory power of the holy, but did not, I think, destroy it. After all, divine justice is not the same as the finite justice which seeks to emulate it. Divine justice belongs to the *mysterium tremendum* of the Godhead, and numinous experience intuits the possibility of this 'wholly other' justice in its sense of the overwhelming love and wrath of the numen, a great compassion and a great anger which together, held in balance, constitute justice.

Otto does not preach a Gnostic dualism. On the contrary, in *Mysticism East and West* he recognizes the dual evaluation made by religion of the world as a glorious creation *and* as a sphere of antagonism to God which must be overcome.[96] And in *India's Religion of Grace* he rejects any view of religion

---

[93] J. Mahoney, 'Holiness', in J. Childress and J. Macquarrie (eds.), *A New Dictionary of Christian Ethics* (London: SCM Press, 1986), 270. Cf. *IRG* 74.

[94] M. Buber, *Tales of the Hasidim: The Later Masters* (New York: Schocken Books, 1961), 281. The idea that humanity could take on the otherness of God is explicitly rejected by Otto as 'something more than religion or theism could afford to permit' (*MEW* 119).

[95] See e.g. *IH* 35, 166 f.; *KGSM* 50, 128; *IRG* 13; *MEW* 24, 27, 57, 147 f., 204, 207, 268; *RE* 42 f.　　　　　　　　　　　　　　　　[96] *MEW* 110.

whose *only* truth lies in the relation of God and the soul in abstraction from creation. Indeed, he there affirms that holiness consists in both solitary spiritual communication with God *and* moral service to humanity.[97]

Even so, the narrowness of his concept of holiness should be acknowledged and discussed. Towards the end of his life, when he was writing *The Kingdom of God and the Son of Man*, Otto was convinced that 'the inner logic which binds the elements of existence with the elements of value is this, that holiness or righteousness are not possible in the present, earthly, fleshly, worldly existence, or in an existence and situation of an earthly kind'. In the Germany of the 1930s his pessimism is perhaps forgivable. He goes on to say that sanctification is not possible in 'an earthly form of existence', but only in the 'wholly other' transfigured existence 'in heaven'.[98] And where Otto reads Isaiah as demanding that holiness be expressed primarily in social morality, he insists that the latter is not to become an end in itself, but is merely a sign that one has entered a higher state and has been 'appropriated to Yahveh' as part of a 'sanctified group withdrawn from the world'. Otto finds the holy best symbolized by the notion of a covenantal relationship: 'the state of complete mutual possession', where God and humankind are bound together in a community of will and purpose.[99]

None the less, if 'the world' is a sphere of alienation from God that is manifest in alienated political and economic relationships, it is possible to reread such statements as promising liberation from alienation into new, blessed communities. For it is precisely this mutual possession which alone has the transformatory power to overcome the alienation of human value from divine value (the holy) which, as the story of exile from Eden suggests, diminishes and destroys God's creation.

---

[97] *IRG* 75–80; cf. *NR* 364–70. However, Otto is clearly undecided in his evaluation of the world as a means to holiness. In *IRG* 66 he promotes a Platonic dualism in which the present world is merely a shadow of an ideal 'real world'.

[98] *KGSM* 49. See also *KGSM* 41, 54. Otto is far from breaking with tradition here: mountain tops, caves, and deserts, as transcendentalist symbols of separation and exclusion from the finite social order, are often treated in the Bible not only as sacred places but as loci of decisive spiritual transformation.

[99] *RE* 40, 41.

So even the exclusive intimacy suggested by Otto in the binding together of human and divine wills has, in fact, profoundly beneficent political ramifications. If sin is a symptom of a lost original state of relation to God in holiness, then salvation, as the expression of divine justice and the gracious forgiveness of sin, can be envisaged as an eschatological restoration of that holy relation. That primary holy relation, once symbolized as 'Eden', precedes and excludes the possibility of immorality or hubris, since hubris is possible only under conditions of estrangement from the divine and exile from Eden.

As a Protestant, Otto understands salvation as the gift of divine grace. Salvation cannot be earned by moral works alone. We have seen that the works of the Christian saints are largely ignored by Otto, who refers in passing only to the numinous impression made by their personal presence.[100] But this Lutheran affirmation of grace is also subject to Otto's numinous hermeneutic. Grace is depicted as the 'scheme' of the *fascinans* element of the holy, tempering the *tremendum* of divine wrath and holding out the possibility of salvific reunion.[101] Holiness may then be understood as a gift of vision that divines what is good and what is defiling.[102]

For Otto salvation is not the reward of a strenuous moral will. This contrasts with Kant, who postulates immortality as a means of prolonging and rewarding the moral endeavour —though this seems more a formal than a religious device. Otto's resistance to the reduction of God to a moral overseer may have been in opposition to Kant's postulation of religion as a regulative ideal for morality, where a rewarding and punishing God would underwrite moral commitment. Although Otto must insist that wickedness is incompatible with salvation, he would none the less deny that salvation is the reward of virtue. In fact, Otto establishes the role of the moral will (and therefore the will to justice) firmly within his own religious meta-ethic. In *Mysticism East and West* he praises Meister Eckhart's 'wonderfully liberating ethic' in

---

[100] See *IH* 82 f., 157 f.   [101] *IH* 140; see also *IH* 132 f.
[102] See Mahoney, 'Holiness', 270.

which essential righteousness is won through unity with holy being. It is in the surrender of the will to mystical union with the numinous source of all holiness, *before* the exercise of the moral will in works, that Otto finds the true freedom of the will. He believes that the unification of the will with that of God is the same as union with God, so that holy empowerment becomes the spiritual, non-rational basis of the moral disposition.[103]

We have seen that Otto's conception of the relationship of holiness and morality developed over his lifetime. By the end of his life, Otto finds that numinous experience confirms the essential value of the divine will because it recognizes a mysterious object of incommensurable value, to which all that is known of value in the mundane sphere is analogous. On the one hand, Otto attempts to retain the logical autonomy of right and wrong; on the other, he also wants to say that all value is logically dependent on God as creator of the immanent and metaphysical realm. He incorporates both positions by the theological affirmation that all true value known to creation is a reflection of the numinous divine essence: holiness. Moral value reflects numinous value, which is itself the essence and ground of God's holiness. The holy is not merely the transcendental ideal of natural morality. It is the radicalization of morality, for moral value originates in God's holy will. Furthermore, the holy will itself originates in the numinous depth of the Godhead, where all value is sublated in and by the ineffable mystery of divine holy being.

In moving on from his early theory of a schematic relation between holiness and morality, and in the further theological amplification of his concept of holiness in *Freiheit und Notwendigkeit*, Otto can be interpreted as having established the following. First, as a value system operating for the good of created social structures, morality is wholly desirable and entirely compatible with the religious desire to serve holy value. Deriving originally from the divine will for holiness, finite socio-historical morality is a source of divine satisfaction, and falls, like all other goods, within the will

---

[103] *MEW* 225 f.

and jurisdiction of the Creator. None the less, Judaism and Christianity believe that God wants humanity to be moral and more—that is, to be holy.

Second, and consequently, religious morality can be understood as a response to the experience of holiness as the origin of all value, and as obedience to the divine imperative to value (love and respect) creation, which is of infinite value to God. But finite social morality stops short of such an absolute justification of its acts, and can operate as an intelligible end in itself. Holiness, however, as the medium of the salvific relation between humankind and the divine, goes further. Obedience to the holy imperative not only results in good acts, but also, by overcoming the profanity of sin, determines the peculiarly religious content of the ontological transformation wrought by reunion with God. Otto's mystical vision of salvation implies an ontological translation from the sphere of the profane to that of the holy. Inclusion in the sphere of holiness will not exclude the moral righteousness of good acts, but in the 'wholly otherness' of holy value will sublate moral righteousness into itself. This is reflected in Otto's concept of God. Here holiness applies both to God's ontological distinction as numinous and to the holy righteousness of his will and action. Therefore God's command that humanity should become holy like himself takes the form of both a moral and a more inclusive ontological transformation.

6

Numinous Experience

Perhaps the best-known sentence of *The Idea of the Holy* is Otto's request to those who have not had any 'deeply felt religious experience' to 'read no further'.[1] Audaciously, he selects his own readership from those of an already spiritual orientation; his philosophical ambitions do not extend beyond the intensification of religious sensibilities and of experiences his readers can recall for themselves. As a theologian and a phenomenologist of religion, Otto did not feel himself required to participate in the debate over whether the intentional object of numinous experience 'really' exists as the cause of the experience.[2] Neither is it my intention to argue for the existence of the numen, or God; no philosophical argument can give knock-down proofs or disproofs of the veracity of a claim to have had an experience of God. The positivists' view that such claims are empty nonsense and the reductionists' confidence that such experiences can be explained away as mere psychological or sociological projections are no longer fully persuasive. The debate over veridicality is of course not over, but is conducted in far subtler forms than during the period of the Vienna Circle and its fifty-year philosophical legacy. The current late modern or, as some would prefer, postmodern climate offers more interesting ways to assess the worth of numinous experience than by reviving old quarrels between logical positivists and theologians. The constructivism exemplified in (but not invented by) Steven Katz's well-known paper 'Language, Epistemology,

---

[1] *IH* 8.

[2] Yandell, *Epistemology of Religious Experience*. This book argues that 'strong' numinous experience (i.e. full-blown numinous experiences such as those of Isaiah, Arjuna, and Moses) provide some irreducible evidence for the existence of God.

149

and Mysticism'[3] a paper directly relevant to Otto's claims for numinous experience, deliberately brackets issues of veridicality. And in the present chapter I too shall assume that since numinous experience is at least in part constructed by a received concept of holiness, it probably cannot offer wholly independent evidence for the existence of a numen. But to reject Otto's claim that the numinous is a *sui generis*, immediate experience, unconditioned by its context, does not mean that numinous experience is thereby vacated of meaning and a function in theology.

In the first part of this chapter I shall ask whether Otto was successful in framing an adequate typology of primary religious experience or whether, in fact, Ninian Smart, amongst others, was right to argue that numinous experience is not as phenomenologically comprehensive a category as Otto believed it to be. Since the present study is concerned with Otto's place in Judaeo-Christian theology and, more specifically, his contribution to the concept of holiness, I will consider only whether numinous experience is sufficiently comprehensive to encompass reported Western encounters with the divine—particularly mystical experiences. I shall then turn to the related epistemological objections to the notion, typified in Otto's work, that the diversity of religious experience can be reduced to one 'pure' experience regardless of its historical, conceptual, and linguistic context. Constructivism (a term that here summarizes arguments against the possibility of mystical experiences having an unmediated, non-relative core, and for their having been contextually constituted) represents a direct threat to Otto's claim for the immediacy of numinous experience. Constructivism asserts that context and experience are mutually informing, and in response to this (quite reasonable) claim, I will examine why Otto was methodologically committed to giving priority to experience over doctrinal interpretation, and why, indeed, such a division between event and interpretation was made in the first place.

[3] In S. Katz (ed.), *Mysticism and Philosophical Analysis* (London: Sheldon Press, 1978).

Numinous Experience and Mystical Experience

Otto's claim that numinous experience is the unmediated core or primary datum of all religious experience, thereby making theology subsequent on numinous experience, is phenomenologically, epistemologically, and theologically controversial. Let us begin with the phenomenological dispute over numinous experience. Otto was convinced that numinous experience lay at the heart of all types of religious experience. So when scholars of mysticism such as Ninian Smart and William Wainwright denied that mystical experience could be subsumed into the category of numinous experience, this appeared to weaken Otto's position considerably. After all, Otto considered mystical experience to be the least conceptual of all religious experience, and therefore more purely numinous than experience structured by monotheistic dogma (what Smart calls 'theistic experience'). For Otto, 'mysticism is the stressing to a very high degree, indeed the overstressing, of the non-rational or supra-rational elements in religion; and it is only intelligible when so understood.'[4]

But of Otto's main commentators, only Philip Almond and Leon Schlamm have accepted and defended Otto's identification of numinous and mystical experience. They are both aware of their anomalous position. As Schlamm recounts in his paper, scholars from Friedrich Heiler at the beginning of the century through to Smart, Wainwright, and Peter Berger have all drawn a phenomenological distinction between mystical and numinous experience, which latter is classed as theistic.

It is customary for scholars to contrast 'prophetic' or devotional religion, where there is a clear subject–object relation between a person who submits to a personal God, with the mystical spirituality in which the mystic seeks absorption in the being of the Godhead. In numinous experiences the human being is brought into an unbidden and often alarming confrontation with the divine. The numinous takes the subject, so to speak, by surprise. Thus Smart: 'The numinous

---

[4] *IH* 22.

experience so brilliantly described in Otto's *The Idea of the Holy* has an outer and thunderous quality not characteristic of the cloud of unknowing within. For this reason it is best to draw a distinction between numinous and mystical experience.'[5] Accordingly, Smart argues that numinous experience is too narrow a category to include the mystical, which may or may not be theistic, but is above all a methodical, disciplined 'quest, through contemplation, for inner insight and peace'.[6] Smart recognizes that 'the sense of the terrifying mystery of the divine' in numinous experience 'implies a converse sense of one's own inadequacy and lack of holiness'. Here self-identification with the divine would be 'blasphemous and absurd'.[7] And as the *tremendum* element is undeniably prominent in numinous experience, Smart is at least superficially justified in saying that the numinous is very unlike the contemplative and beatific elements of mystical experience.

Almond and Schlamm, by contrast, feel that this division of religious experience into two separate categories is a misreading of Otto's contention that non-rational numinous and rational theistic accounts should be interpreted 'as complementary forms of religious life, each to be understood in the light of the other'.[8] Both Almond and Schlamm examine the *Idea of the Holy* and *Mysticism East and West*, and find that Otto is not as oblivious to mysticism as Smart accuses him of being.[9] In brief, Almond and Schlamm attempt to show that the three 'moments' of numinous experience— the *mysterium, tremendum et fascinans*—can each correspond to the tone or vocabulary commonly associated with mysticism. Of course, it might be expected that the *mysterium* and the *fascinans* elements of numinous experience could be akin to experiences found in any broad typology of mysticism. In

---

[5] Smart, 'Understanding Religious Experience', in Katz (ed.), *Mysticism and Philosophical Analysis*, 13.   [6] Smart, *Philosophers and Religious Truth*, 113.
[7] Ibid. 112.
[8] L. Schlamm, 'Rudolf Otto and Mystical Experience', *Religious Studies*, 27 (1991), 392.
[9] See Almond, *Mystical Experience*, esp. chs. 3 and 5; Schlamm, 'Rudolf Otto', 392–5.

the experience of the numen as *mysterium,* the divine is both utterly beyond knowing, yet at the same time inseparable from the mystery of one's own being. And the *fascinans* and *energicum* elements have, as Otto himself was aware, clear associations with voluntaristic mysticism, where the mystic is consumed with love for the divine and by the love of the divine for the mystic.

But what Schlamm finds more interesting is Otto's 'discovery of examples of the *tremendum* in mystical experience'.[10] For example, where Smart would categorize 'creature-feeling' as numinous/theistic, in that it compels the subject to worship a majestic divine object, 'creature-feeling' for Otto and Schlamm could also denote the radical self-depreciation felt by mystics before the supreme plenitude of divine being.[11] Or again, the horror of the *tremendum* might resemble the Christian mystic's experience of the 'dark night of the soul'.[12] Otto would not have said that either of these two experiences were identical, but that they are rather different stages of the same continuum in which experiences pass from the non-rational to the conceptual.

Like Almond, I see no reason to deny that there are phenomenological disparities between religious experiences and that Otto would have accepted those too.[13] But what Smart has not appreciated, Almond claims, is that Otto did not put the theistic and the mystical together on phenomenological grounds. The fusion of the two is, instead, a function of Otto's Friesian metaphysics. I shall return to his epistemology later; suffice it to say here that Otto understood the working of *Ahndung* as revealing 'the disposition to religion in the spirit of man in general, the hidden source of all its manifestations in history, the ground for its claim to be true, to be indeed the supreme and ultimate Truth'.[14] In short, Otto's confidence that both theistic and non-theistic religious experience have a fundamental unity in the numinous is not a result of his phenomenological investigations,

---

[10] Schlamm, 'Rudolf Otto', 392.
[11] Ibid. 392; *IH* 21 f.
[12] Schlamm, 'Rudolf Otto', 393.
[13] Almond, *Mystical Experience,* 113.
[14] Ibid. 116; *PR* 223.

which in view of lacunae such as his ignorance of Jewish and Islamic mysticism, are hardly thorough. It is more that Otto's use of the Friesian notion of *Ahndung* means that structural, phenomenological differences in religious experience are not decisive, since all religious experience comes from a universal psychological source.[15] So whether or not the Friesian epistemology is *true* or can guarantee the veridicality of claims to unmediated religious experience, it does at least provide some epistemological grounding for Otto's claim for an unmediated core religious experience. The mere fact that Otto used a particular mystical epistemology does not thereby make Otto's position (or, for that matter, Almond's reading of Otto) unassailable.[16] The importance of Almond's point is that the philosophical substructure of Otto's phenomenology of religious experience is such that criticism which interprets Otto's account of numinous experience on phenomenological grounds alone is bound to be wide of the mark.

However, there may, none the less, be key structural differences between numinous and mystical experience, especially in their more pronounced forms. For example, I am not convinced that the subject–object dualism that is so much a part of the logic of numinous experience can ever be simply translated into an experience of mystical identification. After all, numinous experience is an experience of the reality of divine holiness, a holiness that the subject wishes to share in. Such a relationship requires an ontological and axiological distinction between the two subjects, divine and human. The concepts of revelation and theophany require a similar distinction.

Indeed, Otto's own idea of holiness, the conceptually completed numinous, belongs to prophetic biblical religion, and drives towards a particular eschatological *telos* of wholeness or reunion. He knew, for example, that Sankara's mysticism and theistic Christianity cannot be assimilated to one another,

[15] See Almond, *Mystical Experience*, 116 f.; *PR* 93.
[16] Almond's claim that Friesianism holds together Otto's phenomenology and theology has been questioned. Williamson's review of *RO* 473 asks whether this is truer of Almond's own religio-philosophical convictions than those of Otto, 'in which case the book asserts far more than has been established'.

as the former seeks a passive serenity, whilst the latter seeks the active relationship established by holiness.[17]

Yet, whilst structural differences may mean that in the end mystical and numinous experiences have a different theological dynamic or tone, this does not mean that the experiences do not overlap in a number of respects. And the numinous state of mind, as an emotional reaction to a divine presence, may, like mystical experience, appear to be less culturally specific than the completed 'holy', which is freighted with biblical reference.

I suspect that those authors who have excluded numinous experience from mysticism have been somewhat arbitrary in their delimitations of the latter. Although Otto's account of numinous experience as both mystical and theistic may fall into the opposite trap of being overly inclusive, it is at least less arbitrary. Numinous experience when broadly defined may not be typologically neat; yet, putting the mystical and numinous experience together on one continuum does reflect the reality of many people's actual religious experience, in which the mystical and the theistic are often combined according to mood and circumstance. The mystical and numinous may indeed be continuous with one another if we accept that mystical experience is as mediated as any other type of religious experience, and that it requires and inherits certain conceptual frameworks in order to occur at all. Furthermore, the majority of religions, whether predominantly theistic or mystical, contain both types of experience in their traditions. It is not, therefore, unexpected that the numinous, as a fluidly emotional reaction, would straddle both the personal theistic and impersonal mystical categories.[18] For example, in some contemporary forms of nature mysticism the *sensus numinis* is awakened by an aesthetic appreciation of the sublimity of nature, which might then be articulated as an experience of the immanent holiness of God in creation spirituality and ecological theology and praxis.

So Smart's contrast between the two forms of experience

---

[17] *IRG* 94–110, *passim.*
[18] See Barbour, *Myths, Models and Paradigms,* 80 f.

may be, as Schlamm observes, little more than 'a hermeneut-ical tool which resembles the kind of ideal type-distinctions that sociologists of religion tend to construct in order to study religious institutions'.[19] In actuality, people's religious experiences are more likely to represent a synthesis of their previous knowledge and experience. The argument over the relation of numinous and mystical experience may, then, be something of a typological storm in a teacup.

Whether an experience of the divine is called numinous or mystical is not particularly important if one relinquishes Otto's global claim that numinous experience is a founda-tional religious experience of which all other religious experi-ences are variants. It seems more likely that numinous and mystical experiences share a number of features such as in-effability, a putative freedom from dogma, and a peculiarly heightened state of awareness. It would, I think, be fair to say that all numinous experiences have mystical elements, but not all mystical experiences have numinous elements. Experi-ences in which the mystic deliberately attempts to achieve a form of contentless consciousness are very far indeed from the passionate intentionality associated with a numinous experi-ence. And if the structural dynamics of numinous experience are as dogmatically informed as I will find them to be, then numinous experience cannot be the primary religious experi-ence that Otto claimed it to be (though it might function as such for the discourse community which provided its con-text). In this case, Otto's contention that any religion begins with, and is founded upon, essentially common numinous experience faces far more serious obstacles than those posed by the phenomenology of religion.

The Constructivist Critique of Unmediated Religious Experience

Otto and other scholars of religion in his era nearly all assumed that a raw experience could be isolated from its

---

[19] Schlamm, 'Rudolf Otto', 398.

post-experiential report. Yet the constructivist position has made it seem almost common sense that all experience, including that of gods, is mediated, organized, and conditioned by a context of complex conceptual structures which are what enable us to identify an experience in the first place. It is not that Steven Katz is saying simply that beliefs create experience, and that the sense of objective divine presence is therefore illusory. Rather, there is what Katz calls a 'two-directional symmetry', in which the two are in reciprocal relation.[20] Although Katz does not engage with Otto's work in any detail, the implications of his argument are clearly relevant to any assessment of Otto's claims for numinous experience as a perennial, unmediated, core religious experience. For if all experiences are, in fact, mediated historically, then religious experiences might be expected to be as culturally and historically disparate as their contexts.

Otto theorized in an intellectual environment that was accustomed to taking what postmodernists have dubbed 'a view from nowhere'; he was largely oblivious to the relation of a metaphysical stance to the cultural and ideological presuppositions that have shaped it. But for Otto, the immediacy of numinous experience is not just incidental to his theory: numinous experience has to be immediate. The *sui generis*, irreducible quality of the numinous demands that no language, concept, or natural object provide an intervening medium between the numen and the numinous consciousness. Metaphorically speaking, religious language does no more than cloak a naked experiential moment. The function of immanent objects is merely to excite numinous apprehension, after which concepts can provide an a posteriori account of the character and meaning of the experience. Whilst, for Otto, the experiential moment is ineffable, the special feelings aroused suggest predications for the numinous which may be expressed in symbolic or analogical language. This then provides an indirect account of what the divine is like. And it is in these early articulations of numinous

---

[20] Katz, 'Language, Epistemology', 41. Cf. W. Proudfoot, 'Religious Experience, Emotion and Belief', *Harvard Theological Review*, 70 (1977), 344, 367.

experience, whose crudity is progressively refined,[21] that Otto discerned the birth of the concept of God. It is worth emphasizing that, unlike Schleiermacher's 'feeling of absolute dependence', the sense of the numen as present is not an inference from a set of emotions, where the numen is posited as an appropriate explanation of those emotions. Otto argued the reverse: religious experience has 'immediate and primary reference to an object outside the self'. For numinous feeling 'can only arise in the mind as accompanying emotions when the category of "the numinous" is called into play'.[22]

The question at issue is whether Otto can justify his contention that one essential numinous experience precedes its various rationalizations in the theologies of the world's religions. He assumes that indifferently of history, culture, and geography, religious experience postulates a numen whose presence elicits an essentially similar state of mind, but which is variously named. Whilst Katz cannot disprove this kind of claim by an a priori argument, he convincingly demonstrates that the writings of different mystics, when read in their own context of belief, are structurally and theologically disparate. And if this is true of mystical experiences, it will also be true of numinous experiences.

It seems likely that the experience and the terms in which it is reported are mutually informing. A Jewish mystic, for instance, participates in an entire system of values, images, and beliefs which, according to Katz, 'define, *in advance*, what the experience *he wants to have*, and which he does then have, will be like'. As Jewish monotheism precludes Jewish mystics losing their personal identity in ecstatic union with God, the ultimate mystical experience is reported as a 'clinging to God' (*devekuth*), suggesting intimacy with the divine object, but not to the extent of overcoming the ontological and axiological duality between God and human beings. On the other hand, Christians, who have already accepted that divine and human elements have, historically, been mixed in the incarnate Christ, are permitted an absorptive mysticism of the sort found in the writings of Meister Eckhart.[23]

---

[21] *IH* 132–5.   [22] *IH* 10 f.
[23] Katz, 'Language, Epistemology', 33–6, 41.

Of course, Katz's argument has not gone uncontested,[24] and it does not rule out the logical possibility that a religious experience could transcend its context or be the same across a number of traditions. However, the kind of relativism Katz is proposing, even if only in the form of an a posteriori argument, would not be acceptable to Otto, who precisely avoided any such possibility by saying that the numinous was *sui generis*. Accordingly, we find in *The Idea of the Holy* an anthology of experiences as disparate as those of Goethe and Arjuna. Numinous experiences are collected together not just on the grounds that they *sound* similar (an accusation often unfairly levelled at Otto), but because they are all experiences of an unconditioned reality. Katz—rightly, I think—rejects any such move as a failure to respect contextuality. If a Jew or a Buddhist uses the phrase 'ultimate reality' of *devekuth* or *nirvana*, the meaning of the phrase is not structurally or teleologically equivalent.[25] So too, the intentional object of these experiences: God, Atman, nirvana, or even 'Being' are probably not just different titles for one unitary reality common to all religious people's experience, but are instead, as Katz puts it, 'descriptions, or at least disguised descriptions, and carry a meaning relative to some ontological structure'.[26]

If this is correct, then it seems to me that there are two implications for Otto's use of the term 'numen'. Either this putatively non-specific divine object is far more culturally constructed than Otto realized, or it is a redundant generic term applying accurately to none of the accounts of divine realities named in the various traditions. But if the former is more likely, and Otto's account of numinous experience is far more culturally specific than he would have wanted to acknowledge, this is not to deny its legitimate role in clarifying what it makes sense to say about holiness within the grammar of theism.

---

[24] See R. Forman (ed.), *The Problem of Pure Consciousness* (New York: Oxford University Press, 1990). This volume consists of a variety of attempted refutations of Katz's position. For a scathing response to Forman's collection, see M. Bagger, 'Ecumenicalism and Perennialism Revisited', *Religious Studies*, 27 (1991), 399–411. [25] Katz, 'Language, Epistemology', 46 f. [26] Ibid. 56.

The Context of Otto's Theory of Numinous Experience

Although Leon Schlamm admits that 'no experience is entirely unmediated', he rightly points out that the 'contribution of religious tradition to numinous experience is relatively insignificant', and varies according to the different moments of a given numinous experience. The *tremendum* and *fascinans* moments of numinous experience will be influenced to a far greater degree by tradition than would the *mysterium* moments of the experience.[27] Moreover, the object of numinous experience is unconceptualized; its gender is not yet linguistically delineated, and by itself it carries no institutional authority or imprimatur.[28]

All the same, there is little doubt that Otto's concept of holiness would have been biographically and socially determined to some degree (though that would not necessarily detract from its importance). The very religion Otto confessed committed him to basing theology on experience. In his retirement lecture from Marburg, Otto declared himself a 'Lutheran in respect of his recognition of the objective grounding of revelation; but a pietist in that this recognition was based on the universal capacity of each human individual to have genuine and real religious experience'.[29] Otto grew up with a pietistic Protestant theology in which salvation was dependent neither on moral works nor on spiritual disciplines, but on a personal experience of grace through faith. As such, he might well have been predisposed to understand religion primarily as a private experience rather than a system of rational credal assent in which the sacred is approached through priests and teachers. Otto's Protestant sense of personal sinfulness clearly emerges in his description of 'creature-feeling' and the correlative emotional reaction that the divine is *tremendum*. He certainly would have brought a Lutheran hermeneutic, however shadowy, to his texts.

Moreover, the Prussia in which Otto grew up was a particularly authoritarian, stratified society, even for the times.

---

[27] Schlamm, 'Numinous Experience', 548.
[28] Raphael, 'Feminism, Constructivism', 516.
[29] Almond, 'Rudolf Otto', 311.

In Europe, until the second half of the twentieth century, piety and punishment were often closely allied as a form of social control, so it might be expected that Otto's God would take a dictatorial form. And it is surely not coincidental that Nathan Söderblom, another Northern European Protestant, contemporary with Otto and of similarly pietistic background, whose concept of holiness was similar to Otto's, himself felt the reality of God in terms of what Otto would call a numinous experience. Writing in the third person, Söderblom describes an experience he had in 1893, twenty-one years before he became Archbishop of Uppsala. Returning from church one Sunday,

> There came over him what might be called a direct perception of the holiness of God. He understood what he had long felt indistinctly, that God was far stricter than he could imagine or that anyone can really comprehend. God is a consuming fire. This apprehension was so powerful, so shattering, that he was unable to stay on his feet. Had he not collapsed into a chair with his head on the table, he felt that he must have fallen onto the floor. He moaned and groaned under this mighty grasp.[30]

It may be that as human relations become increasingly informal (superficially at least), as children are less intimidated by parents and teachers, and as the media demystify the power held by political leaders by their repeated exposure to the public gaze, such experiences will become increasingly rare.

Rather differently, it is also worth noting that the context of a person's numinous experience will colour, and even make having such an experience more likely than at other times. As Keith Yandell points out,

> one is at least more likely to have had a numinous experience (or its counterfeit) if one has ingested certain substances and is in a religious setting (seated in a high-ceilinged chapel, say, before stained glass windows, with Handel's *Messiah* being played on a good pipe organ).[31]

---

[30] From Sharpe, *Nathan Söderblom*, 44. See also ibid. 212.
[31] Yandell, *Epistemology*, 226.

It is evident from the text of *The Idea of the Holy* that, for Otto, certain sorts of aesthetic stimuli are productive of the *sensus numinis* and others are not. Otto is not indifferent to contextuality, even if he does not accept that natural stimuli constitute an element of the numinous experience itself.

As with most academic enterprises, there were other factors governing Otto's insistence that the numinous be given priority in the history of religion and in the personal religious history of the individual. These factors were not purely theological. Otto's insistence on the autonomy of religion was, in part at least, necessitated by the advance of secular thought which granted no privileged status to religious claims, and was predicting its eclipse by science. Or again, in the context of marked international tension in the years preceding the First World War, Otto might have hoped that numinous experience would provide a kind of pre-dogmatic experiential lingua franca between members of different faith communities, and so make the contribution to world peace that he later believed his Inter-Religious League could do.

The Ineffability of Numinous Experience

If one is prepared to concede that numinous experience is dogmatically coloured, not merely in its 'schematization' but also at the moment of experience itself, then such an admission must preclude the possibility that the experiential moment is genuinely ineffable. Yet it is clear that Otto's theological and phenomenological integrity demand that he present numinous experience as ineffable and therefore 'pure', or unadulterated by reason. Theologically, he insists that divine reality cannot and should not be compassed by language, and phenomenologically, he notes that those who have experienced divine reality want to use circumlocutions when they attempt to describe it. So in his fidelity to religion he wants to say that the numinous is 'wholly other', hence ineffable and a-conceptual, meaning that there can be only a contingent relation between the experience and its interpretation.

The effect of this is to keep numinous experience safe from reductionists who want to explain it away. Yet its being safely out of reach of reductionism exposes it to the charge of being epistemologically vacuous. It demands a lot of the critic to have to accept that an experience cannot be described *and* that this same experience is at the heart of all other religious experiences. Logically, the ineffability of numinous experience deprives us of any apparent means to identify it as a particular sort of religious experience, or to check whether two or more experiences are both numinous experiences. And if one numinous experience cannot be assumed to be comparable or continuous with another, they cannot carry the theological and philosophical claims Otto makes for them.[32]

Moreover, if numinous experience is truly ineffable, then it cannot form part of a phenomenology of experience, since there is no necessary content with which to compare it. Worse, if the interpretation of the content of numinous experience is contingent, it cannot provide a foundation for theology and the revelation whose meaning theology articulates. (Yet, if the interpretation of numinous experience is forced to satisfy particular theological criteria, the unconditioned quality of the numinous is eliminated.) So too, the plurality and diversity of religious experience and expression that contemporary religious studies and the inter-faith movement celebrate, is choked by Otto's claim that all religious experience is ultimately 'reducible' to numinous experience.

Religious leaders of any revelation community might also be suspicious of any experience which promised direct, unsanctioned access to a divine being not yet named by the hierarchy. In general, the concept of an unspecified divinity present to consciousness has been found to be too vague for use in positive theological discourse. As it stands, the *numen praesens* does not seem to provide enough evidence of the function and quality of its existence to satisfactorily complement the developed personalism of Judaeo-Christian

---

[32] S. Sutherland draws this conclusion about a-conceptual religious experience in 'Religion, Experience and Privacy', *Religious Studies*, 20 (1984), 132.

theology. Before John Oman's well-known critique of Otto in the early 1930s, in *The Natural and the Supernatural*, F. K. Feigel had dismissed numinous experience as a foundation for Christian religion on the ancient grounds that numinous experience could come indifferently from God or the devil.[33]

Oman, in his turn, finds that the emotions evoked by the numinous object might equally be evoked by the presence of ghosts, awesome natural phenomena, or sub-theistic supernatural (possibly demonic) persons or gods.[34] In his paper 'The Sphere of Religion', Oman admits that the numinous is a common sensation in religion, but as mere feeling it is difficult to distinguish between the awed sense of the holy and the lower types of numinous dread.[35] The merely 'shuddery, spooky feeling' which awakens the *sensus numinis* is, for Oman, the basis of magic and superstition, not religion. Indeed, the only way that these feelings can be distinguished is to look at the *values* they attend or that of the objects to which they refer.[36] Feelings themselves incorporate other ideas; they do not have a purely independent subsistence. So for Oman the sense of the holy achieves clarity by its being stirred only by what is valued as sacred. And what is conceived as sacred is that which is understood to belong to an environment which 'awakes absolute reverence and imposes absolute obligation'.[37] If unrelated to moral value, Oman fears that the sense of holiness may attach itself to a crude undifferentiated (pagan) sacred, with no inward necessity of attribution to the source of true value and the highest object of worship: the God of prophetic religion.[38]

Oman's criticism seizes upon the logical gap between supra-rational numinous experience and rational or conceptual theology, where Otto is at his most problematic. It looks

[33] Feigel, *Das Heilige*, 133.

[34] See Oman, *Natural and Supernatural*, 61, and e.g. J. C. A. Gaskin, *The Quest for Eternity* (Harmondsworth: Penguin, 1984), 81 f., 86 f., 90; A. Galloway, *The Cosmic Christ* (London: Nisbet, 1951), 222, 227; R. W. Hepburn, *Christianity and Paradox* (London: C. A. Watts, 1958), esp. 205–9.

[35] In Needham (ed.), *Science, Religion*, 288.

[36] Oman, *Natural and Supernatural*, 62.   [37] Ibid. 212.

[38] Ibid. 66. Cf. Davis's account of quasi-numinous experiences of evil, in *Evidential Force*, 51.

to Oman as if Otto's theological interpretation of numinous experience is something of a schematic afterthought. It is the diffuseness of the impression of the *unheimlich* that is at issue. For Otto can be no more explicit than that numinous experience provides the obscure sense of a transcendent 'something'. But of course, for Jewish and Christian theologians an undelineated 'something' does not adequately identify God.

An Ottonian Response

There is little doubt that on the epistemological front Katz has inflicted serious damage on Otto's thesis. And even if Otto was right about the unconditioned quality of numinous experience, Oman's criticism, although mounted well over half a century ago, remains a serious theological critique of the consequences of postulating an ineffable, non-historically specific object of all religious experience. However, the criticism of Otto that I have outlined, although damaging to Otto's larger claims for numinous experience, is in many ways exaggerated, and misses much of the subtlety of his thinking. So whilst I accept the basic constructivist insight that contexts shape experiences, which in turn shape and are shaped by theory, making numinous experience as conditioned as any other sort of religious experience, the problem of the non-referential quality of numinous experience can, I think, be resolved on more or less Ottonian terms.

Since epistemologists and theologians, albeit from different perspectives, both attack the 'wholly otherness' of numinous experience, I will begin by examining this contentious phrase. It may be that, as noted previously, the phrase 'wholly other' has been taken too literally. When Otto says that numinous experience is 'wholly other', he means that the divine cannot be defined as other objects can, because it cannot be known as it is in itself. This does not reduce Otto to silence. On the contrary, numinous experience is reported volubly, but only in and through analogies—that is, not directly by description. Indeed, Otto contends that the 'mysterious obscurity of the numen is by no means tantamount to unknowable-ness'.[39] As the numen reveals itself to feeling, it becomes intelligible and recognizable to the religious consciousness.[40] Revelation is the outcome of bringing the inconceivable into the realm of the conceptual, but it is in the experience of the peculiar quality of the numinous object that 'knowing' and 'understanding' are separated:

Something may be profoundly and intimately known in feeling for the bliss it brings or the agitation it produces, and yet the understanding may find no concept for it. To *know* and to *understand conceptually* are two different things, are often even mutually exclusive and contrasted. . . . Assuredly the '*deus absconditus et incompre-hensibilis*' was for Luther no '*deus ignotus*'.[41]

Otto feels that 'numen' is a felicitous term for this object, 'simply because one cannot say exactly what (it) is'.[42] Otto seems to be ambivalent here. He finds it both necessary and desirable that the experienced numen be schematized as 'God',[43] so to represent the totality or culmination of meaning that is the mark of a superior religion.[44] Yet he constantly resists this process as taking away something of the original, spontaneous sense of what the divine is *really* like, both in itself and in experience. In fact, Otto's theological minimalism persisted long after the publication of *The Idea of the Holy*: the rigid doctrines formulated in dogmatics remained, for him, a denial or surrogate of the mystery proper to religion.[45]

It could be said that Otto obscures his position by refusing to elaborate on the nature or mode of presence of the numen beyond its being simply 'there'. He limits positive predications to the realm of analogy, itself acknowledged as having more symbolic than substantive significance. He fears that ordinary language would endanger the *sui generis* quality of the affective response to the numen as underivable from and irreducible to the rest of conscious natural experience. However, there is a sense in which Otto's experiential

[39] *IH* 135.   [40] *IH* 134.   [41] *IH* 135.
[42] Otto, 'Sensus Numinis', 420.   [43] *IH* 110.   [44] *IH* 1.
[45] *RE* 70-3.

theology is not as radically agnostic as it might appear. The concept of the 'wholly otherness' of the numen may be more rhetorical than strictly prohibitive of linguistic expression. If we can use analogies to predicate finite qualities to the numen, then we must at least be aware of what makes the symbolic amplification of those predicates applicable in the case of the divine. Conversely, if Otto prohibits positive predications of the numen, that entails that we must in some way be aware of what it is in the numen that resists language and concept. So the *quale* of the numen derives from the positive experience of its presence and the negative language used in its evocation. Otto was probably wrong, then, to consider numinous experience a-conceptual. Numinous experience is unlike the contentless experiences which, for Smart at least, characterize mysticism.[46] As a specific form of reaction to a divine presence, it is full of (implicit) content, which, even if not thought out, does not make the content a-conceptual.

Philosophically, this may not take us all that far. As Almond, for all his sympathy with Otto, points out, the positive experience of the holy and the negative language used to describe it 'do bear some analogy to each other; yet it is impossible to determine the exact nature of this relation, or how far this analogy extends'. Earthly analogies are both radically unlike, as well as similar to, their transcendent forms. Therefore Otto gives a 'complex accounting of divine attributes with a large amount of uncertainty about what these attributes mean when applied'.[47] Whatever Otto is prepared to say about God is based only upon a sense of a divine *mysterium* which is valuable in a unique way. This mystical reticence alone may not seem a promising foundation for a positive theology. Otto knows that the rationalization of mystery is necessary to the daily practice of a given religion, yet at the same time he resists the way in which religions form a carapace of tradition over experience of the living numen/God.

---

[46] N. Smart, 'Interpretation and Mystical Experience', *Religious Studies*, 1 (1965), 75.　　　　　　　　　　　　　　　　　　　　[47] *RO* 67.

None the less, after the publication of *The Idea of the Holy*, Otto translated many of its speculative, philosophical contentions into a more explicitly biblical, theological form.[48] Here we have evidence that, as Almond puts it, the numinous can be expressed theologically as a revelation of grace. It reveals by 'creature-feeling' 'the lack of value inherent in human existence by simultaneously revealing that which is of supreme value'.[49] Valuelessness is thereby overcome by a numinous excitement that makes the spiritual appropriation of grace possible. Even Rudolf Bultmann (for whom Otto is said to have been something of a *bête noir*[50]) recognizes the profound theological significance of the numinous, remarking that Otto's stress on 'the inner connectedness of the aspects of the *tremendum et fascinans* is an analogy, by no means superficial, to the doctrine of the inner unity of the knowledge of judgement and grace'.[51]

Numinous experience, for Otto, is the beginning of salvation, and it precedes any codification of it into a body of communal knowledge or revelation. He even treats the Bible as a primary source: a collection of instances in which individuals' numinous experiences drive the narrative of salvation history forward or, in the case of Jesus, are a personal manifestation of the numinous. Otto has a low Christology. Jesus's salvific meaning does not principally lie in the incarnation, cross or the resurrection, but more in 'the quality of his inner life', the 'nimbus of the numinous' around Jesus which was attested by his own followers.[52]

It is in the confrontation of numinous value with creaturely 'disvalue' that humans feel their worthlessness and seek to 'cover' themselves from the wrath of the numen by certain rites which later acquire the connotation of moral consecration. If the holy is crudely conceived as a charge or power, then to be put back in right relation with it is to be empowered for the struggle against the structures of sin.[53] Rituals of atonement and sanctification mark a person's will to move

---

[48] See esp. *RE* chs. 1–5.   [49] *RO* 70.
[50] Recounted by Eliade in *No Souvenirs* (London: Routledge & Kegan Paul, 1978), 263.   [51] Quoted by Lattke, 'Rudolf Bultmann on Rudolf Otto', 355.
[52] *KGSM* 242, 164 f.   [53] See *IH* 51–7; cf. *ROR* 93.

into ontological alignment with the divine. By entering the sphere of the holy (often staked out as a sacred space), a new relationship with the divine is established whereby profanity is overcome.[54] Describing the Ottonian process of transformation, Davidson writes: 'not only did the sinner himself recognise his changed status in the vibrant rapture and bliss of such an experience; he was often for the same reason set apart from his fellows as a "holy man".' So human finitude is transcended in the purging experience of the *sui generis* value of the numen, and once purged by the realization of one's being as 'creature', one is made acceptable to the divine and ready to begin the process of mystical inclusion in its value. In a person's new ontological status of holiness, she or he begins 'to participate in the transcendent worth and dignity, indeed in the very holiness of God'.[55] This is salvation.

So salvation history is, for Otto, more a series of mystical experiences than an eschatological event. And the mechanisms of atonement, although ritualized, are also mystical, since they allow an ontological reunion with God, rather than satisfying any quasi-legal demand for restitution. In *The Idea of the Holy* salvation becomes less a communal, eschatological beatitude than a blissful absorption within the numen that can be experienced in the present life of faith.[56] Again, for Otto, it is above all aesthetic meditation on the person and passion of Jesus as the earthly manifestation of the numinous *par excellence* that leads to salvific absorption in the numen. In short, Ottonian theology begins and ends with presently available direct experience which is not dependent on texts or priests.

It now becomes possible to see a central flaw in Oman's criticism of Otto. Charles Campbell rightly protests that 'it is the merest caricature of Otto's position' to define the numinous solely by the *tremendum* at the expense of the *fascinans*: 'the *fascinans* is that in virtue of which the numinous

---

[54] For further discussion of the link between the sense of divine presence in what Kellenberger refers to loosely as 'numinous' experience and the discovery of relationship to the divine, see J. Kellenberger, *The Cognitivity of Religion* (London: Macmillan, 1985), 116.　　　　　　　　　　　　　　[55] *ROR* 95.

[56] See e.g. *IRG* 13 f.; *KGSM* 128 f.; *MEW* 57, 147–8, 207, 268; *RE* 42–4.

consciousness is enraptured and entranced by the transcendent *worth* or *value* of the numen.'[57] The desire to be united with the numen points to its transcendent goodness. While such goodness cannot be fully conceptualized, it can be tentatively articulated in the language of moral value.

In sum, the moment of numinous experience is ineffable, in that it defies description. But where the emotional response to the *numen praesens* is one of awe and an overwhelming desire to be united with it, that might be sufficient for a Jew or Christian with a concept of God as awesome and transcendently good to identify the numen as worthy of the name 'God'. Of course, this does not rule out the possibility that the numen one experiences may in fact be attractive but evil. Traditional Western theology has always lived with this possibility. Satan, or in Judaism the *sitra achra*, is often depicted in cunningly benign disguises. However, numinous experience, as Otto describes it, offers no opportunities for hubris, but rather compels prostration of the self before the object of worship. Moreover, numinous experience does not take place within a vacuum: the nature of the experience will also be known by its fruits.

Ahndung *and the Self-revelation of God*

Otto is more ambitious for numinous experience than its being a merely instinctual reaction to any supernatural presence. His Friesian epistemology backs up his theological conviction that God reveals his holiness immediately to the individual.[58] In his theory of numinous experience Otto postulated a human psychology, in the oldest sense of that word, which (potentially) allows individuals unmediated religious

---

[57] Campbell, *On Selfhood and Godhood*, 343.

[58] However, Bastow, 'Otto and Numinous Experience', 171, denies that the Friesian system is suited to Otto's purposes. Bastow claims that it has no formal similarities to Otto's phenomenology of religion, and does not reflect 'the dualism of an emotional reaction' to 'the numen as a distinct entity'. According to Bastow, Otto realizes that his connection with Fries is tenuous, and therefore deliberately omits explicit reference to Fries in *IH*.

experience. Jacob Fries follows Kant in denying the possibility of positive knowledge of God. But he goes beyond Kant in positing presentiment (*Ahndung*)—in distinction from knowledge and faith—by which a person can feel what God is. This is held to be an ineffable, non-conceptual experience. By using Fries, Otto is able to link *Ahndung* and numinous experience, to allow a unified form of knowledge of the divine. This transcendental psychology is based on Otto's philosophical conviction that God can be experienced only pre-conceptually. Since the numen is not caused by a perceptual object, the Kantian categories of pure and practical reason cannot deal with the sense of a supernatural numen as *praesens*.[59] Otto is then compelled to posit (or resort to, depending on one's sympathies) a non-natural faculty of the soul on the fringes of consciousness and experience to accommodate the categorical correlate of the soul: the numinous.[60]

It is Otto's fundamentally dualistic belief that the sense of holiness unlocks the 'eternal reality' which breaks 'through the veil of temporal existence' and reveals it to the 'unlocked heart'.[61] Otto posits religion as a self-sufficient category: its object, its value, and the perception thereof form an independent unity belonging to a real world 'which is a world free from the laws of nature, free from mathematics and mechanics, a world of spirit . . . a "realm of grace", a world of God'.[62] The sphere of the holy belongs, then, to a 'wholly other' reality, to which all natural judgements are inapplicable. Access to this transcendent dimension of reality, 'the eternal and true world of spirit',[63] is only possible by a dualistic ontology whereby the natural, finite body is inhabited by a soul with the capacity to recognize the manifestations of the eternal world by a form of anamnesis or recollection, which occurs by the operation of the religious a priori. For

---

[59] For the sense in which Otto's account of numinous experience is a 'thorough-going and culminating expression' of Kant's *sui generis* categories of judgement dependent on sufficient a priori conditions, see J. Bowker, *The Sense of God* (London: Oxford University Press, 1973), 168.

[60] Ibid. 11, 112–13. Cf. G. M. Jantzen, 'Mysticism and Experience', *Religious Studies*, 3 (1989), 296. [61] *PR* 93.

[62] *PR* 42. [63] *PR* 93.

this to happen, Otto needs to employ a mystical ontology by which to posit a *sui generis* category, the numinous, *and* the means of its transcendent understanding:

In the case of the non-rational elements of our category of the holy we are referred back to something still deeper than the 'pure reason', at least as this is usually understood, namely, to that which mysticism has rightly named the *fundus animae*, the 'bottom' or 'ground of the soul' (*Seelengrund*).[64]

The key to Otto's epistemology is his vigorous assertion that 'the divine transcends not only time and place, not only measure and number, but all categories of the reason as well. It leaves subsisting only that transcendent basic relation which is not amenable to any category.'[65] So it is only through awareness of holiness that we can say anything about God, and what we say can only be analogical. This entails that, epistemologically, Otto can begin theology only when the numinous has been made manifest. He cannot read back ideas about God into experience, because such knowledge would be impossible through reason alone.

In the process of divination by presentiment, or to use Otto's term, *Ahndung*, the religious a priori is active in the *Seelengrund*, grasping the presence of the holy or numinous object by a pure numinous impression.[66] The faculty of divination is central to Otto's transcendental psychology. It performs two functions. First, divination has a receptive role, 'picking up' or sensing a numinous presence. Second, it has an interpretative role, discriminating between purely natural stimuli and those which have a value sufficient to suggest holiness beyond the realm of appearance. In which case, the numen is first sensed as a *mysterium*, and later 'translated' into the definite rational attributions that form the basis of belief rather than the diffuse, but powerful

---

[64] *IH* 112; see also *IH* 194–5.   [65] *IH* 87.

[66] See *IH* 112–16, 136–42, 175–7. See also e.g. *RO* 88–97; *ROR* 159–71; Bastow, 'Otto and Numinous Experience', 170–4; Campbell, *On Selfhood and Godhood*, 333–5, 374–6; England, *Validity of Religious Experience*, 203–6; *MEW* 161, 196, 204, 275–80; *RO* 121; Haubold, *Die Bedeutung*, 58. On *Ahndung*, see *IH* 145–7; *PR*, esp. 93–135; *NR* 74 f.; *IRG*, App. I, p. 119; *MEW* 42; *RO* 45, 52–4; *ROR* 133–5; Streetman, 'Some Later Thoughts', 381 n. 4.

intuitions of *Ahndung*. But belief, as a system of positive predications of the divine, is contingent on the context of the experience. The infinite object itself must, by its nature, remain rationally incomprehensible; it is only by divination that it is recognized.

If *Ahndung* forms an epistemological bridge between these two separate realities, the finite world and the eternal world of holiness, then it becomes clear that Otto did not simply collect a set of phenomenal responses and randomly infer their cause. On the contrary, there is a unified categorical relation between the sense of the holy and the holy itself. At the moment of numinous intuition, the sense of the holy moves *out* of history into the sphere of the holy. And at the moment of numinous revelation, the sphere of the holy moves *into* the finite world of historical religious sensation: the numinous intuition. For Otto, then, faith is no Kierkegaardian leap into the darkness, but the workings of a particular psychological faculty. As Almond puts it so succinctly, 'faith and the category of the Holy are the respective theological and philosophical expressions of means by which the action of the numen—grace—towards man is appropriated.'[67]

This may or may not be a convincing formulation. But it at least indicates that Otto was concerned to offer an account of how numinous experience actually works. We have, in his psychology, an account of how the mind discriminates between holy and profane objects and a means by which he can say that all human beings are ontologically equipped to experience the numinous, regardless of context. Whilst the epistemological idiosyncrasies of Otto's scheme may not be entirely persuasive, they do, on their own terms, justify his bifurcation of private experience and theological interpretation and his assigning temporal and theological priority to the former.

It is not the aim of this book to show that every claim Otto made for holiness was correct. It is more important to look at how Otto found holiness, theorized about it, then left it for future theologians. And since numinous experience

---

[67] *RO* 84.

is not as 'wholly other' or removed from other types of experience as Otto believed it to be, it can provide the experiential foundations for conceptual structures to accommodate and shape the experiences on which theology is based. In the logic of Otto's system it may be legitimate to give at least a notional priority to experience over theology. But it probably does not damage the cause of holiness overmuch to conclude that the concept of holiness and experiences of divine holiness are mutually informing.

There are, to conclude, biographical, soteriological, metaphysical, and psychological reasons for Otto's belief that theological discourse should be founded upon religious experience, and numinous experience in particular. In terms of both his own system and the logical requirements of monotheism I hope to have shown that Otto's experiential basis for theology does have its own inner logic and coherence. But it would hardly be a recommendation of numinous experience to say that, like dreams, it has its own logic. To function theologically, numinous experience must be a ground of meaning, value, and praxis within present, lived experience, and the way in which it can be so is the subject of my final chapter.

7

Holiness and Liberation

The distinction between holy and mundane or natural value has dominated twentieth-century holiness discourse. Contemporary theology and religious studies are generally less interested than they once were in the value of the holy in abstraction, and prefer to theorize in the context of its historical application. With the rise of emancipatory and immanentist theologies over the last thirty years, it is now the sharpness of Otto's differentiation of natural value from that of the holy that is most contentious. The earth is now, in all senses, the terrain on which holiness discourse is conducted. Otto's numinous disvaluation of the natural is especially problematic in an age in which the natural is under threat from nuclear devastation. But if there is an ecological problem with his theology, it is one shared by most Christian theologies. For it is widely agreed among emancipatory theologians that the Western Graeco-Christian heritage of transcendental theology and ascetic devaluation of matter has evacuated nature and the bodies of subject people of sacrality. To have placed nature outside the sphere of religious meaning is also to have left it at the disposal of modernity's economic and ideological projects. As Margaret Miles (among numerous others) has observed, the history of Christian spirituality has been characterized by its dependence on two pervasive ascetic assumptions:

that there exists a spiritual world whose permanence, beauty and worth infinitely outweigh anything associated with the material conditions of human life, bodies, objects, and the natural world; and that individuals must resolve to identify and exercise the spiritual aspect of themselves, extricating their loyalties from other human beings, society, and 'the world'. Both of these assumptions represent dangers for the practice of Christianity in the nuclear world.[1]

Moreover, as Miles points out, transcendentalism has 'contributed to creating the nuclear world, a world more literally "despised" than even the harshest medieval mystic could have imagined'.[2] Theologians once used the word 'natural' as a virtually pejorative term for what lay beyond the sphere of Christian revelation. But contemporary theology is now more likely to use the word 'natural' to refer to the threatened natural environment that is of absolute value and which biblical religion has played a significant part in degrading. Denise Carmody's view, that 'until we re-establish [the natural world] as a holy presence of divinity we shall have no radical measure to counter ecological exploitation',[3] is that held by emancipatory theology as a whole.

Rather than recapitulating arguments against desacralization which are familiar and, to many, almost self-evident, this chapter is intended to bring the present study's discussion of the twentieth-century contest over the nature and location of holiness into the present day. On the boundary of a new millennium that may well be humanity's last, it seems important to ask whether Otto's concept of holiness, and his account of numinous experience in particular, can provide a point of departure adequate to the ecological and spiritual crisis that is the context of contemporary theology.

Sacramental theology has always affirmed that material substances like bread, wine, and water can be transformed, within the terms of a given salvific narrative, in such a way as to reveal and therefore communicate God. The ecological implications of sacramentalism are clear,[4] but recent emancipatory theologies have sought to restore an even more comprehensive sacrality and theological consequence

---

[1] M. Miles, *The Image and Practice of Holiness: A Critique of the Classic Manuals of Devotion* (London: SCM Press, 1988), 176.   [2] Ibid. 177.

[3] D. Carmody, *Christian Feminist Theology* (Cambridge, Mass.: Blackwell, 1995), 93.

[4] See e.g. John Habgood, 'A Sacramental Approach to Environmental Issues', in C. Birch *et al.* (eds.), *Liberating Life: Contemporary Approaches to Ecological Theology* (Maryknoll, NY: Orbis, 1990), 47.

to embodiment and to creation as a whole. In doing so, they have had to weaken or dissolve the sacred–profane distinction in order to rid materiality and organic change of their traditional stigma of profanity. Emancipatory theology is profoundly suspicious of the separateness and alterity that constitute the Ottonian concept of holiness—the very characteristics which, in the second half of this chapter, I will argue to be necessary elements of a liberative theology. Indeed, I want to propose that numinous consciousness can be a significant experiential dynamic of the prophetic criticism of modern desacralization.

Emancipatory Criticism of the Sacred–Profane Opposition

Perhaps the most influential account of holiness since that elaborated by Otto in *The Idea of the Holy* has been a sacramental monism, all forms of which are opposed to Otto's differentiation of the holy from the natural as 'wholly other'. The social dimension of sacramental monism is best exemplified by John G. Davies's book *Every Day God*. This was published in 1973, and looks for the meaning of holiness in what Davies is happy to call a secular, technological, desacralized, 'hominized universe', finding it to be a product of love for one's neighbour.[5] In this book, Davies articulates what may be the strongest argument against the numinous otherness of the holy: the Christian doctrine of the incarnation of God in the man Jesus. For Davies, the life of Jesus abolishes the old model of the holy as separate and 'wholly other' to the profane world. The Incarnation bridged the gulf between the divine and the human: 'the holy is no longer the unapproachable but that which has drawn near.'[6] When, in the Gospels, Jesus says 'I am among you as one who serves' (Luke 22: 27), his presence is the antithesis of a blinding, purifying theophany. Although the Gospels testify to the numinous fear and amazement which Jesus's teaching and

---

[5] Davies, *Every Day God*, esp. 3–241; see also Kreider, *Journey towards Holiness*, 42.   [6] Davies, *Every Day God*, 53.

miracles could evoke, and despite Otto's claim that Jesus suffered numinous dread in the garden of Gethsemane,[7] Davies argues that the New Testament departs from the Old Testament in replacing numinous dread with the good news that 'God is love, and he who abides in love abides in God, and God abides in him' (1 John 4: 16).[8]

Indeed, for Davies, the Incarnation, and the New Testament as a whole, interrupt all holiness discourse. Paul states that nothing that is in Christ is unclean or common in itself except for those who merely think it is unclean (Rom. 14: 14). So too in Luke's Gospel and in Acts Jesus's life and death have rendered all foods clean (Luke 11: 41; Acts 10: 14 f., 10: 28). In Christ the old division of the sacred and the profane is ended, 'for the holy has come down to the level of the profane so that what is common may be elevated to the level of the holy'.[9] On these grounds, Davies claims that the profane cannot be a meaningful category to Christians; he will not allow theology to construct a model of the holy from a general phenomenology of religion, as he (mistakenly) feels Otto has done, but from the particularity of God's self-revelation in Christ.[10] This view has now become widely accepted among feminist and ecological theologians, who also claim that after about 300 years, the early Church's drive to

abolish distinctions of holiness within a universal community of creation was deeply contradicted by an opposite influence on Christianity from gnosticism which viewed the whole material creation, and especially sexuality, as a realm of fallenness separated from God.[11]

Alongside the strongly immanentist Christianity that Davies's work represents, another type of sacramental monism emerged during the 1960s and early 1970s. Under the influence

---

[7] *IH* 84 f.   [8] Davies, *Every Day God*, 59.   [9] Ibid. 60.
[10] Ibid. 62.
[11] R. Radford Ruether, 'Women's Body and Blood: The Sacred and the Impure', in A. Joseph (ed.), *Through the Devil's Gateway: Women, Religion and Taboo* (London: SPCK, 1990), 15. See also e.g. S. McDonagh, *To Care for the Earth: A Call for a New Theology* (London: Geoffrey Chapman, 1986), 115. Here McDonagh also refers to Jesus as a taboo-breaker.

of American 'process' and 'death of God' theology, holiness
came to be regarded as generally suffused into existence as
a whole. Throughout these two decades, scholars of religion
were objecting to modern desacralization, but also trying
to engage with modernity on its own terms by producing
'secular' concepts of holiness—that is, making the profane
or secular an object of religious celebration. In 1971 Nathan
Scott, for example, wrote that he did not wish to live in a
desacralized, mechanized world, but wanted his whole existence to be 'a conduit' of sacredness.[12] For him, 'the gen-
ius of the sacramental principle is to break down partitions
between the sacred and the quotidian.' Refusing to resort
to what he calls (following John Robinson) 'supranaturalist
projections', he locates the numinous outside the cultic or
conventionally religious sphere of reference—in effect, with
the profane (here used as a synonym for the secular):

Objects, actions, places belonging to the ordinary sphere of life
may convey to us a unique illumination of the whole mystery of
our existence, because in these actions and realities . . . something
numinous is resident.[13]

Similarly, Sam Keen's 'Manifesto for a Dionysian Theology'
represents a concept of holiness typical of its time. Like Scott
and Thomas Altizer, Keen claims that the God of supernatural agency, whose special revelations have segregated the
holy from the everyday, is dead. Now, God is 'the creative
power at the heart of all things',[14] and holiness is to be seen
as natural and, in the widest sense, erotic. Keen envisages
the holiness of human life as a nexus in which all dimensions of reality converge. Only when a person iconoclasti-
cally casts aside the fallacious opposition between material
profanity and the metaphysical realm of ideal value can he

[12] N. Scott, *The Wild Prayer of Longing* (New Haven: Yale University Press,
1971), 44, 47.
[13] Ibid. 49, also 54, 57–60, 75. See also H. Smith, 'The Reach and the Grasp:
Transcendence Today', in H. Richardson and D. Cutler (eds.), *Transcendence*
(Boston: Beacon Press, 1969), 1–17. Cf. the rejection of this position by J. Hitchcock,
The Recovery of the Sacred (New York: Seabury Press, 1974), p. ix.
[14] S. Keen, 'Manifesto for a Dionysian Theology', in Richardson and Cutler
(eds.), *Transcendence*, 45.

or she be liberated for joyous, Dionysian participation in the holiness of the ordinary. Like Otto, Keen argues that the holy alerts us to the mysterious; but, contrary to Otto, Keen seeks to wrest the holy from a transcendent, monarchical God, and in a revolutionary redistribution of power attempts to return holiness to the world, where it can be 'homogenised into the quotidian'. After this spiritual *coup d'état* the only relevance left to God is semantic: 'God' becomes a word by which to interpret earthly experience.[15] Keen's claim that the holy is the awesome primal power 'which provides meaning, value and dignity' to human life,[16] has, like sacramental monism as a whole, fed directly into contemporary ecological and feminist spirituality, in which the deliberate shift away from anthropocentrism and androcentrism has extended holiness to the whole biosphere.

Since the 1960s, the tone and focus of monistic (that is, anti-dualistic) theologies have changed. Emancipatory theology has postulated a passible God suffering in ontological and political solidarity with the oppressed. In short, the dualistic division of the sacred and the profane that underpins Otto's axiology has been put into question by theologies which insist that only a God who is immanent in creation and the sufferings of creation can guarantee the value and hence the future of life. Politically and aesthetically, contemporary Christian spirituality tends to experience holiness in the processes of political praxis, in the luminosity of the everyday world (especially when this honours the traditional conditions of most women's lives), and in the ecological connections between natural systems (not vertical historical relationships between earthly and celestial agents).

The late modern theological and spiritual reaction against high modernity's alienation of matter and spirit and against older alienatory traditions of monarchical theism has entailed that conceptions of divine–human relations are not commonly characterized by numinous dread. (Some Jewish

---

[15] Ibid. 31–52.
[16] S. Keen, *Towards a Dancing God* (New York: Harper & Row, 1970), 103. See also S. Sutphin, *Options in Contemporary Theology* (Lanham, Md.: University Press of America, 1987), 13.

theologians would, in any case, claim that the holy is set apart (*hikdish*) in so far as certain obligations and forms of behaviour are due to it; but, *contra* Otto, it produces 'no inward shuddering, no sense of the eerie . . . and no feeling of one's numinous disvalue or unworth'.[17]) Contemporary theology does not quake and cringe before God. Jürgen Moltmann's criticism of the monotheistic God as a patriarch wielding absolute power over his dominion has been an influential voice in the move away from the more traditional, unapproachable, numinous concept of God. Moltmann's Trinitarian model of God as a dynamic community of reciprocally engaging persons, of which non-hierarchical communities of equals are an eschatological reflection,[18] is both a product of, and a stimulus to, the relational theological turn. Ecological theology criticizes the modern Lutheran (especially Barthian) separation of nature and creation on one side and humanity and God on the other, leaving creation the mere 'external basis' of salvation history, and thereby exhausting its meaning and value as nature.[19]

Christian panentheistic models of the world of the sort proposed by Jay McDaniel and Sallie McFague[20] also leave little room for the apprehension of numinous alterity. The traditional privileging of the holy and the concomitant separation of natural ecology into benign, useful elements and profane harmful elements such as poisonous plants and insects has been identified by Wendell Berry as precisely constituting our 'fallenness'.[21] Believing that contemporary Christianity is complicit in modern desacralization, Berry urges that until there is an affirmation of the holiness of all

---

[17] Leiser, 'Sanctity of the Profane', 88.

[18] See J. Moltmann, *The Trinity and the Kingdom of God* (London: SCM Press, 1981); *idem*, *God in Creation* (London: SCM Press, 1985).

[19] See C. Halkes, *New Creation: Christian Feminism and the Renewal of the Earth* (London: SPCK, 1991), 78–80, for a criticism of the traditional Protestant distinction between nature and creation.

[20] See S. McFague, *The Body of God* (Minneapolis: Augsburg Fortress, 1993); J. McDaniel, *Earth, Sky, Gods and Mortals* (Mystic, Conn.: Twenty-Third Publications, 1990), esp. 183.

[21] W. Berry, *Sex, Economy, Freedom and Community* (New York: Pantheon Books, 1992), 97.

creation as God's presence in all things, history will consist in 'evil, in separation and desecration'.[22]

Creation spirituality, like ecological theology in general, is also strongly inclined to be critical of the sacred–profane distinction and the fear associated with the Ottonian numinous. Matthew Fox, the foremost proponent of creation spirituality, seeks to reignite the capacity for awe and wonder that modernity has all but extinguished. But as creation spirituality is a form of nature mysticism, that awe and wonder are not produced by numinous consciousness of God's awesome transcendental agency. Here awe is primarily a reaction to nature, in which *dabhar*, the immanent creative energy of God, flows through all things.

Whilst Fox does not wish to relinquish the concept of holiness in so far as it denotes the capacity for reverence in which modernity is so spectacularly lacking, he argues that holiness is dangerous as an incitement to a non- or antinatural perfection. Holiness has been perverted, he claims, by the myth of original sin that profaned nature's once perfect (holy) state. Instead of rejecting creation's imperfection as its profanity, Fox wants us to understand holiness in two ways. It is to be seen, first, as a process of personal ripening or becoming whole, and second, as God's offering us 'cosmic hospitality' at the great banquet of creation, at which he is both welcoming host and (in the Incarnation) guest.[23]

Creation spirituality shares a good deal of its politics and content with feminist spirituality and theology, though the latter represents a more systemic emancipatory critique than the former. Central to all recent feminist theory has been its criticism of gendered binary oppositions (such as light and darkness, reason and chaos), where the negative, disordering 'feminine' element merely serves to reinforce the value of the positive, ordering, normative 'male' element. As the sacred–profane distinction is one of the most fundamental of gendered oppositions, it is also a primary target for deconstruction. The marginalization of women in institutionalized religion

---

[22] Ibid. 101.
[23] M. Fox, *Original Blessing: A Primer in Creation Spirituality* (Santa Fe, N. Mex.: Bear & Co., 1983), 112 f.

is seen as a function of the man-made categorical boundaries which logically divide the (male) sacred 'A' from the
(usually female) profane not-A by the law of the excluded
middle, casting not-A as that corrupting element which must
be excluded to protect the well-being of A.[24] Contemporary
emancipatory theologies of relationship have largely aban-
doned the category and practices of religious separation as
merely sacralizing alienation. Penelope Margaret Magee argues
that since philosophers, theologians, and clerics have put the
sacred and the profane to war with one another to secure
their own advantage, feminists should not 'sell arms to the
combatants' by uncritical use of the traditional (Durkhei-
mian) opposition, but should instead subvert its very terms
in the interest of religious and sexual equality:

The politics of subversion will be a dangerous undertaking—the
pleasure of keeping our shoes on and striding towards the burning
bush. If 'Being in their place is what makes [things] sacred' . . . 'but
so, equally, does their being *out* of place' . . . who knows what disorder might result?[25]

Over the last twenty years, feminist religious studies has
carefully documented the harm done to women and nature
not only by modern desacralization but also by pre-modern
ascetic concepts of holiness which denigrate all embodiment,
and female embodiment in particular, because it is subject
to cycles of organic ('profane') change: birth, growth, multiplication, and decay that are oblivious to the linear processes of salvation history. With few exceptions, the world's
religions have cast femaleness as a sexual (and by extension,
moral) impediment to (male) holiness. The reproductive
female body is tabooed or profanized and separated from the
male body (whether by screens, veils, or seclusions of one
form or another) as constituting a threat to the good order
and peace of holy living.[26]

[24] See N. Jay, 'Gender and Dichotomy', in S. Gunew (ed.), *A Reader in Feminist Knowledge* (London: Routledge, 1991), esp. 93.
[25] P. M. Magee, 'Disputing the Sacred: Some Theoretical Approaches to Gen-
der and Religion', in U. King (ed.), *Religion and Gender* (Oxford: Blackwell, 1995),
117.   [26] See Ruether, 'Women's Body and Blood', 13.

As such, feminist theology and spirituality cannot proceed without first criticizing or dispensing with practices and discourses proposing the absolute dualism of the sacred–profane opposition, especially as framed by Otto and Eliade. In many respects, religious feminism is right to do so. There is no doubt that, as a form of power, holiness is peculiarly susceptible to political misuse. If holiness is a manifestation and mediation of divine power, then those who control access to the holy can disempower others by its monopolization. Fencing off subject categories of being from the holy renders them profane by definition. And in the politics of institutional religion (to which Otto was largely indifferent) the maintenance of privileged access to the sacred and the right to stake out its spatial sphere can be means by which an élite calls a community to order and establishes dominance over the subjected, profaned other.[27] As profane, the other is deprived of the privileges of protection and conservation to which holy things are entitled.

Perhaps feminist theology's greatest contribution to prophetic theology has been its judgement of patriarchy as a state of sin, thereby making sin a historical or political condition rather than an ontological or biological one. Patriarchy, as the paradigmatically sinful historical state, is a second-order reality, not a created given; that is feminist theology's locus of hope. Patriarchy is sinful in that its exploitative hierarchies break the relationality that constitutes God's being with the world and the ecology of creation. In all emancipatory theology relationality is not only a pre-condition of healthy spirituality, but also a transformatory power, which, in the collective power of its connections, overcomes the sinful political structures that impede social justice.

Otto, however, understands sin as an ontological condition that differentiates creature and divinity, not as a historical particularity. Numinous unworth, he writes, is 'given with the

---

[27] See J. S. Hawley and W. Proudfoot, Introduction to their edited volume *Gender and Fundamentalism* (New York: Oxford University Press, 1994), 27; G. Sahgal and N. Yuval-Davis, 'Fundamentalism, Multiculturalism and Women in Britain', in their edited volume *Refusing Holy Orders: Women and Fundamentalism in Britain* (London: Virago, 1992), 8–9.

self's existence as "creature" and profane natural being'.[28] Although these words show Otto's anthropology at its most severe, for feminist theology, this kind of holy–profane distinction is sinful, in that as practice and as scholarly discourse it is both a symptom and a cause of separation and disconnection. Mary Grey, in *Redeeming the Dream*, rejects Otto's account of numinous experience, as a form of spiritual humiliation that is 'totally opposed to what women have experienced'.[29] Whilst conceding that numinous consciousness can be experienced as the sublimity of nature, Grey feels that numinous experience sunders the interconnectedness of God and nature that defines feminist theological, ethical, and spiritual values. For Grey, the Ottonian model of God as *mysterium tremendum et fascinans* produces a sense of separation from God: 'the deeper the experience the greater the awe and terribleness of God as wholly other. Spirituality will then consist in recognizing that one is dust and ashes before the deity.'[30]

The Holy–Profane Opposition as a Mark of Prophetic Opposition

Historically, theology has undoubtedly been commandeered by oppressive ideologies, and has also assimilated and propagated them, particularly those which uphold the dominance of men over women as patterned upon God's dominion over the world. But if justice is a numinous value, a mystery of God's love and purposes rather than their mere instrument, then so too the suffering or witnessing to injustice can

---

[28] *IH* 55.

[29] M. Grey, *Redeeming the Dream: Feminism, Redemption and the Christian Tradition* (London: SPCK, 1989), 44.

[30] Ibid. Although it is clear that women suffer under what appear to be broadly similar marginalizations and exclusions from the sacred as defined, controlled, and dispensed by male priestly castes, the question of whether women generically, rather than historically, have religious experiences which are 'totally opposed' to the Ottonian numinous experience is unanswerable. Much will depend on the religious temper of the individual woman. By contrast, Kathryn Allen Rabuzzi, in *The Sacred and the Feminine: Towards a Theology of Housework* (New York: Seabury Press, 1982), esp. 56–61, uses Otto's numinous aesthetic from *The Idea of the Holy* to frame a (rather conservative) feminist theology of housework.

arouse numinous emotions. Otto's work can thus take religio-political criticism into a new discursive arena without compromising his insistence on the radical otherness of the sacred. Indeed, a prophetic judgement on the numinous horror of desecration reads the numinous as resistant to its own desecration *by virtue of* its otherness.

Our reading of numinous experience will be different to that of Otto at the turn of the century; but that does not mean that emancipatory theologians (among whom I would number myself) have to jettison the basic structure and terms of numinous experience. This chapter is not intended to criticize emancipatory theology as a project for the restoration of *shalom* to the whole of creation, but rather to question the monistic concept of holiness it usually assumes. Whilst any theology should urge the nurturing of relationships in the ecology of all living things, it should also cast judgement on those sinful structures which institutionalize non- or anti-relation. That is, in order to restore relationship, theology must first isolate and name those structures of power which, having broken relationship, are profane and have no place in creation until their transformation by judgement and repentance. Undifferentiated holiness is a genuinely religious ideal, but lacks the transformatory dynamics of models of God and divine–human relations which institute justice as a prerequisite of *shalom*, and, as such, require clear differentiation and demarcation of the holy and what sins by profaning the holy.

Rather than reject numinous experience out of hand, holistic criticism of numinous experience needs to recognize, then, that numinous experience does not take place in a vacuum, but in a world where relationships between humans and all other created things have been politically degraded. Here the numinous does not compound the alienation of created things from God: that has already been completed by political structures of economic, sexual, and environmental alienation. Rather, numinous self-depreciation reminds us that we are not God, that creation is not at our disposal. Moreover, in the numinous event, two ontologically and axiologically distinct forms of being come together in an encounter which is not, according to Otto, only one of terror but also, in its *fascinans* element, one of mystical joy.

Although Otto has relatively little phenomenological interest in the separation of holy things from profane things, his insistence on the otherness of the holy supports the principle of a transcendental division between the holy and what he understands to be the profane, 'the impure which is unable to assume the worth of holiness or to come into its presence'.[31] Admittedly, Otto's concept of profanity as the ontological state of creatureliness is in danger of consigning immanence as a whole to intrinsic unworth. Like other feminist theologians, I would want to say that sin and therefore profanity are historical rather than ontological. But if, in the context of modernity's desacralization of creation, one understands the profane first as that which is impure or unfit for God's presence *because* it has been defiled (metaphorically sacked from the temple—*profanum*—to which it belongs and distributed as spoils for common use), and second as the agency which is guilty of the profaning, then the opposition of the holy and the profane takes on a new, prophetic meaning. The separation of what is *sacer* (consecrated to the divine) and the profane (what *has been made* available for common use) draws a line that represents the necessity of a moral, hence political, choice or alignment between two attitudinal worlds. The holy becomes that which is in absolute historical–political opposition to the processes that have made 'natural' objects profane, and recasts the actual profane as that which has done the profaning.

In this context, the otherness of the sacred offers no licence for religious withdrawal from engagement with the world. The opposition of the sacred and the profane is not a purely formal configuration, but also in the existential world an opposition that necessitates a religio-moral engagement whose social expression will be political in character. Prophetic withdrawal from 'the world' (as the sum of what profanes) must, however, hold up its separation as a sign. The boundary between the sacred and the profane is a mark of

[31] *IH* 91.

prophetic alignment and choice. Such boundaries can take visible forms, as when protesters occupy or picket natural spaces threatened by 'development' and attempt to forbid trespass upon them. Those who are complicit in desecration and violently break their lines stand under the judgement of the holy. The holy carries its own juridical principle: in Jewish tradition, whoever uses a product of God's creation without pronouncing a benediction—that is, without acknowledging its source—should be called a thief. And whatever the manifest ecological shortcomings of the biblical tradition of human stewardship over creation, that tradition does at least imply that creation's goods are of limited access, in that they are stewarded, not owned. In Ottonian terms, then, whatever oversteps those limits and assumes absolute ownership of creation has not only failed to show proper reverence, but has above all forgotten its creaturehood. Such persons are, literally, transgressors, and are therefore exposed to numinous wrath.

Yet if, as in strongly immanentist or monistic theologies, everything is holy, then holiness is everywhere and nowhere. If there is no principle of division that names religio-ethical transgression, then there are no frontiers to halt the advance of those political structures of alienation from God whose very purpose is to parasitize/profane whatever lies within their reach. The division of holiness and profanity produces an urgent, purposive model of history, whereas the problem of modernity is precisely that it robs history of any *telos* beyond that of the final mastery of nature.

The Ottonian distinction between the holy and the profane reminds us that if we refuse to name anything profane, then we cannot, within the logic of this pair of words, name anything holy either. The one word presupposes the other, and in most languages implies that the two things should be separated. So if nothing is profane, the sacred is voided of content, and everything is, in effect, made available. If nothing is enclosed or fenced off as taboo or forbidden, closed to economic colonization or scientific reduction, then there is no obstacle to modernity's Baconian unveiling of creation's mysteries. Everything in creation is exposed to the light of instrumental reason, and all its goods are laid out for consumption.[32] Holiness cannot be understood as whatever is merely not profane: it is whatever is in proximity to God, and therefore in a state of limited access, and therefore, of integrity.

Theists believe that all things in the cosmos were made by God, and are therefore, at least originally and potentially, holy. But the salvific narratives of Christianity and (less so) Judaism show that between the genesis and the *telos* of creation, history has gone awry. Jewish theology, without a doctrine of original sin, has a more optimistic anthropology than Christianity. But for both Judaism and Christianity the reality of evil demands that spiritual and ritual boundaries be erected to protect the holy and to provide means of crossing from profane, polluted states of being or consciousness to those fostering the likeness of divine holiness. The prophetic voice cries out in the wilderness (now of modernity's making) that history must prepare a passage for the holy into the world. Biblical theism recognizes that history is a witness to human lostness as well as the medium of salvation, making the cartography of the sacred indispensable to the salvific process. When traditional theology speaks of sinners as 'the lost', this may be understood as referring to the 'lostness' of those political structures which, having severed the relationship between themselves and the whole cosmos for the sake of personal or collective power and profit, have also alienated themselves from a cosmos whose created ontological character is interrelational. In the end, having transgressed the boundaries of creaturehood and the sacred times and spaces that bound God's self-revelation, the profanizers become— in the formlessless and turmoil of their vast conurbations, ceaseless trading, and global (mono)culture—the profane.

In the biblical texts, God sets limits, rings, or empty spaces around that which reveals him. These boundaries demarcate and protect the historical and physical spaces in which revelation takes place, and also frame their meaning. In

---

[32] See Halkes's discussion of Bacon's desacralizing rhetoric in *New Creation*, 29 f.

Exodus 19: 10–12 Moses is told to tell the people to wash their clothes in readiness for the theophany on Mount Sinai, and to set a boundary around the mountain, ensuring that no one approaches.[33] It is not that holiness requires, metaphorically speaking, electrified or barbed wire to protect itself. The 'keep off' sign borne by tabooed objects symbolizes how, if the whole earth is God's holy mountain, the place of his self-revelation, nothing must interpose itself between the revelation and its object without attention to its risks. It is *because* the holy mountain is repulsive to those who would profane it that it is also an eschatological image of the cessation of violence: 'They shall not hurt or destroy in all my holy mountain; for the earth shall be full of the knowledge of the Lord as the waters cover the sea' (Isa. 11: 9). Numinous consciousness, as a divination of the inviolability of divine things, is the pre-condition of *shalom*. For when the earth is 'filled with the glory of the Lord'—that is, when the image of God in all things is restored—they will be holy. And to be holy is to be inviolable, and therefore safe from the destructive 'touch' of violence and exploitation. But until that eschatological *kairos*, not everything in the world is holy. Indeed, there is very little left that modern science and economics has not exposed to its desecratory touch.

The holiness of God, and by extension all that he has created with the intention that it should be holy as he is holy, means that far from devaluing creation, an Ottonian model of the holy can (re)sacralize creation as having a value that is 'wholly other' to those mercantile values which the profane 'world' attributes to it. Numinous apprehension warns us that the *tremendum* of divine wrath will fall on those who disfigure, pollute, or extinguish the created diversity of life,

---

[33] The human conceptualization of these religious boundaries is of course problematic. In Exod. 9: 15 the men of Israel are also ordered to prepare themselves for the disclosure of holiness by keeping away from women for three days. In *Standing Again at Sinai: Judaism from a Feminist Perspective* (New York: HarperSanFrancisco, 1990), 25–6, Judith Plaskow argues that the exclusion of women at the central event of Judaism means that 'the Otherness of women finds its way into the very center of Jewish experience'. If women did not enter into the covenant as men did, this would prompt Rachel Adler's question, 'Are women really Jews?'

which as Otto points out in relation to the Book of Job, has a marvellousness that testifies to the numinosity of its creator.[34] Otto may seem to devalue creation in so far as he insists on the non-naturalness of the numinous. But this is a way of accentuating God's holy/wholly otherness, rather than judging God's creation to be bad in itself. Indeed, it is precisely for feminist and ecological reasons that I would invoke numinous wrath as a mark of God's absolute opposition to whatever has profaned his image by establishing a free market in the human and non-human goods of creation (especially one established in his name). This understanding of the concept of holiness as a principle of judgement need not be alien to immanentist concepts of holiness. John Davies notes that when we witness the pollution of nature, 'the holy addresses us'; we have to 'confess our responsibility and we experience judgement'.[35] God's wrath is a measure of the absolute seriousness of the desecratory offence. Desecration is not merely having mixed up cultically clean/unblemished things with unclean/blemished or decaying things. It is an act of colonization that parasitizes creation's creative energies, and, more, deprives God of a sphere of self-manifestation. The desecrator refuses to be holy, and worse, refuses to let the desecrated object be holy, as God has willed it to be.

Otto's opposition of the 'world' and the holy (particularly in the *Religious Essays* and *The Kingdom of God and the Son of Man*) need not be read, then, as a gnostic rejection of the created natural order as such. On the contrary, to theologize about holiness as that which constitutes divine transcendence is not to insist on God's severance from nature; after all, if God creates in his own image—even in transcendence—God suffers desecration through that of his creation. Rather, to transcendentalize holiness is to direct attention to the axiological possibilities that are, evidently, not yet fully realized in the world. Moreover, as a stimulus of the *sensus numinis*, Otto concedes that the natural and the supernatural are at least aesthetically related, so that the natural *qua* creation can hardly be a matter of spiritual regret. More importantly,

[34] *IH* 79.   [35] Davies, *Every Day God*, 187.

in his earlier, less pessimistic work, the dualistic depreciation of the flesh is regarded as numinous self-disvaluation
'carried to its extreme'; that is, it is not the normative element of creature-feeling, but an excess of creature-feeling.
For it is not that the creature is profane in his or her self,
but that in the presence of the numen, experienced as the
'all-in-all', 'the creature with his being and doing, his "will-
ing" and his "running" (Rom. IX.16), his schemes and his
resolves, become nothing'.[36] That is, numinous experience
puts the human project into perspective; and, more, when
that project has eclipsed or displaced God, stands in judgement upon it.

The essential dualism of Otto's work is a function of the
concept of holiness itself: namely, as an instrument of religious differentiation and distinction. The proper contemporary differentiation of the holy from the profane is one that
is well summarized by Altizer's words: 'the meaning of the
sacred is reached by inverting the reality created by modern
man's profane choice.'[37] In the Ottonian view, holiness frac-
tures mundane reality by 'the eruption of something utterly
different from the world'.[38] Holiness disrupts the compla-
cencies of the *status quo*, and beckons towards new conditions of possibility.

The *self*-revelation of God has its own *kairos*; it is an
eschatological unveiling of the holy of which the modern
scientific exposure of creation through atomic blasts, open-
cast mining, and deforestation, is a dangerous parody. The
numinous episteme, by contrast, is a way of knowing the
world without subjecting it to the interests of the knower.
For numinous experience impels a crisis of values at the
point at which the profane is differentiated from the holy in
a manner more basically emotional than a rational acknowledgement of their difference. To develop Otto's thinking in
a more explicitly prophetic direction, it could be said that
this process of the radical devaluation of profane values occurs

[36] *IH* 89; see also 81.
[37] T. Altizer, *Mircea Eliade and the Dialectic of the Sacred* (Philadelphia: Westminster Press, 1963), p. 45.
[38] Evdokimov, 'Holiness in the Orthodox Tradition', 147.

in the divination of the holy as of 'wholly other' value to the world (that is, the sphere of alienation from God) in which values are attached to its goods as prices the powerful can pay to expand their own sphere of operation.

This century, more than any other in the modern period, should have taught us the meaning of the profane and the necessity of (re)naming the profane *in order to* preserve the conditions of the sacred. And it may be the case that until history reaches its *telos*, the holy and the profane will belong to distinct and opposing categories of religio-political value whose dissolution would have an eschatological rather than strictly historical character. But, phenomenologically, the *naming* of the profane is not predetermined; it is historical, and has changed and may change again. Sexuality, for example, no longer profanes the body in contemporary spiritualities. Here profanity is, rightly, no longer something inherent in human or natural embodiment. Instead, the body is profan-*ized* in suffering the damage of invasive pollutants like car exhaust and pesticides. Ideograms for the numinous are also subject to change. For example, in a noisy, over-developed world, hushed, empty spaces may well produce a yet more numinous impression than they did for Otto on his travels before the First World War, and certainly than they might have done before industrialization.[39]

Thus Arnold van Gennep: 'Characteristically, the presence of the sacred (and the performance of appropriate rites) is variable. Sacredness as an attribute is not absolute; it is brought into play by the nature of particular situations.'[40] Phenomenologically, the naming of the sacred and the profane pivots, and may even reverse under particular historical and ideological conditions.[41] Although the numinous has formal, definitive elements, and the otherness of numinous value and the sanctity of God's creation are non-relative, the phenomenological configuration of relations between the

[39] Cf. *IH* 68–9.
[40] A. van Gennep, *The Rites of Passage* (London: Routledge & Kegan Paul, 1965), 12.
[41] See my study of the post-Christian feminist reversal of female profanity and sacrality: *Thealogy and Embodiment*, esp. 21–74.

sacred and the profane is historically conditioned. This process of change is sometimes led by theological and aesthetic trends, but also belongs to the character of the sacred as that which, as *mysterium*, eludes conceptualization, and as that which belongs to the character of revelation as a historical process.

Wherever a religion invokes a sacred–profane opposition, the constant renegotiation of that opposition will, to some extent, have structured its historical development. In the West, theology and spirituality derive their momentum from critical engagement with the sacral universe bequeathed by the Bible and the centuries of elaboration upon its meaning. And, rather than the abolition of the sacred–profane distinction, it is its critical reconfiguration which keeps religious discourse alive.

For example, whilst Davies's and others' monistic readings of holiness in the Gospels are legitimate, it is also possible to read the Gospels as intending the reverse: namely, as being founded upon a holy–profane opposition for their very meaning. For in the Gospels God has, in effect, profaned himself by his incarnation in Christ among the cultically outcast of the time. Christ's holiness may, then, consist precisely in his sacrificial willingness to accept defilement for the sake of humanity's purification from sin. In the Gospels Jesus did not teach that nothing was profane, but urged the recognition of an *authentic* distinction between holy and profane things. He urged people to see the actuality of uncleanness —not in bodily fluids, particular foods, disease, or sexual misdemeanour, but in the estrangement of the human heart and will from God.

Moreover, the dramatic irony and tension of the Gospels rest on the paradoxically lowly circumstances of the Messiah and Son of God. From beginning to end, God's self-revelation in the life of Jesus was characterized by the conditions of the profane. Jesus was born in the straw among the animals; he had close friendships with women; he accepted a blessing from a sinful woman (Luke 7: 36–50); he washed his disciples' grimy feet; he suffered the 'unclean' touch of the haemorrhissa and blessed her for it (Mark 5: 25–34 and parallels);[42] he commissioned the Samaritan woman to preach, although she was doubly unclean as a woman and as a Samaritan (John 4: 7–26); he made his Messianic entry into Jerusalem on a donkey; and he touched lepers and ate with sinners.[43] These stories are all evidence of the numinous tension between the holy and the profane in Jesus's life. Jesus's death on a rubbish dump outside the walls of Jerusalem, the holy city, may represent the final and ultimate sublimity of a sacrificial holiness that is mediated by the profane.

This model of holiness, as a prophetic reversal of the established sacred–profane distinction, seems to reinforce more than abolish that distinction. Above all, the scene of the crucifixion excites numinous horror at the absolutely inglorious end of God's incarnation on earth. The sacrificial meaning of the crucifixion relies upon the shock of witnessing the ultimate profanation of God by human sin. For a Christian, the cross represents not only the suffering of God in Christ and all who suffer, but also the absolute guilt of the world in its degradation of God. The cross shocks its witnesses into repentance. But Jesus is not left nailed to the profanity of the cross. In the resurrection Jesus's holiness is vindicated by his ascension (whether real or metaphorical) to God's right hand in heaven—the paradigm sphere of the holy.

Obviously, these references to the role of the profane in the Gospels are not intended to provide an exhaustive account of their meaning; rather, they are to illustrate a process in which religious truth is revealed through the use of sacred–profane distinctions, whether maintaining them with

---

[42] This narrative, regularly cited as evidence of Jesus's indifference to the holy–profane distinction, is notably ambiguous. In *Theology and Feminism* (Oxford: Blackwell, 1990), 88–9, Daphne Hampson notes that Jesus merely heals the haemorrhissa of what, like his contemporaries, he calls a 'disease'. Jesus nowhere challenges the menstrual taboo; nor does he call for the admission of women to the inner courts of the Temple. Both she and Judith Ochshorn find Jesus's teaching on the superiority of the life of the spirit over that of family ties insensitive to the spiritual depth of women's lives, especially as mothers.

[43] In 'Women's Body and Blood', 14, Rosemary Ruether interprets Jesus's relations with women as expressions of his will to break customary taboos. I read these pericopae as renegotiating their meaning, not abolishing them.

reverence or prophetically subverting them. Moreover, within the framework of the New Testament renegotiation of the meaning of the holy, further and continuous negotiations have taken place. One example of this process might be the nineteenth-century evangelical proto-feminists who enlarged the sacral sphere of motherhood by manœuvring within the existing evangelical ideology of femininity, in which moral and domestic hygiene were the pre-conditions of feminine sanctity. Through conceiving philanthropic praxis as a natural extension of the maternal vocation, women like the 'social purity' campaigner Ellice Hopkins and Florence Nightingale 'purified' the unclean public sphere of ruthless capitalism, vice, illness, and squalor by bringing order and hygiene to its institutions. In doing so, the public sphere was reformed into a (quasi-domesticated) version of the female redemptory private sphere. This had the religious effect of letting women live out their activist Christian theology and the political effect of justifying their intervention in public affairs.

Or again, in late modernity, a reconfiguration of the sacred–profane opposition that is almost the reverse of that of evangelical feminism can be found in Mary Daly's post-Christian philosophy. She uses the Ottonian numinous to construct a prophetic critique of the sacred *by* the sacred. Her work is indicative of the adaptability of the Ottonian scheme, here used in a theoretical context absolutely foreign to that of *The Idea of the Holy* itself. Whilst being critical of Otto's androcentric world-view, she relies on his evocation of the numinous to imagine a politicized (feminist) sacred: a dreadfully other energy that is *profanum*—before or outside the precincts of the patriarchal establishment—and, as outcast(e), subversively indifferent to its *status quo*. 'Holy Hags' are prophetic feminists who are ' "wholly other" to those who are at home in the kingdom of the fathers'.[44] Quoting from Otto's own analysis of the numinous as *mysterium*, Daly writes that 'Dreadful women are "quite beyond the sphere of the usual, the intelligible and the familiar." . . . The mythic wholeness/

[44] M. Daly, *Gyn/Ecology: The Metaethics of Radical Feminism* (London: Women's Press, 1991), 50.

holiness of Dreadful women unmasks the estranged State of Patriarchy.'[45] Here, the authentic sacred recalls an untouchable (unavailable) biophilic 'free time/space', also termed the 'Background' [*sic*] or 'wild realm' of 'wholeness and integrity' that existed before patriarchy and still exists beyond the boundaries of customary (that is, truly profane) 'foreground' patriarchal values. Daly's controversial feminization of the holy is less significant here than her conviction that sacred power precedes and stands over against its ideological distortion into an instrument of coercion, and that it empowers acts of judgement, liberation, and healing.

To some extent, Otto has already laid the foundations for a prophetic theology based on numinous consciousness. He regards the numinous as an experiential correlate of the outworking of salvation history. He presupposes that Mosaic religion marks the beginning of an evolutionary process by which the progressive rationalization and moralization of the numinous culminates in the prophets and the Gospels.[46] And he reads the biblical texts through a numinous episteme, finding that 'while the feelings of the non-rational and numinous constitute a vital factor in every form religion may take, they are pre-eminently in evidence in Semitic religion and most of all in the religion of the Bible'.[47]

Few theologians today would be confident in making such a claim. There is no doubt that the holiness of God is a central biblical theme, whose tradition goes back to the early or pre-monarchic biblical period (see 1 Sam. 2: 1–10 and Exod. 15: 1–7 respectively).[48] But in the last fifty years Old Testament studies have regarded holiness as a central and unifying concept of the Old Testament, though not the only one.[49] So too, postmodern hermeneutics have made theology aware that magisterial pronouncements on *the* biblical message or assertions of a unitary biblical tradition that transcends economic, ethnic, or gendered difference are to some extent biographical in their assumption of epistemic centrality and interpretive privilege. (However, it is worth noting that it is

---

[45] Ibid., quoting *IH* 26.   [46] *IH* 75.   [47] *IH* 72.
[48] See Gammie, *Holiness in Israel*, 104.   [49] Ibid. 74, 197.

precisely because biblical texts do not provide an unmediated religio-ethical norm that numinous consciousness can be so significant to the interpretation of prophetic texts. For it is the situation where the text is 'heard' or received as revelation by numinous consciousness that provides the ethical norm, not the authority of the text itself.)

Although contemporary biblical scholars have mixed feelings about adapting Otto's work to the interpretation of holiness texts (particularly those of the Priestly writings),[50] John Gammie has, none the less, made fruitful use of Otto's analysis of holiness as 'a starting point and constant frame of reference' for his reading of Old Testament holiness theology.[51] For Gammie, 'holiness in Israel was a summons to Israel to aspire to the justice and compassion characteristic of her summoning God.'[52] As he notes of the biblical writers,

Priests, prophets, and sages were united in awareness that the holiness of the very God of Israel called for cleanness. They differed, of course, in their vision and understanding of what cleanness this awesome God required, but at many points they also shared judgements on the prerequisites of purity.[53]

The inspiration of Otto in Gammie's reading is clear. Otto's understanding of 'creature-feeling' is strongly associated with the biblical concept of cleanness.[54] Sometimes Otto seems to be saying that one must experience creature-feeling simply by virtue of being human, not divine. But he speaks most eloquently of creature-feeling in the context of his theology of atonement. For Otto, when a person has defiled others,

---

[50] Jenson, *Graded Holiness*, 43.

[51] Gammie, *Holiness in Israel*, 6. Gammie is not the only biblical scholar to deploy an Ottonian hermeneutic; see e.g. S. Terrien, *The Elusive Presence: Toward a New Biblical Theology* (San Francisco: Harper & Row, 1978), and *idem*, 'The Numinous, the Sacred and the Holy in Scripture', *Biblical Theology Bulletin*, 12 (1982), 99–108.   [52] Gammie, *Holiness in Israel*, 195.

[53] Ibid. 8.

[54] In *Purity and Danger* (Harmondsworth: Penguin, 1970), 67, Mary Douglas observes that Levitical 'holiness is exemplified by completeness. Holiness requires that individuals shall conform to the class to which they belong.' This is, in part at least, the point Otto is making about 'creature-feeling' as the realization that the exercise of pseudo-divine power is a transgression against God and the created order.

he or she knows that 'even holiness itself may be tainted and tarnished by his presence'; that in his ' "profaneness" [he] is not *worthy* to stand in the presence of the holy one'.[55] In *The Idea of the Holy* guilt and remorse over moral transgression are only analogous to numinous self-depreciation. But at the same time he recognizes that

alongside this self-depreciation stands a second [feeling], which while it may have reference to the same action as the other yet avails itself of definitely different categories. The same perverse action that before weighed upon us now *pollutes* us; we do not accuse ourselves, we are defiled in our own eyes. And the characteristic form of emotional reaction is no longer remorse but *loathing*. The man feels a need, to express which he has to recourse to images of *washing* and cleansing.[56]

It is precisely creature-feeling's numinous sense of the absolute 'cleanness' of the divine being that furnishes the knowledge that modern desacralization is not only sinful in its alienation from God but has, in its alienation from nature as creation, spiritually and physically contaminated us, making the world repellent to God.[57] Despite this, the numen is a *numen praesens*, experience of which has the character of *fascinans*, theologically construed as the gift of grace.[58]

The value of John Gammie's Ottonian reading of the Old Testament as, in a number of ways, summoning Israel to cleanness is its implicit acknowledgement that numinous consciousness feeds a collectively transformative concept of holiness (unlike the more typically psychologizing discussions of

---

[55] *IH* 54.   [56] *IH* 55.

[57] Cf. Douglas's influential account of the atoning function of purification rituals in *Purity and Danger*, esp. 12–13. She argues that dirt is not shunned because of 'dread or holy terror'. Purification eliminates the dirt that is, according to Douglas, 'matter out of place' and that offends against a community's sense of order and the unity of its experience. But Otto's 'dread and holy terror' at uncleanness (to which she does not directly refer) is not directed towards material dirt; nor is it a function of the need for a stable or tidy social order. For Otto, uncleanness is a symbol of an ontological and moral state which is, only secondarily, a sign and a product of social disorder. Douglas claims that 'ideas about separating, purifying, demarcating and punishing transgressions have as their main function to impose system on an inherently untidy experience.' (ibid. 15.) Otto's view would be that if numinous consciousness *does* provide social stability, that is its effect, not its purpose.   [58] See *IH* 140.

numinous experience as private religious emotion). Gammie's reading of Isaiah of Jerusalem (and also of Isaiah of Babylon and Isaiah of the Restoration[59]) is particularly helpful to the present purpose of demonstrating the prophetic, political consequences of numinous consciousness. Otto believed that 'the capital instance of the intimate mutual interpenetration of the numinous with the religious and moral is Isaiah'.[60] Admittedly, the Isaianic prophecies have a tendency to degenerate into numinous apocalyptic, whose punitive imagery is too reminiscent of the atrocities of war to be helpful; but Isaianic holiness theology can, none the less, be read as an exemplar of the close relation of numinous consciousness and justice. In the words of primo-Isaiah, for whom justice is a function of God's holiness, 'The Lord of Hosts is exalted in justice and the Holy God shows himself holy in righteousness' (Isa. 5: 16). Isaiah puts earthly powers in perspective; it is not these that are to be dreaded but 'The Lord of Hosts, him you shall regard as holy; let him be your fear and let him be your dread' (8: 13). As Gammie writes, 'the prophet proclaims that the reverential fear of God has a freeing effect: potentially threatening political machinations should not, and will not, become the object of dread if the people would but keep in mind the holiness of God.'[61] Numinous consciousness produces religious dread, but the holiness of God also consists of the mysteries of love and justice, which produce a numinous consciousness that is infinitely more transformative than ordinary experiences of fear.

God's justice is a purgative justice (to use Gammie's term) that produces the cleanness that is prerequisite to the restoration of the glory of his presence on earth. Isaiah teaches that the sacrificial cult, the established mechanism of atonement, is not a sufficient means to holiness; where 'we have all become like one who is unclean' (64: 6), God's holiness also demands (and empowers) the transformation of the moral consciousness: 'Wash yourselves; make yourselves clean; remove the evil of your doings from before my eyes; cease

---

[59] These latter two writers are perhaps more usually referred to as deutero- and trito-Isaiah, the authors of Isa. 40–55 and 56–66 respectively.   [60] *IH* 75.
[61] Gammie, *Holiness in Israel*, 82. Cf. Isa. 30: 15, 31: 1.

to do evil, learn to do good; seek justice, correct oppression; defend the fatherless, plead for the widow' (Isa. 1: 16–17).[62] Gammie argues that 'throughout his career [Isaiah] clung to the notion that sin defiles but holiness requires cleanness'. Exploitation of the poor and defenceless (1: 16–17, 3: 14–15, 10: 1–4) and indifference to the poor and hungry (32: 6–7) require a social, legal, and, above all, divine justice that exposes self-exaltation as more than vanity, but as moral and spiritual uncleanness. Indeed, for Isaiah, human justice is a manifestation of divine holiness. As Gammie puts it, '*God manifests the divine holiness by moving human beings to perform righteous acts.*'[63]

Holiness and cleanness are inalienably associated, yet distinctions between the clean and the unclean cannot be used without painful consciousness of recent demonic misappropriations of the concept of cleanness in the Stalinist and Hitlerian rhetoric of ideological, racial, and genetic hygiene. For many, recent history is a good reason not to use the language of purity at all. Organicist postmodernism is acutely aware of the anti-ecological nature of eliminative purity. It celebrates instead mixed or hybrid identities; what Maria Lugones refers to as the 'curdled', pluri-vocal identities-in-process inhabiting a cross-cultural space that is 'in the middle, anomalous, deviant, ambiguous, impure. It lacks the mark of separation as impurity.'[64] In the post-Holocaust, but newly and dangerously nationalistic era, to mix is a proper subversion of Fascistic separatism or apartheid. Creation is no one's *Lebensraum*. There can be no separatist spaces without deportations and sealed ghettos on their perimeters. The mixing of national and ethnic categories anticipates eschatological reconciliation; it has nothing to do with pollution which should be theologically understood as the defacing of God's image in creation through the infidelity of human ideology and social organization to his will for justice and *shalom*. It is a task of prophetic theology to reclaim the metaphor of cleanness (as a numinous ideogram for justice) from

---

[62] Gammie, *Holiness in Israel*, 83–5.
[63] Ibid. 85; emphasis original.
[64] M. Lugones, 'Purity, Impurity, and Separation', *Signs*, 19 (1994), 462.

those who have used it to erase ethnic, religious, or intellectual difference in the interests of a demonic purity.

So too, modernity's uncleanness must be named as more than a moral offence. It is the sin of profiting from desacralization and the wasting and contamination of the human and non-human lives which suffer its effects. It produces and rewards those whose social and intellectual ambitions entail positioning themselves in I–it anti-relations with available objects, whether these be members of the labour force, natural (treated as 'free') resources, or objects of the kind of scientific experimentation that values 'knowledge' over all other goods. Modern hubris forgets its creaturely status; that is its uncleanness. In this context, numinous consciousness of what it means to be a creature is not only an emotional reaction to the devastation brought upon all creatures by modern hubris, it is also, completed as the feeling of the holy, an epistemic principle by which modern desacralization of the value of life and of all living things is judged to be sinful through a total reaction of mind and body.

Conclusion

The biblical religions have always tried to balance a sense of God's love with their hopes for his justice. Salvation without justice is a cheap salvation, passing over radical evil and the suffering of its victims. Yet justice without love holds out no possibility of reconciliation, leaving human history with wounds that can never be healed. Human reason cannot conceive the balance of love and justice in God; its intimation belongs to the *fascinans* element of the holy.

However, love is less readily associated with the numinous than justice (and that of a somewhat retributive kind). Otto's heavy reliance upon the ancient catastrophic metaphor of consuming fire to evoke the numinous energy of divine presence can hardly recommend itself to late modern theology: the second half of the twentieth century has seen too much go up in smoke. It has witnessed the belching chimneys of Auschwitz, the atomic mushroom cloud, the oil-fields set ablaze during the Gulf War, and the tropical rain forests napalmed or set alight for clearance. Here life has been wasted and laid waste to by fire and dispersed as smoke. The rapid combustion of the world's fossil fuels is bringing about a potentially devastating global climatic change and poisoning the air that all living things breathe. With the smell of burning in our nostrils—especially that of the (pseudo-) sacrificial burnt offering, or holocaust, of six million Jews—the self-manifestation of the numen in smoke, fire, darkness, and cloud (even if only metaphorical) may seem not only unhelpful, but part of the problem.

But this is to forget that the awesome power of the *energicum* element of the numinous represents the quality of God's wrath at the extent of human sin and the quality of his love.[1] The analogy of numinous power to consuming fire must be clearly and responsibly differentiated, then, from human awe at our own technological capacity for almost unlimited destruction, such as was expressed by Robert Oppenheimer's famously numinous quotation of the *Bhagavadgita* ('Behold, I am become Death, the destroyer of worlds') when the first atom bomb was exploded in 1945. The conduct of twentieth-century warfare may, in its scale, arouse the *sensus numinis*, but it is not, in itself, the numinous, which is a quality of divine, not human, acts. Oppenheimer's words demonstrate how human hubris has arrogated not only divine creative power, but the language in which religion has imagined its exercise. This is ideology, not theology. Yet, if ideologues commandeer numinous metaphors, and *theologians* cease to use them, there will be few imaginal resources left by which to express religious anger at sins against the created ecology (where 'ecology' is interpreted socially as well as environmentally as an originally just, balanced division of labour and resources). Moreover, numinous ideograms of God's wrath reaffirm the freedom of the human will to have done otherwise, and remind those who have power over the immediate history of nature that they are accountable to the extent of their responsibility.

The development of numinous consciousness into a given concept of holiness is therefore of more than intellectual interest; it is an index to a society's religio-political values,[2] and is, as Walter Brueggemann writes, 'urgent in the face of profanation, which empties life of larger passion and dignity', and 'urgent in the face of pervasive brutality, which trivialises God's purpose and abuses God's world'.[3] Peter Slater has similarly observed that late modern history has tragically expanded the horizons of the profane:

---

[1] *IH* 24.

[2] In *Original Blessing*, 110, Matthew Fox writes that '"holiness" is a word worth retrieving. One of the most telling questions that can be asked about a period's spirituality is, what is its understanding of holiness? A people's grasp of what constitutes holiness will affect its entire way of living, of question, of celebrating.'

[3] 'Editor's Foreword' to Gammie, *Holiness in Israel*, pp. xi f.

We find that we too have our moments of wonder and awe but not in the context of cloisters or pagodas pointing our eyes towards heaven. In the stories of our times we find that what has been profaned is not the sanctuary of some tribal deity but the sanctity of individual human life. Not only the body as the temple of the spirit, but the spirit itself has been denied all possibility of a dignified death.[4]

Pelagia Lewinska, a non-Jewish survivor of Auschwitz, experienced how closely profanization is related to annihilation. During the Holocaust, the Nazi rhetoric of social hygiene was realized as 'truth' in that, under conditions of absolute deprivation, Jews became verminous and filthy, a threat to the purity and health of the Aryan race, visually justifying the necessity of what has recently, and demonically, been called 'ethnic cleansing'. The Holocaust was perpetrated by people from a culture with a reputation for cleanliness. The chaotic living/dying conditions at Auschwitz—the absence of washing facilities, the 'ditches, the mud, the piles of excrement behind the blocks'—were not, therefore, a bureaucratic oversight. Indeed, in a testimony to which brief quotation does an injustice, Lewinska writes that it was the latrines which pointed towards the true purpose of the camps: 'They had condemned us to die in our own filth, to drown in mud, in our own excrement. They wished to abase us, to destroy our human dignity.'[5] As the editorial comment on Lewinska's memoir notes, 'when conditions of filth are enforced, befoulment of the body can be experienced as befoulment of the spirit.'[6] Those who were able to maintain the struggle for the most notional personal cleanliness did so as an act of spiritual and political resistance.[7]

To be pushed into the mud between the barracks at Auschwitz was often to die in it. And if one did not, then

---

[4] P. Slater, 'The Transcending Process and the Relocation of the Sacred', in A. M. Olson and L. S. Rouner (eds.), *Transcendence and the Sacred* (Notre Dame, Ind.: University of Notre Dame Press, 1981), ed. 49.

[5] P. Lewinska, 'Twenty Months at Auschwitz', in C. Rittner and J. Roth (eds.), *Different Voices: Women and the Holocaust* (New York: Paragon House, 1993), 87.

[6] Ibid. 85. [7] Ibid. 90.

'what rose to its feet was no longer human but a ridiculous monster of mud'.[8] In one passage, Lewinska remembers being in the men's camp and seeing how 'some inmates were dragging a man by his legs, the rest of his body covered with mud, tracing a great furrow in the black mire'. She asks her readers how they would feel if, as wife or mother, they had seen 'their love and joy in such a state'?[9] (And how great, too, would be the grief of the mother/father God who lovingly created that child in the image of divine holiness only for its life to end in brokenness and filth.)

Yet it was here at Auschwitz, the paradigm case of modern profanization, that there were also paradigm instances of cleansing that illuminated the meaning of God's grace. When a woman had been pushed or had fallen into the mud and did not have the strength to pull herself out again, whoever came to her aid was performing a salvific act in every sense. To wade into the heavy mud was to take the sacrificial risk of sinking in it, and to sink in the mud was to risk being set upon by dogs or thrown on to the piles of corpses irrespective of whether one was dead or alive.[10] Lewinska writes of the oaths that were made between women never to leave one another dying in the mud; it was a mark of absolute devotion for one inmate to help another rise from it. Here Lewinska's record alerts us to the ways in which pollution of consciousness, human embodiment, and nature belong together, so that the metaphor of 'washing' can be reclaimed as a metaphor of a reconsecration that is at once political, spiritual, and practical. Her record testifies that numinous horror is not, properly, the *product* of the failure of human rationality, but a reaction of horror to the profanation of creation. And in that numinous horror moves the subject to praxis, it also feeds a theology of hope; the gracious 'washing' of one woman by another that Lewinska describes was an instance of the practical and symbolic relation of purification and reconsecration to resurrection.

This is not to say that moments of human grace redeemed Auschwitz; the justification of Auschwitz is not—and, morally,

---

[8] P. Lewinska, 'Twenty Months at Auschwitz', p. 90.
[9] Ibid. 87.   [10] Ibid.

should not be—available to the finite theological imagination. It is, perhaps, even for God, unredeemable. The Contemporary theology cannot, and perhaps should not, come to terms with the Holocaust and other twentieth-century enormities in which the numinous has evoked less the majesty of God than the mystery of his averted face (what has long been known to Judaism as *hester panim*). The numinous element of the holy offers no easy reassurances. Otto's concept of holiness is grounded in the experience of dread and fascination: the ancient ambivalence of the holy. As Umberto Eco has observed, two ideas of God have peopled Western history. There is the personal, omnipotent, righteous Lord of Hosts. And there is a shadowy divine *alter ego* known to mystical and negative theology: the 'God who is not', the vortex, the silent abyss, the God who turns his back. 'This is the God that the sense of the sacred feeds upon, ignoring the institutionalised churches, as Rudolf Otto described it more than fifty years ago in his famous *Das Heilige*.'[11] The scale of twentieth-century evil is such that if we are to be left with a God who is morally worthy of worship, justificatory accounts of his will should not be available to theological reason. The great value of the numinous is that as *mysterium tremendum*, it reminds us that theodicies which attempt to rationalize evil away are epistemologically futile (if not morally redundant). The numinous is at once the naming and the unnaming of the mystery of divine being. Numinous consciousness is a falling silent, a recognition that theology and theodicy cannot yield answers beyond what it makes sense to say of and hope from a particular, historical model of God.

Admittedly, there is a risk that in certain political conditions a numinous anti-theology can support the abolition of absolute ethical standards and, as in Nazi Germany, clear the stage for moral havoc. But carefully articulated, the mysteriousness of the numinous does not justify antinomianism. On the one hand, the *mysterium* of the numinous sets a limit

---

[11] U. Eco, 'The Gods of the Underworld', in *Faith in Fakes* (London: Secker & Warburg, 1986), 93.

on human knowledge of God, and therefore a limit on the power of the anthropomorphic constructions of God that underwrite worldly power. Without this numinous humility, or 'creature-feeling', civilization's exercise of rational omnipotence can overreach itself and fall into madness, as it began to do at the end of Otto's life. (As Richard Rubenstein has wisely remarked, 'the Holocaust bears witness to *the advance of civilisation*.'[12]) On the other hand, if numinous consciousness were to guarantee only the futility of theology, its relevance would be limited to the more radical of negative theologies. However, Otto did, finally, hold together the rational and the non-rational elements of his concept of holiness, and because the numinous, as the mystery of God present to consciousness, always has a historical-political content, it can also mark the beginning of a prophetic—that is, a *sui generis*—religio-moral engagement with the contemporary world.

This study has supported Otto's will to preserve the holy from colonization by human values and interests; but it has also made deeper connections between numinous value and the value of creation than Otto might have done. I have wanted to distinguish between the holiness of the world as created and the profanity of the world constructed by the patriarchal project, a distinction which allows the correlation of numinous experience and its most important effect— prophetic witness to the abuse of God's world—the medium and locus of the *numen praesens*.

Numinous experience is a private reaction to the mystery of divine presence; but in its completed form as a prophetic witness to the holy, it inaugurates collective responsibilities of reconsecration and proclamation. In Acts 1: 3–10 the apostles have a series of numinous (or what Otto calls 'mystical') experiences of the risen Christ, in which Christ makes prophecy a direct consequence of numinous experience, saying, 'But you shall receive power when the Holy Spirit comes upon you; and you shall be my witnesses in Jerusalem and in all Judaea and Samaria and to the end of the earth' (1: 8). So

---

[12] R. Rubenstein, *The Cunning of History* (New York: Harper Books, 1978), 91.

too, Isaiah's vision of Yahweh's holiness and, by contrast, his numinous consciousness of the profanity of worldly power, were at the same time a call to prophecy: 'Woe is me! For I am lost; for I am a man of unclean lips, and I dwell in the midst of a people with unclean lips; for my eyes have seen the King, the Lord of hosts! . . . Then I said, "Here am I! Send me." And he said, "Go and say this to the people"' (Isa. 6: 5, 9).[13] It is, above all, where numinous consciousness of the *tremendum* of the holy becomes the affective dynamic of prophetic theology, and where, as *mysterium*, the holy beckons to the future and to 'wholly other' possibilities of meaning and value, that Otto's concept of holiness will best serve twenty-first-century theology.

[13] See *IH* 223 f.

APPENDIX

Freedom and Necessity
A Conversation with Nicolai Hartmann about the Autonomy and Theonomy of Values

Translated by Dr. Thorsten Moritz

Nicolai Hartmann concludes his admirable work *Ethics* (Berlin, 1926) with a series of antitheses between *autonomist ethics* and *religion*. They are probably the most severe statements that have ever been made regarding the much treated topic 'Ethical Autonomy or the Law of God'. He, himself, sees the main contrast in the 'antinomy of freedom', being that ethics strictly demands freedom, whereas religion destroys all freedom. One might disagree with this claim. In any case, it seems to me that the problem of *ethical autonomy versus God's will*, could be treated in its own right and in fact that it needs to be dealt with. It is striking that Hartmann, despite his sharp polemic against the religious trespassing into the field of ethics continues to speak of the 'antinomy between ethics and religion'. As soon as religious convictions are regarded as wrong, there is no need to mention or to discuss antinomies any more. This means that, in contrast to Hartmann's subtle discussion, the details of the religious position become irrelevant and are allowed to disappear in a void. And yet despite his sharp objections to so-called real religious claims, Hartmann often continues to speak in ways that suggest that he regards a 'philosophy of religion' as possible. He even defines tasks which need to be accomplished not by speculative ethics but by central philosophy whilst curious to get to know the entire framework for what the author has to say, and to find out whether 'ethical' verdicts are the last word, or whether, despite its categorical delineation, there remains something which one way or another forms that which is 'beyond'.

His attacks on and his delimitation of the so-called trespasses of 'religion' (which is essentially understood as the Christian typology of redemption and at the same time as the *predestinarian* bondage of human will) are far reaching. In what follows, I can comment on only some of them.

I have pointed out the general misunderstandings regarding the basic religious idea that humanity is inherently unable to 'achieve salvation' (and, at the same time, the mistaking of specifically religious myths with matters of psychology). Luther, among others, maintains the sufficiency of grace for salvation, and rejects religious *synergies* by examining the psychological question of freedom or bondage of the will, according to categories of determination or indetermination, and by teaching the 'bondage of the will'; something Hartmann also had in mind. Certainty in these areas is only possible when it is understood that God alone can provide 'salvation', not because our will is weak but because 'salvation' is not essentially something that falls within the sphere of what our human will can achieve. This is something that needs to be discussed in its own right. Furthermore, Hartmann uncritically and one-sidedly regards the predestinarian vantage point as the normal. From a religious point of view, an equally valid understanding would be that God creates *free* beings with the capacity for salvation or being lost, and that they should bear the responsibility for any lack of salvation. Yet, despite all the severe objections, even the most committed and one-sided predestinarians do not wish to deny that sin entails the notion of *guilt* and, therefore, of an individual's responsibility. It has to be said that here we have a very real 'antinomy', a term used a great deal by Hartmann, but that this antinomy is not between a religious and an ethical vantage point, but is quite evidently rooted in the religious sphere itself. Predestinarian preachers of repentance may be deterministic in theory; in practice, however, they are indeterministic, for it is they who appeal powerfully for a decision—repentance and a change of heart—by confronting people with guilt and responsibility. In any case, deterministic notions are unchristian, if they can be shown to be no more than the state of Kismet in Islam. Christian determinism is not fatalistic. The truth is that genuine religious attitude is itself antinomian. Nowhere is responsibility, and particularly one's own responsibility, more important and in greater tension than in the Christian call to repentence and conversion. *Mea culpa, mea maxima culpa!* Where this realization has not well and truly come to the forefront, there can certainly be no genuinely religious attitude. But as far as *culpa* is concerned, the realization of guilt is not possible without that which Hartmann regards as the criterion of a sense of freedom, that is without the very clear and non-negotiable realization: 'You should have acted differently and you could have acted differently.' On the other hand, the religious experience of grace does lead in the direction of predestination. But it would be fatal for the purity of religious experience if, by emphasizing grace, the fact that there had to be genuine personal responsibility and an experience of guilt was overshadowed. These two trajectories are related as genuine antinomies. This is what Hartmann himself has to say about antinomies on p. 737: 'Antinomies do not disprove the real co-existence of that which is separate, even if they are genuine antinomies, i.e. if they are irreconcilable. All they prove is the inability of human thinking to understand this co-existence.'

It would be possible to object to many of the antinomies which Hartmann, according to p. 737, finds between religion and ethics. The first alleged antinomy is that of the overall direction, or that between this-worldly and other-worldly tendentiousness: religion is supposed to be wholly other-worldly, its underlying assumption being that the 'this worldly' has no intrinsic values. In favour of an aesthetic, world-denying religiosity, such a claim ignores the basic principle, at least in Christianity, that God is the creator and that the world is his creation, in fact his good creation, and that the 'this worldly' is very much *focused on* the 'other worldly' as the place of testing in view of the genuinely 'this worldly' task set by God. The Good Samaritan's act of loving his neighbour was truly this-worldly and ethical. This is how Christ understood it and this is how it functions as an example. Loving one's neighbour as something completely this-worldly, that is as an act of humanity, does not exclude the notion that in so doing and generally in the this-worldly ethos, God's will is being followed and done, in other words, that something of a higher quality is being done. It is true that the primary and essential response to the 'holy' call from Above to repentance and conversion, consists of a very thorough and penetrating letting go of the this-worldly and being focused on to a goal which is purely other-worldly and which can only be expressed in emotive language. But this happens precisely when any monkish asceticism is being overcome, in such a way that, after becoming independent from this world and overcoming the world as the enslaving idol, the world appears before the religious eye as a valued creation from God's hand in which and through which God serves and operates. On the other hand, Hartmann's thesis about the imminence of all ethics ('for ethical pursuits, transcendence has a perceptive ring') raises the question: What can be said about the individual who, as part of the ethical pursuit in this world, reaches the conclusion that all imminence, even that of the most profound depth, is destined to be *transitional* and subject to verification? Such a person will recognize that one's understanding of all transcendence as having a deceptive ring is itself deceptive and that the connections between the this-worldly ethic pursued and other-worldly goal needs to be considered; a goal witnessed to by all higher religion.

Hartmann himself finds the strongest and most profound antinomy in the notions of 'redemption, grace, and forgiveness', which are unknown to ethics and must remain so. The central concept here is 'forgiveness' and the desire for forgiveness, because this denotes that which Hartmann regards as fatal; namely the sense of dealing with sin and guilt.

It seems to me that here we find a remarkably striking mistake in Hartmann's overall conception. This sense of paying-off, this desire for release that is absolution or forgiveness, being excused and freed from debt, the pardoning and the setting free of the conscience, removing the pressure of guilt, appears not just in religion but at the very centre of ethics, the core of ethics—at that point where ethics becomes the most profound. It happens at the very point where ethics deals with the most profoundly ethical relationships, the relationship between two individuals, the demands which people place on each other, however graded and varied these might be, depending on the intimacy of the fellowship experienced by the various partners. It even happens more generally where the sense of intimacy is of a peripheral and weak nature, that is where people deal with each other. Where there is lack of gratitude, or injustice has been done, it does not suffice to provide external compensation, because the conscience as such demands and asks for the heart-felt *forgiveness* of the other person, not least for the sake of its own sense of release and purification. This is a very essential and genuine part of the most characteristically moral feelings such as regret and embarrassment. Wherever it is missing, the realm of genuine personal morality has been left behind.

An 'ethical standard' can be compromised, but it cannot forgive. The kind of ethics which places a one-sided emphasis on values does not allow room for forgiveness. It also makes no provision for the even higher and more substantial concepts of propitiation. This is true of Hartmann for he finally understands even personal attitudes as ethical standards. However, 'injustice' cannot be done to a value-system, only to a person, and it does not consist of the fact that a standard was compromised: although that is true, it is a separate matter. Rather it consists of a violation of an individual's personal rights and this cannot be rectified by re-establishing a value system. What is needed is a sense of regret, the willingness to admit guilt, and the acceptance of the victim's accusing sentence of judgement and forgiveness. Hartmann precipitately and almost mechanically construes the so-called antinomy, whereas the sacred ethos involves a new and superior insight, one which incidentally is beyond the realm of the profane, namely that any trespassing is not only a violation of an ethical standard or a person, but at the same time, a sin against God, the highest person. Persons can forgive one another, they can annul debts, they can restore the fellowship which was adversely affected by the conflict. Whether they are obliged to do so is another matter. Perhaps they are not and perhaps forgiveness among people has always been a matter of free giving. What is actually needed, however, is an attitude of regret, coupled with a desire for forgiveness, on the part of the guilty person.

It seems to me that of all the so-called antinomies which Hartmann piled up like a tower, the only real one, the one that has been recognized throughout history, the one which has not yet been resolved, and the one which, in my opinion, essentially cannot be resolved on the level of human thinking, is his third antinomy on pp. 738 ff. It is the age-old antinomy between the autonomy of that which is good in and of itself and the theonomy that is the establishment of all 'legal frameworks' by God. It is the antinomy between 'ethical law and God's will', between autonomous and authoritative ethics, or whichever traditional designation one might wish to use. 'The thesis that ethical values are autonomous, that is, that they exist in and of themselves, that is, not for the sake of someone else, and that their value derives intrinsically (as was shown), is the bare essential for any ethical framework which is worth the name; . . . that they are not based on some sort of authority, or on an authoritative pronouncement or a will—otherwise, their rationale would not be absolute and a priori . . . but that it is something intrinsic that proves their irreducibly ethical character' (p. 739).

The difficulty is that the validity of all demands cannot be conveyed to the conscience as a matter of volition, but has always necessarily, by definition, and irreversibly been rooted in *natura rerum*.

This, at any rate, is one of the difficulties. What about the substance? Does the fact of the intrinsic validity of objective values relegate God to the sidelines? Let us start with the following observation: experts in moral theory tend to be excellent phenomenologists and they respect that which Goethe called the primeval phenomena. One such phenomenon is *the sense of the holy* (something which specialists in moral theory undoubtedly regard as a sense of *moral value*). This is something which, at least on the level of experiential actuality cannot be disputed. We can go even further. When specialists in moral theory, in a remarkable display of objectivity and in contrast to naturalistic biases, genuinely open themselves up to the rather meek and gentle testimony of our often dark sense of morality, one which according to their own theory suffers from significant tensions and even antinomies, and when at this point they recognize a basis for scientific insights, they will also have to take seriously ancient moral perceptions of holiness. What does this awareness add up to?

First, it involves an extension of the realm of ethical imperatives, well beyond the actual field of ethics. Secondly, it undoubtedly means a depth and urgency of demand far beyond that of a purely this-worldly ethical standard. Thirdly, there must be a reorientation of all acts of service on the basis of external values. To have an ethical awareness does not mean that all standards are based on transcendental values or ideals, but initially it implies a subjection and service of all possible tasks under the highest tasks, i.e. those that are thoroughly transcendental. This reorientation may not amount to a *foundation* of all values, but it comes close to it.

To sense what is holy and, therefore, to possess the possibility to sense what is sinful, are categories which, as I have attempted to show elsewhere, apparently are not legitimate in so-called pure ethics. The fact that they force their way, so to speak, into the latter, prove their inevitability for any profound sense of truth. Even Hartmann has to use the term 'sin' although, strictly speaking, he should only talk of transgression, mistake, or trespass. For the inner witness, that is our religious conscience, some *particular* ways of understanding sin are initially more realistic until with time our conscience has become subtle enough to extend the character of sin to *all* ethical transgression. In so doing, all of ethics is subjective under the idea of the holy and its opposite, that which is sinful. At this point, a clear teleology emerges.

It is a sense of sin (not *Weltangst* or existential dilemmas) which marks the point of departure for Christian preaching. Sensing that which is sinful and its dark implication and precondition—without which it would not be possible—is the idea of the holy which forms the 'religious a priori' especially of Christianity. Where the Christian message is made explicit, the Holy Saviour God emerges as the one who judges sin and who seeks the sinner. Where this has happened, there is very clearly no longer just teleology of all values in their orientation towards that which is holy, rather the Holy One himself becomes the foundation, origin, and enabler of all real and potential values in this world and above. This is true, not just in terms of professed teaching, but indeed on the experiential level of a genuine and deep meditation. This fact has to be taken seriously, at least phenomenologically. It does not matter how difficult it might be theoretically to regard values which are rooted autonomously in the *natura rerum* of those who embody them, as having a further foundation in God. This is a claim which in view of its experiential, meditational evidence ought to be taken seriously by phenomenologists who should be careful not to favour precipitately one type of experience, namely that of their own narrow experience of values.

The fact that the directive is embedded in its own autonomist value system, that is the intrinsic quality and reasonableness of that which is demanded, is part of the naivety of experience. This is shown by word from Amos: 'You, the people, have been told that which is good and which the Lord asks of you.'

It is characteristic of the religious experience of values that it does not eliminate the ability to make objective judgements, something which we refer to as conscience. Instead it is intimately interconnected with a sense of awe in sight of God's will, hence the prophet regards the two as synonyms. God's imperative is not a command and especially not the command of a despotic individual who requires blind obedience. To the Christian, God's will in no way involves blindness, or to put it differently, the Christian is not blind in sight of God's will, before understanding, and the directives implied in God's will are in and of themselves comprehensible in terms of their validity. They are not understood as the judgement of the threatening Almighty One, nor are they adhered to as the verdict of an individual who uses promises as a means of persuasion. Where they are followed properly, it is the result of a heartfelt affirmation of the validity of the received directive. This is true whether it is one of the Ten Commandments or Christ's commandment to love others or, as sometimes happens, a particular call which confronts one in a particular situation resounds in and according to my predicament and which, although this may not be the rule, is especially fitting and challenging. The accompanying sense of insight is one of emotional understanding. It is the consent, not of the mind, but of one's feelings. It is an insight that God does not only make demands as a mighty ruler, and as one whose superior power and the associated fear forces recognition; rather it is the deepest conviction that it is right to expect of God that the demands he makes are irrevocably justified. At the same time, the phenomenological experience has two essential components. First, that, unlike human goodwill, God is not bound by an external and superior law, and secondly, that his will is not 'contingent' (that previous concepts of 'freedom' transcend ideas of *necessitas* and *contingentia*). This corresponds to the religious concepts of repentance and shame. Characteristically, they emerge strongly whenever God's directives are ignored, but there is certainly not only the painful realization of having transgressed the arbitrary will of a despotic ruler and of now having to face punishment. Rather, it is the recognition that that which was demanded has a deep and intrinsic value and that its violation characteristically leaves the sinner with a sense of non-value. God's will was not simply that which the Mighty One desired. Rather it was intrinsically good and holy. To withstand it was therefore not 'existentially' dangerous, but it was genuine sin, truly and objectively of non-value, something that weighs down the transgressor and that causes a sense of repentance and shame.

Yet there are truly autonomous values which have the intrinsic characteristic, *ex natura rerum*, to make demands on our conscience. To damage someone else's sense of worth, to let oneself go in a display of moral depravity, to prefer lying to truth: these are intrinsically bad or evil and that which is evil must not be. It ought not to exist for its own sake. (Correspondingly, the same is true of our so-called rights which we are going to distinguish from pure values). Are there any gods alongside God, or has God decreed through his creation that lying is evil and truth is good, rather than the other way round? Did that, which today and from our perspective is given as a matter of *rerum natura*, depend on his creator-will? Could God have decreed that love is evil and hatred good? Could that which, from our limited human perspective, appears to be an unchangeable principle beyond the reach of any law perhaps be a *parte Dei* contingency, so that the normative principle which we encounter derives its validity only from a *parte intellectus nostri* and is an ordination of the God who is free of contingencies, who is not restricted or affected by anything. Should we not conclude that God's greatness demands such a scenario? Does this not become more likely and possible in the light of the most recent scientific considerations? If even mathematical axioms begin to look doubtful in terms of their absolute inherent indispensability, if the principle of causality is no longer determinative, and if even the foremost logical principles turn out to be little more than intellectual exercises, it follows that the absolute validity of such problematic constructs called 'objective values' is perhaps even less secure and that their foundation in the will of the Almighty God and his ordination is far more preferable and more plausible than a foundation in developmental-theoretical or biological contingencies. It even appears that God only really becomes God when he is seen as the one who operates in a totally contingent fashion and, therefore, is the one who is entirely free.

However, as I tried to show elsewhere, contingent action is genuine not only in the realm of the gods, but even humans. But it would be wrong to press it into the service of enabling the kind of moral freedom which manifests itself in our own reasonable actions because contingent action is at the same time thoroughly, and at its very root, worthless action. It is inconceivable how on the basis of will, which is worthless, a world might be created which manifests values which are in some sense valid. Such a worthless will can only generate, if anything, that which is wholly devoid of meaning and values.

Contingency is excluded primarily by that foundational religious principle which undoubtedly precedes all of God's statements: 'You shall be holy, because I am holy.' The term 'holy' is essentially derived from the axiological sphere; it is a term which denotes ultimate, and at the same time, unique value or 'hyper value'. Holiness as a moral value is best captured on an experiential level. Elsewhere, I have attempted to point out the characteristics of one's subordination under the corresponding determinator of moral values (that is, if, in this context, we are justified in distinguishing between value and the one embodying it, in other words, if they are not identical). We have already discovered that the one who embodies holiness remains entirely irrational, hidden behind a screen of rational terminology, yet in line with the depth of his being and his relationship to the world which he sustains. Those who deny this insight are unlikely to have possessed a genuine sense of holiness and are therefore incapable of accounting for it. This irrationality is part of his nature and such categorizations as contingency and necessity are not applicable to him. Should one wish to think along such lines, however, one would find that initially Christian thinking undoubtedly favours the latter category. For a holy will cannot possibly have emerged from the empty void of total indeterminacy and a completely arbitrary will; rather it rests on a being, on a holy being, and this holiness determines a priori that this will is not contingent, but one which is characterized from the outset by its moral value.

The picture that emerges is not one of arbitrariness, of overpowering decisions made on the hoof, of a domineering, despotic, and moody individual. Rather the emerging picture is one of the quiet depth of a moral value; a value which is self-motivating and self-extracting. On the strength of its will to demonstrate love and on the strength of the creative awareness of meaning and value, it takes on the quality of a creator, but also the redeemer of the creation which finds itself at odds with the central objectives. It creates a world full of 'value systems' which are like rays of primeval origin and which though autonomous are but reflections of theonomy itself, that is the primeval autonomy of the morality which characterized the creator and which permeates his creation. Just as, speaking idealistically, the essence of all things derives from God and embodies the primeval divinity in the narrow sphere of the world as creation by way of endless deflections and gradations, so God's creation is characterized by his imprint of divine morality, again, in endless deflections and gradings with a diversity of distance and differentiations, compared with the undeflected, and in this way the autonomy of creation has been absorbed by theonomy.

To use the image of human psychology, creation corresponds to the nature of the creator as his expression, something which itself denotes volition because it emerges not by way of a natural emanation, but on the strength of the evidence of a revelatory will; a will which decided to reflect its 'glory' in creation; a will which has in store grace for the 'children'. Because of its shiny character and because of God's will, divine morality finds its reflection in its counterpart. This is demanded autonomously by the rays of moral value, but in making this demand, God's own morality and will is reflected.

It hardly does justice to God to point out contingencies and upheavals in the world order. Thus to create space for God, Clarke maintained in 'The imperfection of the world', that the world's imminent causes do not suffice to sustain its order. It seemed that a self-sufficient world no longer needed God, nor had any place left for him. Leibniz rightly replied to Clarke that the latter made a distinction between natural law and God's involvement and that this trade-off favours God. There is a similar problem with the attempt to compromise the autonomy of world imminent values with a view to creating space for theonomy. In the former instance, we find the paradox that a world which originated with its creator, ought to reflect this fact as little as possible. The more perfect and self-sufficient it is for its own purposes, the greater its worthiness of God. Marquis Posa put it like this: '. . . He humbly conceals Himself in his own eternal laws. When the free spirit sees them it says 'the world suffices for itself' and no pious praise will praise him more than the free spirit's blasphemy.' We are incapable of explaining the relationship between world and creator God. In the world we are referred to laws and more recently to principles of probability and yet we cannot make God the partner of these principles. Nor can we explain how God, despite these laws, rules the world one way or another. At the same time, pious awareness subjects the world experientially to the ruling creator God. Our awareness of morality points us to worldly values and our responsible conscience calls on us to obey the demands of these values. In their midst we can hear God's demand, a demand which we experience as one of morality and volition. Again, we will not resolve the tension between the 'this-worldly' and the 'beyond', but in view of the immediacy of naïve experience, we are not aware of an enigma. Instead, we think that we understand that which appears to be self-evident, when in our conscience we clearly recognize the language of worldly values and by virtue of being, so to speak, led by the spirit, detect God's demand in it. We support the development of a picture, such as the one mentioned above, a picture of primordial divine values moving into creation, the theonomy of which appears in the latter in the guise of autonomous values. We know that this too is a picture, but it is one which does not appear empty to our quest for truth. Rather it points in a direction in which a solution might be found, even if it is located somewhere in infinity.

Other pictures and teachings with which we are familiar point in the same direction, sometimes by way of conscious inclusion of our argument and sometimes apart from it. They do not resolve the problem entirely but they allow a glimpse of its approximate solution.

It has frequently been pointed out that the relationship between God and his creation, resembles that between an artist and his creation. Not only in the sense that the artist has developed it as a mental picture, that it emanated from his spirit and, therefore, relates differently to him than the mere relationship between cause and effect but also in the sense that the piece of art which originated with the artist as the imprint of his character and nature creates a reflection of these in itself. It reflects the ingenuity, depth, value, and honour of the creator spirit, and the so-called values are those of the artist as they are reflected.

At a deeper level, there is the speculative teaching of the creation, having been brought about by the eternal *logos*, which was in God and which was God, and which at the same time is the principle that gives being, meaning, and value to the world and the things in it. According to Augustine, the *logos* is that which emanated in eternity from God, the thought that rests in God and through which God thinks about and recognizes himself according to the riches and fullness of his being. It derives its own identity from being this counterpart. It is precisely God's thinking about himself, which now functions as the principle behind the world and its meaning and character in so far as the *logos* becomes a creation principle of the world. Whatever meaning, being, and value is present or possible in the world derives from the depth of meaning and value of the godhead itself, albeit it involves endless distance and is by no means exhaustive. All the essentials of this world are to be seen in analogy to God's being and the value which rests upon each of them is an emanating spark of God's moral glory. This is approximately how we can restate the old teaching. If this is so, then the values which challenge or attract us in the world are no longer separate or competing entities *vis-à-vis* God's eternal meaning and morality; they are almost their extension into the world. The term 'almost' is deliberate here, because we cannot expect to penetrate any further into this picture and parable. At least they suffice to bring to the light of day a little bit of that of which we are entirely convinced within our concealed awareness.

Needless to say, that which until now we have referred to as God's 'will' is initially a human expression for the challenge and demand which corresponds to the eternal value and its reflection in creation. In so far as God the Creator *wants* this permeation of all that is with 'his glory', that is with a reflection of his own glory, and in so far as this suggests his own plan for the world and his challenge to obedience, the moral demand and that of his volition become one.

Bibliography

ALLCHIN, A., 'Holiness in the Anglican Tradition', in M. Chavchavadze (ed.), *Man's Concern with Holiness* (London: Hodder & Stoughton, 1970), 35–58.

ALMOND, P., *Mystical Experience and Religious Doctrine* (Amsterdam: Mouton, 1982).

—— 'Mysticism and Its Contexts', in R. Forman (ed.), *The Problem of Pure Consciousness* (New York: Oxford University Press, 1990), 211–19.

—— 'Rudolf Otto: The Context of his Thought', *Scottish Journal of Theology*, 36 (1983), 347–62.

—— 'Rudolf Otto: Life and Work', *Journal of Religious History*, 12 (1983), 305–21.

ALTIZER, T., *Mircea Eliade and the Dialectic of the Sacred* (Philadelphia: Westminster Press, 1963).

ARMSTRONG, J., *The Idea of the Holy and the Humane Response* (London: Allen & Unwin, 1981).

ATKINSON, J. BAINES, *The Beauty of Holiness* (London: Epworth Press, 1953).

BAGGER, M., 'Ecumenicalism and Perennialism Revisited', *Religious Studies*, 27 (1991), 399–411.

BAILLIE, J., *The Interpretation of Religion* (Edinburgh: T. & T. Clark, 1929).

—— *Our Knowledge of God* (London: Oxford University Press, 1939).

BARBOUR, I. G., *Myths, Models and Paradigms* (London: SCM Press, 1974).

BASTOW, D., 'Otto and Numinous Experience', *Religious Studies*, 12 (1976), 159–76.

BEARDSWORTH, T., *A Sense of Presence* (Oxford: The Religious Experience Research Unit, 1977).

BENNETT, C. A., 'Religion and the Idea of the Holy', *Journal of Philosophy*, 23 (1926), 460–9.

BERKOVITS, E., *Faith after the Holocaust* (New York: Ktav Publishing House, 1973).

BERRY, W., *Sex, Economy, Freedom and Community* (New York: Pantheon Books, 1992).

BILANIUK, P., 'The Ultimate Reality and Meaning Expressed in Eastern Christian Icons', *Ultimate Reality and Meaning*, 5 (1982), 296–313.

BOOZER, J., review of *Rudolf Otto*, by P. Almond, *International Journal for Philosophy of Religion*, 23 (1988), 43–5.

BOWKER, J., *The Sense of God* (London: Oxford University Press, 1973).

BRAYBROOKE, M., 'Religious Studies and Interfaith Developments', in U. King (ed.), *Turning Points in Religious Studies* (Edinburgh: T. & T. Clark, 1990), 132–41.

BREGMAN, L., *The Rediscovery of Inner Experience* (Chicago: Nelson Hall, 1982).

BRODY, B., 'Morality and Religion Reconsidered', in P. Helm (ed.), *Divine Commands and Morality* (Oxford: Oxford University Press, 1981), 141–53.

BROWN, P., *The Cult of Saints* (London: SCM Press, 1981).

BRUNNER, E., *Man in Revolt* (London: Lutterworth Press, 1947).

—— *The Mediator* (London: Lutterworth Press, 1934).

BUBER, M., *The Legend of the Baal-Shem* (Edinburgh: T. & T. Clark, 1985).

—— *Tales of the Hasidim: The Later Masters* (New York: Schocken Books, 1961).

BYNUM, C. WALKER, *Holy Feast, Holy Fast: The Religious Significance of Food to Medieval Women* (Berkeley: University of California Press, 1987).

BYRNE, P., *Natural Religion and the Nature of Religion* (London: Routledge, 1989).

CAILLOIS, R., *Man and the Sacred* (Glencoe, Ill.: Free Press, 1959).

CAMPBELL, C. A., *On Selfhood and Godhood* (London: Allen & Unwin, 1957).

CARMODY, D., *Christian Feminist Theology* (Cambridge, Mass.: Blackwell, 1995).

CLARK, S., *The Mysteries of Religion* (Oxford: Blackwell, 1986).

CLAYDON, W. A., 'The Numinous in the Poetry of Wordsworth', *Hibbert Journal*, 28 (1930), 29–30.

COATS, R. H., 'Holiness: New Testament and Christian', in J. Hastings (ed.), *Encyclopaedia of Religion and Ethics* (Edinburgh: T. & T. Clark, 1913), vi. 743–50.

COMSTOCK, W., 'A Behavioural Approach to the Sacred: Category Formation in Religious Studies', *Journal of the American Academy of Religion*, 49/4 (1981), 625–43.

COUSINS, E., 'Spirituality in Today's World', in F. Whaling (ed.), *Religion in Today's World* (Edinburgh: T. & T. Clark, 1987), 306–34.

CUPITT, D., *Taking Leave of God* (London: SCM Press, 1980).

DALY, M., *Gyn/Ecology: The Metaethics of Radical Feminism* (London: Women's Press, 1991).

DANIÉLOU, J., 'Phenomenology of Religions and Philosophy of Religion', in M. Eliade and J. Kitagawa (eds.), *The History of Religions: Essays in Methodology* (Chicago: University of Chicago Press, 1959), 67–85.

DAVIDSON, A. B., *The Theology of the Old Testament* (Edinburgh: T. & T. Clark, 1904).

DAVIES, C. FRANKS, *The Evidential Force of Religious Experience* (Oxford: Clarendon Press, 1989).

DAVIES, J. G., 'The Concept of Holiness', *London Quarterly & Holborn Review*, 185 (1960), 36–44.

—— *Every Day God* (London: SCM Press, 1973).

DAVIS, C., *Body as Spirit* (London: Hodder & Stoughton, 1976).

DAWSON, L., 'Otto and Freud on the Uncanny and Beyond', *Journal of the American Academy of Religion*, 57/2 (1989), 283–311.

—— *Reason, Freedom and Religion: Closing the Gap between the Humanistic and Scientific Study of Religion* (New York: Peter Lang, 1988).

DIAMOND, M. L., *Contemporary Philosophy and Religious Thought* (New York: McGraw-Hill, 1974).

DIAMOND, M. L., and LITZENBURG, T. V. (eds.), *The Logic of God: Theology and Verification* (Indianapolis: Bobbs-Merrill, 1975).

DOUGLAS, M., *Purity and Danger* (Harmondsworth: Penguin, 1970).

DRIVER, T., *The Magic of Ritual* (San Francisco: HarperCollins, 1991).

DUQUOC, C., and FLORISTÀN, C. (eds.), *Models of Holiness* (New York: Seabury Press, 1979).

ECO, U., *Foucault's Pendulum* (London: Secker & Warburg, 1989).

—— *Faith in Fakes* (London: Secker & Warburg, 1986).

EFROS, I., *Ancient Jewish Philosophy: A Study in Metaphysics* (Detroit: Wayne State University Press, 1964).

ELIACH, Y., *Hasidic Tales of the Holocaust* (New York: Oxford University Press, 1982).

ELIADE, M., *No Souvenirs* (London: Routledge & Kegan Paul, 1978).

—— *The Quest* (Chicago: University of Chicago Press, 1969).

—— *The Sacred and the Profane* (New York: Harcourt Brace & World, 1959).

ENGLAND, F. E., *The Validity of Religious Experience* (London: Ivor Nicholson, 1937).

EVDOKIMOV, P., 'Holiness in the Orthodox Tradition', in M. Chavchavadze (ed.), *Man's Concern with Holiness* (London: Hodder & Stoughton, 1970), 145–84.

FARMER, H. H., *Revelation and Religion* (London: Nisbet, 1954).

FEIGEL, F. K., *Das Heilige: Kritische Abhandlung über Rudolf Otto's Gleichnamiges Buch* (Haarlem: De Erven F. Bohn, 1929).

FISON, J. E., *The Blessing of the Holy Spirit* (London: Longman, Green & Co., 1950).

FLESSEMAN, E., 'Old Testament Ethics', *Student World*, 57 (1964), 218–27.

FORMAN, R. (ed.), *The Problem of Pure Consciousness* (New York: Oxford University Press, 1990).

FOX, M., *Original Blessing: A Primer in Creation Spirituality* (Santa Fe, N. Mex.: Bear & Co., 1983).

FREUD, S., *Moses and Monotheism* (London: Hogarth Press, 1964).

GALLOWAY, A., *The Cosmic Christ* (London: Nisbet, 1951).

GAMMIE, J., *Holiness in Israel* (Minneapolis: Fortress Press, 1989).

GARROD, F. W., review of *Naturalism and Religion*, by R. Otto, *Hibbert Journal*, 42 (1943), 698–700.

GASKIN, J. C. A., *The Quest for Eternity* (Harmondsworth: Penguin, 1984).

GENNEP, A. VAN, *The Rites of Passage* (London: Routledge & Kegan Paul, 1965 [1908]).

GREY, M., *Redeeming the Dream: Feminism, Redemption and the Christian Tradition* (London: SPCK, 1989).

GRIFIN, D. R., *The Reenchantment of Science: Postmodern Proposals* (New York: State University of New York Press, 1988).

GROSSMAN, A., 'Holiness', in A. A. Cohen and P. Mendes Flohr (eds.), *Contemporary Jewish Religious Thought* (New York: Free Press, 1988), 389–98.

GULCZYNSKI, J. T., *The Desecration and Violation of Churches* (Washington: Catholic University of America Press, 1942).

HABGOOD, J., 'A Sacramental Approach to Environmental Issues', in C. Birch *et al.* (eds.), *Liberating Life: Contemporary Approaches to Ecological Theology* (Maryknoll, NY: Orbis, 1990), 46–53.

HALKES, C., *New Creation: Christian Feminism and the Renewal of the Earth* (London: SPCK, 1991).

HAMPSON, D., *Theology and Feminism* (Oxford: Blackwell, 1990).

HARDY, A., *The Divine Flame* (London: Collins, 1966).

HARVEY, D., *The Condition of Postmodernity: An Enquiry into the Origins of Cultural Change* (Cambridge, Mass.: Blackwell, 1990).

HAUBOLD, W., *Die Bedeutung der Religionsgeschichte für die Theologie Rudolf Ottos* (Leipzig: Leopold Klotz, 1940).

HAWLEY, J. S., and PROUDFOOT, W. (eds.), *Gender and Fundamentalism* (New York: Oxford University Press, 1994).

HAY, D., 'Scientists and the Rediscovery of Religious Experience', in U. King (ed.), *Turning Points in Religious Studies* (Edinburgh: T. & T. Clark, 1990), 232–41.

HEPBURN, R. W., *Christianity and Paradox* (London: C. A. Watts, 1958).

HICK, J., 'Is God Personal?', in F. Sontag and M. D. Bryant (eds.), *God: The Contemporary Discussion* (New York: Rose of Sharon Press, 1982), 169–80.

HITCHCOCK, J., *The Recovery of the Sacred* (New York: Seabury Press, 1974).

HODGSON, L., *The Place of Reason in Christian Apologetic* (Oxford: Blackwell, 1925).

HUGHES, G. E., 'An Examination of the Argument from Theology to Ethics', *Philosophy*, 22 (1947), 3–24.

HUXLEY, J. S., *Religion without Revelation* (London: M. Parrish, 1957).

JAMES, W., *The Varieties of Religious Experience* (London: Fountain Books, 1977; orig. pub. 1902).

JANTZEN, G. M., 'Mysticism and Experience', *Religious Studies*, 3 (1989), 295–315.

JAY, N., 'Gender and Dichotomy', in S. Gunew (ed.), *A Reader in Feminist Knowledge* (London: Routledge, 1991), 89–106.

JENSON, P., *Graded Holiness: A Key to the Priestly Conception of the World* (Sheffield: JSOT Press, 1992).

JUNG, C. G., and VON FRANZ, M.-L., *Man and his Symbols* (London: Aldus Books, 1979).

KANT, I., *Critique of Practical Reason*, trans. T. K. Abbott (London: Longman, Green & Co., 1898).

KATZ, S., 'Language, Epistemology, and Mysticism', in S. Katz (ed.), *Mysticism and Philosophical Analysis* (London: Sheldon Press, 1978), 22–74.

KEEN, S., 'Manifesto for a Dionysian Theology', in H. Richardson and D. Cutler (eds.), *Transcendence* (Boston: Beacon Press, 1969), 31–52.

—— *Towards a Dancing God* (New York: Harper & Row, 1970).

KELLENBERGER, J., *The Cognitivity of Religion* (London: Macmillan, 1985).

KIECKHEFER, R., *Unquiet Souls* (London: University of Chicago Press, 1984).

KREIDER, A., *Journey towards Holiness* (Basingstoke: Marshall, Morgan & Scott, 1986).

KRISTENSEN, W., *The Meaning of Religion* (The Hague: M. Nijhoff, 1960).

LATTKE, M., 'Rudolf Bultmann on Rudolf Otto', *Harvard Theological Review*, 78 (1985), 353–60.

LEENHARDT, F. J., *La Notion de saintété dans l'Ancien Testament: étude de la racine QDhSh* (Paris: Libraire Fischbacher, 1929).

LEEUW, G. VAN DER, *Religion in Essence and Manifestation*, trans. J. E. Turner (London: Allen & Unwin, 1938).

LEISER, B. M., 'The Sanctity of the Profane: A Pharisaic Critique of Rudolf Otto', *Judaism*, 20 (1971), 87–92.

LEWINSKA, P., 'Twenty Months at Auschwitz', in C. Rittner and J. Roth (eds.), *Different Voices: Women and the Holocaust* (New York: Paragon House, 1993), 84–98.

LEWIS, H. D., *Our Experience of God* (London: Allen & Unwin, 1959).

LEWIS, H. D., and SLATER, R. L., *The Study of Religions* (Harmondsworth: Pelican, 1969).

LODAHL, M., *Shekhinah/Spirit: Divine Presence in Jewish and Christian Religion* (New York: Paulist Press, 1992).

LUDWIG, T., 'Otto, Rudolf', in M. Eliade (ed.), *The Encylopedia of Religion* (New York: Macmillan, 1987), xi. 139–41.

LUGONES, M., 'Purity, Impurity, and Separation', *Signs*, 19 (1994), 458–79.

MAGEE, P. M., 'Disputing the Sacred: Some Theoretical Approaches to Gender and Religion', in U. King (ed.), *Religion and Gender* (Oxford: Blackwell, 1995), 101–20.

MAHONEY, J., 'Holiness', in J. Childress and J. Macquarrie (eds.), *A New Dictionary of Christian Ethics* (London: SCM Press, 1986), 269–70.

MARCEL, G., 'The Sacred in the Technological Age', *Theology Today*, 19 (1962), 27–38.

MARETT, R. R., *The Threshold of Religion* (London: Methuen, 1924).

MARTIN, A. D., *The Holiness of Jesus* (London: Allen & Unwin, 1934).

McDANIEL, J., *Earth, Sky, Gods and Mortals* (Mystic, Conn.: Twenty-Third Publications, 1990).

McDONAGH, S., *To Care for the Earth: A Call for a New Theology* (London: Geoffrey Chapman, 1986).

McFAGUE, S., *The Body of God* (Minneapolis: Augsburg Fortress, 1993).

McKENZIE, P. R., 'Introduction to the Man', in H. W. Turner, *Rudolf Otto: The Idea of the Holy* (Aberdeen: H. W. Turner, 1974), 3–7.

MACKINTOSH, H. R., *The Christian Apprehension of God* (London: SCM Press, 1929).

McLAUGHLIN, E., 'Women, Power and the Pursuit of Holiness in Medieval Christianity', in R. Ruether and E. McLaughlin (eds.), *Women of Spirit: Female Leadership in the Jewish and Christian Traditions* (New York: Simon & Schuster, 1979), 99–130.

MACQUARRIE, J., *In Search of Deity* (London: SCM Press, 1984).

—— *Principles of Christian Theology* (London: SCM Press, 1966).

—— *Twentieth-Century Religious Thought* (London: SCM Press, 1981).

MEISELMAN, M., *Jewish Woman in Jewish Law* (New York: Ktav Publishing House, 1978).

MELAND, B., *The Realities of Faith* (New York: Oxford University Press, 1962).

—— 'Rudolf Otto', in M. Marty and D. Peerman (eds.), *A Handbook of Christian Theologians* (Cleveland: World Publishing, 1965), 169–91.

MILES, M., *The Image and Practice of Holiness: A Critique of the Classic Manuals of Devotion* (London: SCM Press, 1988).

MINEAR, P. S., 'The Holy and the Sacred', *Theology Today*, 47 (1990), 5–12.

MOLTMANN, J., *God in Creation*, trans. M. Kohl (London: SCM Press, 1985).

—— *The Trinity and the Kingdom of God*, trans. M. Kohl (London: SCM Press, 1981).

MOORE, J. M., *Theories of Religious Experience with Specific Reference to James, Otto and Bergson* (New York: Round Table Press, 1938).

NEEDHAM, J. (ed.), *Science, Religion and Reality* (London: Sheldon Press, 1925).

OMAN, J., *The Natural and the Supernatural* (London: Cambridge University Press, 1931).

—— review of *The Idea of the Holy*, by R. Otto, *Journal of Theological Studies*, 25 (1924), 275–86.

—— 'The Sphere of Religion', in J. Needham (ed.), *Science, Religion and Reality* (London: Sheldon Press, 1925), 259–99.

OTTO, R., *Aufsätze das Numinose betreffend* (Stuttgart: Verlag F. A. Perthes, 1923).

—— 'In the Sphere of the Holy', *Hibbert Journal*, 31 (1932–3), 413–16.

—— 'The Sensus Numinis as the Historical Basis of Religion', *Hibbert Journal*, 30 (1931–2), 283–97, 415–30.

—— 'Towards the Reform of the Divine Service', *Hibbert Journal*, 29 (1930), 1–8.

—— 'Wert, Würde und Recht', *Zeitschrift für Theologie und Kirche*, 12 (1931), 1–67.

OXTOBY, W., 'Holy, Idea of the', in M. Eliade (ed.), *The Encylopedia of Religion* (New York: Macmillan, 1987), xi. 431–8.

—— 'Holy, [The Sacred]', in P. Wiener (ed.), *Dictionary of the History of Ideas* (New York: C. Scribner's Sons, 1973), 511–14.

PALS, D. L., 'Is Religion a Sui Generis Phenomenon?', *Journal of the American Academy of Religion*, 55/2 (1987), 259–82.

PATON, H. J. (trans. and ed.), *The Moral Law: Kant's Groundwork of the Metaphysic of Morals* (London: Hutchinson, 1948).

PEDERSEN, J., *Israel III–IV* (London: Oxford University Press, 1940).

PELIKAN, J., *Human Culture and the Holy* (London: SCM Press, 1959).

PLASKOW, J., *Standing Again at Sinai: Judaism from a Feminist Perspective* (New York: HarperSanFrancisco, 1990).

POLAND, L., 'The Idea of the Holy and the History of the Sublime', *Journal of Religion*, 72 (1992), 175–97.

PROUDFOOT, W., 'Mysticism, the Numinous and the Moral', *Journal of Religious Ethics*, 4 (1976), 3–28.

—— *Religious Experience* (Berkeley: University of California Press, 1985).

—— 'Religious Experience, Emotion and Belief', *Harvard Theological Review*, 70 (1977), 343–67.

RABUZZI, K. A., *The Sacred and the Feminine: Towards a Theology of Housework* (New York: Seabury Press, 1982).

RAPHAEL, M., 'Feminism, Constructivism and Numinous Experience', *Religious Studies*, 30 (1994), 511–26.

—— *Thealogy and Embodiment: The Post-Patriarchal Reconstruction of Female Sacrality* (Sheffield: Sheffield Academic Press, 1996).

RAUSCHENBUSCH, W., *Theology for a Social Gospel* (Nashville, Tenn.: Abingdon, 1981).

REEDER, J. P., 'The Relation of the Moral and the Numinous in Otto's Notion of the Holy', in G. Outka and J. P. Reeder (eds.), *Religion and Morality* (New York: Anchor Press/Doubleday, 1973), 255–92.

RINGGREN, H., *The Prophetical Conception of Holiness* (Uppsala: Universitets Arsskrift, 1948).

RITSCHL, A. *The Christian Doctrine of Justification and Reconciliation*, trans. H. R. Mackintosh and A. B. Macaulay (Edinburgh: T. & T. Clark, 1900).

ROBINSON, H. WHEELER, *The Religious Ideas of the Old Testament* (London: Duckworth, 1913).

RUBENSTEIN, R., *The Cunning of History* (New York: Harper Books, 1978).

RUDOLPH, K., *Historical Fundamentals and the Study of Religions* (New York: Macmillan, 1985).

Rudolf Otto: Gedächtnisfeier (Berlin: Verlag A. Töpelmann, 1938).

Rudolf Otto: Zum Gedächtnis (Leipzig: L. Klotz Verlag, 1937).

RUETHER, R. R., 'Women's Body and Blood: The Sacred and the Impure', in A. Joseph (ed.), *Through the Devil's Gateway: Women, Religion and Taboo* (London: SPCK, 1990), 7–21.

RYLE, J. C., *Holiness* (Welwyn, Herts.: Evangelical Press, 1976; orig. pub. 1877).

SAHGAL, G., and YUVAL-DAVIS, N., 'Introduction: Fundamentalism, Multiculturalism and Women in Britain', in *idem* (eds.), *Refusing Holy Orders: Women and Fundamentalism in Britain* (London: Virago, 1992), 1–25.

SCHELER, M., *On the Eternal in Man*, trans. B. Noble (London: SCM Press, 1960).

SCHLAMM, L., 'Numinous Experience and Religious Language', *Religious Studies*, 28 (1992), 533–51.

—— 'Rudolf Otto and Mystical Experience', *Religious Studies*, 27 (1991), 389–98.

SCHLEIERMACHER, F. D. E., *On Religion*, trans. J. Oman with an Introduction by R. Otto (New York: Harper & Row, 1958; orig. pub. 1799).

SCHWARZ, H., *The Search for God* (London: SPCK, 1975).

SCOTT, N., *The Wild Prayer of Longing* (New Haven: Yale University Press, 1971).

SHARPE, E., *Comparative Religion: A History* (London: Duckworth, 1975).

—— *Nathan Söderblom and the Study of Religion* (Chapel Hill, NC: University of North Carolina Press, 1990).

—— 'Six Major Figures in Religious Studies', in R. Beaver *et al.* (eds.), *The World's Religions* (Tring, Herts.: Lion Publishing, 1982), 15–16.

SHERRY, P., *Spirits, Saints & Immortality* (London: Macmillan, 1984).

SHIRER, W., *The Rise and Fall of the Third Reich* (New York: Simon & Schuster, 1960).

SLATER, P., 'The Transcending Process and the Relocation of the Sacred', in A. M. Olson and L. S. Rouner (eds.), *Transcendence and the Sacred* (Notre Dame, Ind.: University of Notre Dame Press, 1981), 40–57.

SMART, N., *Dimensions of the Sacred: An Anatomy of the World's Beliefs* (London: HarperCollins, 1996).

—— 'Interpretation and Mystical Experience', *Religious Studies*, 1 (1965), 75–87.

—— 'On Knowing what is Uncertain', in L. S. Rouner (ed.), *Knowing Religiously* (Notre Dame, Ind.: University of Notre Dame Press, 1985), 76–86.

—— *The Phenomenology of Religion* (London: Macmillan, 1973).

—— *Philosophers and Religious Truth* (London: SCM Press, 1964).

—— 'Truth and Religions', in J. Hick (ed.), *Truth and Dialogue* (London: Sheldon Press, 1974), 45–58.

—— 'Understanding Religious Experience', in S. Katz (ed.), *Mysticism and Philosophical Analysis* (London: Sheldon Press, 1978), 10–21.

SMITH, H., *Forgotten Truth: The Primordial Tradition* (New York: Harper & Row, 1976).

—— 'The Reach and the Grasp: Transcendence Today', in H. Richardson and D. Cutler (eds.), *Transcendence* (Boston: Beacon Press, 1969), 1–17.

SMITH, J. Z., *Imagining Religion: From Babylon to Jonestown* (Chicago: University of Chicago Press, 1982).

SMITH, W. CANTWELL, *Towards a World Theology* (Philadelphia: Westminster Press, 1981).

SMITH W. ROBERTSON, *The Religion of the Semites* (London: A. & C. Black, 1927).

SÖDERBLOM, N., 'Holiness: General and Primitive', in J. Hastings (ed.), *Encyclopaedia of Religion and Ethics* (Edinburgh: T. & T. Clark, 1913), vi. 731–41.

—— *The Living God* (London: Oxford University Press, 1933).

—— *The Nature of Revelation* (London: Oxford University Press, 1933).

SPENCER, S., 'Religion, Morality and the Sacred', *Hibbert Journal*, 28 (1930), 343–53.

STEINER, G., *In Bluebeard's Castle: Some Notes Towards the Re-definition of Culture* (London: Faber & Faber, 1971).

STREETER, B. H., *The Buddha and the Christ* (London: Macmillan, 1932).

STREETMAN, R. F., 'Some Later Thoughts of Otto on the Holy', *Journal of the American Academy of Religion*, 48/3 (1980), 365–84.

STRENG, F. J., 'Objective Study of Religion and the Unique Quality of Religiousness', *Religious Studies*, 6 (1970), 209–19.

SUTHERLAND, S., 'Religion, Experience and Privacy', *Religious Studies*, 20 (1984), 121–32.

SUTPHIN, S., *Options in Contemporary Theology* (Lanham, Md.: University Press of America, 1987).

SWINBURNE, R., *The Coherence of Theism* (Oxford: Clarendon Press, 1977).

TERRIEN, S., *The Elusive Presence: Toward a New Biblical Theology* (San Francisco: Harper & Row, 1978).

—— 'The Numinous, the Sacred and the Holy in Scripture', *Biblical Theology Bulletin*, 12 (1982), 99–108.

THOMAS, K., *Religion and the Decline of Magic* (London: Weidenfeld & Nicolson, 1971).

TILLICH, P., *Biblical Religion and the Search for Ultimate Reality* (London: Nisbet, 1955).

—— *The Courage to Be* (London: Nisbet, 1952).

—— *The Protestant Era* (London: Nisbet, 1955).

—— *Systematic Theology* (2 vols., London: SCM Press, 1978).

—— *What is Religion?* (New York: Harper & Row, 1969).

TOULMIN, S., *Cosmopolis: The Hidden Agenda of Modernity* (New York: Free Press, 1990).

TURNER, H. W., *Rudolf Otto: The Idea of the Holy* (Aberdeen: H. W. Turner, 1974).

UNDERHILL, E., *Man and the Supernatural* (London: Methuen, 1927).

WACH, J., *Types of Religious Experience* (London: Routledge & Kegan Paul, 1951).

WEBB, J., *The Occult Establishment*, ii: *The Age of the Irrational* (Glasgow: Richard Drew, 1981).

WEINSTEIN, D., and BELL, R., *Saints and Society* (Chicago: University of Chicago Press, 1982).

WELCH, C., *Protestant Thought in the Nineteenth Century* (2 vols., New Haven: Yale University Press, 1985).

WENDEROTH, C., 'Otto's View on Language: The Evidence of *Das Heilige*', *Perspectives in Religious Studies*, 9 (1982), 39–48.

WHALING, F., *Christian Theology and World Religions: A Global Approach* (Basingstoke: Marshall, Morgan & Scott, 1986).

WHITEHOUSE, O. C., 'Holiness: Semitic', in J. Hastings (ed.), *Encyclopaedia of Religion and Ethics* (Edinburgh: T. & T. Clark, 1913), vi. 751–9.

WILLIAMSON, C., review of *Rudolf Otto*, by P. Almond, *Journal of the American Academy of Religion*, 53/8 (1985), 473–4.

WILLINK, M. D. R., *The Holy and the Living God* (London: Allen & Unwin, 1931).

WINDELBAND, W., *An Introduction to Philosophy*, trans. J. McCabe (London: T. Fisher & Unwin, 1921).

WINDQUIST, C., and WINZENZ, D., 'Altered States of Consciousness: Sacred and Profane', *Anglican Theological Review*, 56 (1974), 181–9.

WOOD, H. G., review of *The Kingdom of God and the Son of Man*, by Rudolf Otto, *Hibbert Journal*, 42 (1943), 87–9.

YANDELL, K., *The Epistemology of Religious Experience* (Cambridge: Cambridge University Press, 1993).

ZAHRNT, H., *The Question of God: Protestant Theology in the Twentieth Century* (London: Collins, 1969).

Index